I Do But I Don't

Walking Down the Aisle
Without Losing Your Mind

KAMY WICOFF

Da Capo Lifelong Books
A Member of the Perseus Books Group

"Girls Just Want to Have Fun" © 1984 Sony/ATV Tunes LLC. All rights administered by Sony/ATV Music Publishing, 8 Music Square West, Nashville, TN 37203. All rights reserved. Used by permission.

Designed by Brent Wilcox
Set in 11.25 point Adobe Garamond by The Perseus Books Group

Library of Congress Cataloging-in-Publication Data
Wicoff, Kamy.
    I do but I don't : walking down the aisle without losing your mind / Kamy Wicoff.
        p.   cm.
    Includes bibliographical references.
    ISBN-13: 978-0-7382-1012-4 (hardcover : alk. paper)
    ISBN-10: 0-7382-1012-9 (hardcover : alk. paper)
    1. Brides—Psychology. 2. Women—Psychology. 3. Weddings.
4. Marriage customs and rites. 5. Women—Social conditions.
6. Feminism. I. Title.
    HQ1206.W65   2006
    392.50973—dc22
                                                                2006009050

Published by Da Capo Press
A Member of the Perseus Books Group
http://www.dacapopress.com

Da Capo Press books are available at special discounts for bulk purchases in the U.S. by corporations, institutions, and other organizations. For more information, please contact the Special Markets Department at the Perseus Books Group, 11 Cambridge Center, Cambridge, MA 02142, or call (800) 255-1514 or (617) 252-5298, or email special.markets@perseusbooks.com.

1 2 3 4 5 6 7 8 9—09 08 07 06

For my mother

"To see what is in front of one's nose needs a constant struggle."

GEORGE ORWELL

CONTENTS

INTRODUCTION   ix

one   The Proposal, Part One   1
           The "I'm-So-Independent" Tap Dance

two   The Proposal, Part Two   35
           The Real Thing

three The Ring   65
           My Baptism by Bling-Bling

four   Home   99
           Weddings Are Women's Work

five   The Dress   133
           My Inner Bride Is Hiding from Me!

six   The W.C., Part One   165
           The Wedding Consumer

seven The W.C., Part Two   187
           Showers, Scan Guns, and Girly Clothes

eight Beauty Day   201
        Walking the White Carpet

nine My Proposal   231
        At Last

ten "Bachelorette" Is Not a Word   235
        . . . And Lollipops Are for Chicks

eleven The Wedding.   267
        The Rest of My Life Will Never Be Long Enough

EPILOGUE   *Mysterium Coniunctionis*   287

REFERENCES   291

ACKNOWLEDGMENTS   297

INTRODUCTION

I will never forget the first time I saw myself in a proper wedding dress. I walked into the fitting room wearing jeans, boots, a T-shirt, and, believe it or not, green underwear. I emerged before a wall of brightly lit mirrors to see . . . *a bride*. The image knocked the wind out of me. Seeing myself clothed that way, with a veil, full skirts, and a long flowing train, seized me with emotions so unexpected, fierce, and complex that I was immobilized. Surprisingly, however, I have since come to value that moment for its clarity. When I walked out of that fitting room, I was totally, unavoidably disabused of the notion—heavily advertised by every modern wedding magazine, website, and guide—that being a bride was about being "myself." (*The Knot's Book of Wedding Gowns* actually calls its shopping chapter "Finding Yourself.") Instead I saw that being a bride was not about being myself, but about finding myself *as a bride*, because a bride is not an individual woman, but an icon of womanhood; a bride is not a person, but a thing.

Seeing myself transformed into a thing so symbolic, so timeless, and so utterly feminine enthralled me in a way I had never anticipated. But for an instant I allowed myself to acknowledge that it unnerved me in a way I'd never anticipated, either. Something about playing the role of bride felt threatening, though I couldn't say what felt threatened, exactly, and I couldn't say why. Face-to-face with this vision of myself in bridal attire, however (recognizable no matter how "unique" the dress may be), a litany of questions rushed into my head for the first time that day. It rushed in with the force of things that have been forcibly held back: *Can I be me and be a bride, too? What does being a bride mean? What is it asking of me? What am I asking from it?*

Tears sprang to my eyes.

"It's the wrong dress," said the friend with me that day, squeezing my hand.

It was the wrong dress. Hers was the voice of reason—or at least of wedding logic—and I welcomed it. I felt wrong in it because it wasn't *me*. In the right dress, I would feel right. I had no desire to dig any deeper than that, and resolutely retreated back into the fog of denial that sustained me (sort of) throughout my engagement. I was determined to have a big, beautiful, mostly traditional wedding no matter what, and I did.

THIS is a book about my experience getting married. It is not a boy-meets-girl story, however. It is a girl (and boy)-meets-culture story—the story of the head-on collision between individuals and societies that weddings bring about, and how American women my age, the daughters of baby boomers, are handling it. It is also the story of what women confront whenever they confront The Bride: a definition of womanhood that is narrower, more traditional, and more troublesome than many of them would like to admit. It is a difficult subject, more difficult than I knew when I began writing about it. For one thing, very few women (and I corresponded with more than eighty, some married, some not, ranging in age from twenty-three to forty-five, as they filled out the series of questionnaires I created regarding all things weddingy) are willing to acknowledge the idea that, in this modern era, any such thing as "a definition of womanhood" exists, and are even less inclined to acknowledge that such a definition has the power to dictate their behavior. In fact, the most fervent, consistently held belief the women I interviewed expressed was that in a post-feminist, post-sexual-revolution world, women are free to define womanhood themselves, making any discussion of the social and cultural pressures women experience as brides irrelevant and even insulting.

Feel funny in a white dress? the thinking goes, *Then don't wear one! And if you do, you've forfeited your right to bitch about it!* Case closed.

It is a testament to the power of this logic that despite having long been somewhat unusual in my continued and public embrace of feminism—the "f-word" now eschewed even by many women who share feminist ideals—I, too, believed I had the power to define being a bride, rather than be defined by it. And this belief kept me quiet—though just barely—as I waited, humiliated, for my boyfriend Andrew to propose to me, because I was unwilling to propose to him. And this belief kept me from asking questions later when, affianced, I spent more money and time on my appearance than I ever had in my life, and was treated as though landing a man was the pinnacle of my career while Andrew's manly, money-making career soldiered on . . . and so much more.

I clung to it largely because when it came to just about everything regarding my engagement and my wedding, I wanted to conform: to do it right, and do it well. I believed I could do this and preserve my modern, independent, feminist self because I was freely *choosing* it. If I "chose" to be a bride-by-the-book, I told myself, it would cost me nothing. Rightly convinced that nobody should tell me how to be a woman or a bride, I failed to see that anti-feminist backlash had ingeniously co-opted this belief to convince me that nobody *could*—and if I "let" them, I had nobody but myself to blame. And falling into this syllogistic trap did cost me. Sometimes it cost me my sanity. More important, it cost me an invaluable chance to see the way I, my husband-to-be, and our relationship were, and always had been, products of our culture, and how we could meaningfully resist, embrace, or reconfigure that relationship for better, not for worse.

At the time, however, convinced that I had both the ability and the right to play the role of bride without buying into the "old" assumptions that underlay it, and convinced that if being a bride threatened my sense of self, my sense of self must be shakier than it should be, I kept the growing, simmering, nagging inner conflict I felt suppressed, buried under piles of things-to-do-lists, wedding magazines, and, in the end, hidden behind a veil. I simply accepted the fact that I was moody, tetchy, and tense most of the time, even as I found myself, with alarming frequency, acting (and feeling) a lot like a twelve-year-old girl. Once, after I apologized to my mother for snapping at her with the same raw agitation I felt in the seventh grade, she said: "Don't be silly! You're a *bride*, sweetheart. All brides are like that!" On that point, she was right.

A shocking number of brides are like that. Harried, stressed, emotional, and moody in varying degrees, women in the midst of the modern wedding experience have brought us the term "Bridezilla," and have made the term "wedding planner" part of the national vocabulary. They have sought professional help in record numbers, not just from wedding planners but from the newly extant ranks of wedding therapists and wedding coaches, too. Most women, of course, are not Bridezillas, nor do they pay professional counselors to guide them through engagement. But extraordinary numbers of ordinary women feel isolated, freaked-out, and in a general state of crisis from the time they start thinking about engagement rings to the time they put wedding bands on their fingers. And this bridal state of mind has deeper roots than any of the existing literature—if it can be called that—begins to address. The fact is that the usual suspects for bridal stress—in-laws, dress panic, financial worries, and incompetent florists—are not what have driven hundreds of thousands of women my age to seek guidance, comfort, and relief wherever they can find it. Instead, a complex range of factors, particular to the post-feminist, post-sexual-revolution world in which these women came of age, have made women of my generation more avid about weddings than ever (fueling an unprecedented, decade-long wedding-industry boom) and more conflicted about them than ever, too.

WEDDINGS are, and always have been, the primary method of communication between a society and its individuals about what adult women and men are supposed to do and be. The first reason all brides are "like that," i.e., like hormonal twelve-year-olds? Being a bride is like being sent back to the seventh grade, and not just because you are supposed to keep a scrapbook and try on eighteen shades of lipstick. Seventh grade is the first time girls run headfirst into a set of cultural expectations for them as *girls* that often clash directly with who they've begun to be as people. Seventh grade is *how-to-be-a-girl* (or else) boot camp. And as Mary Pipher pointed out in her book *Reviving Ophelia*, which I read years before my wedding but which later became an eerily accurate primer for my experience as a twenty-seven-year-old bride, feminism can actually make this collision even more confusing. At twelve, girls find that while society pays lip service to female equality, becoming an acceptable, desirable girl means downplaying your intelligence (even if you still get good grades), getting a boyfriend, and being hot and thin. At twenty-five—the average marrying age for an American woman—women find that although society pays lip service to female equality, becoming an acceptable, marriageable woman means putting your career second to your man's (even if you still work, as you almost surely do), getting married . . . and being hot and thin.

I remember feeling betrayed the first time I collided with this reality as a girl in San Antonio, Texas, in 1985. I was especially angry with my mother, because she'd fought harder than anyone to convince me that the world was completely different than it had been in 1960, when she was twelve. But when she insisted I didn't have to shave my legs or that I could ask boys out I wanted to yell: *Don't pretend what's happening isn't happening! Just tell me how to use Nair!*

Thankfully, back then the world really was different.

"Lip service" to female equality was a great deal more than that. Feminism had made real gains for women, and if I found the messages maddeningly contradictory, at least they *were* contradictory, and not of the uniform, "girls can be wives, secretaries, or spinsters" variety. With my parents' help, and the help of the feminist movement, I mostly recovered from the seventh grade. In college and afterward, not a girl but not yet a wife, I learned how to be a woman and myself in a way that worked for me. It wasn't perfect, but it felt authentic, and falling in love with Andrew was part of it. We helped each other let go of our most stereotypical male/female training, and by the time we were ready to marry, I felt I'd achieved some long-sought, hard-earned balance.

Which is what made the second collision—the second betrayal—such a shock. From the moment I knew I wanted to marry Andrew, which was the moment I realized I wasn't allowed to marry him until *he* asked *me* (a rule far more sacrosanct than boys-ask-girls-out, as evidenced by the fact that my liberated mother made it clear she'd be "concerned" if I "had" to ask him), I was blitzed with a set of tasks, assumptions, expectations, and rituals that were seventh-grade redux. In case I'd forgotten—what with my job, my premarital sex life, my foul mouth, and my freedom—my real job was to be a passive, professionally pretty, self-absorbed party planner, eager to play house and be judged for my success with boys above all else. What was really scary was that this was not the seventh grade. It was preparation for life as an American wife. Weddings, for example, are the double shift's first shift, as the vast majority of brides assume primary responsibility for wedding planning and work full-time, too. Andrew and I fell into this lopsided labor "sharing" even though neither of us, in theory, would have called it fair. But it was much easier to praise Andrew for being involved than to admit that I was doing most of the work because I was The Bride. The power of the bride-and-groom script overpowered us—or perhaps exposed how much we'd internalized the roles after all, and just how precarious the balance we'd prided ourselves on striking really was.

It was not lost on me that exemplary groom status was conferred upon men who did little more than show up at more than one wedding-related meeting and speak when spoken to, while being even an above-average bride meant treating wedding planning like a second full-time job. I simply chose to accept it. Why? Why didn't I speak up or fight back? There were a lot of reasons, but chief among them was that, as a bride, I wanted the guidance and approbation of my culture more than I ever had in my life. I didn't want to pick a fight! I wanted to feel connected, embraced, to participate in something shared. And my desire to do this was so strong that even when being a bride made me feel cut off, not connected, isolated, not supported, pushed around, and not guided, I chose to adjust and accept rather than to resist or to question, which meant my culture had picked the perfect time to have a fight with *me.* The time I was least likely to fight back, the time I was most likely to accept any terms (or spend any amount of money) in order to prove my womanhood and, of course, to make everybody love me.

In *Reviving Ophelia,* however, Mary Pipher urges the adolescent girls she counsels to fight back, even though she knows that fighting back at such a sensitive, difficult time is daunting at best. It is so hard, she suggests, because it is so crucial—the stakes are high, both for individuals and the societies trying to indoctrinate them. In her therapy, Pipher exhorts girls to defend their authentic selves by scrutinizing their cultures' messages with the eyes of an anthropologist, to fearlessly, skeptically question the rituals, customs, and sex roles they encounter. *What are the rules?* Pipher enjoins girls to ask. "It's only after they understand the rules," she writes, "that they can intelligently resist them." I wrote this book because although I failed to question, analyze, or fight back during my engagement—afraid that doing so would "ruin" what was supposed to be the happiest time of my life, unable to see that repressing these questions threatened to ruin it anyway—it is not too late for all the intelligent resistance I can muster. I'm sick of being sent to the self-help section as though *I* am the problem, as though feminism is history and all such talk anachronistic, as though the femininity rules, as Pipher calls them, no longer exist. Certainly the rules for girls are less uniform, less rigid than they were when my mother was growing up. Certainly they are different for women now than they were then, thank god. But what are they now, for women my age? Where do they come from? How do weddings enforce them? And what difference do they make?

WEDDING dress shopping, of course, was only one of many wedding-related things I did as a bride. The website weddingchannel.com lists no fewer than 124 items on its "things-to-do" list, and Andrew and I did most of them. In this we were very like our peers, who over the last decade have helped turn the wedding industry into a one-hundred-billion-dollar-a-year beast. An entire generation pumped full of the mixed motives I felt in that dress—a powerful need to play conformist sex roles to assuage feminist backlash fears, coupled with a powerful sense of entitlement to be an individual—has been brilliantly manipulated by marketers offering this pricey panacea: you can have a wedding just like everyone else's without sacrificing your individuality! Just pay two thousand dollars to buy a wedding dress both traditional *and* uniquely you!

The enormously sophisticated, well-funded members of The Wedding Industrial Complex, in other words, know more about brides' and grooms' anxieties than brides and grooms do. And they have made a special science of profiling the cash cow that is the modern bride. It has been well documented that brides spend more money during their engagement than at any other time in their lives, and since women in general shop and buy far more than men do (women are responsible for more than 80 percent of consumer buying decisions in this country), brides make marketers' mouths water. And so they should. Lately, products ranging from specially packaged "Eye Dew" eye cream to little white monogrammed bags of M&M's fly off the shelves with alarming speed, as brides continue to astonish with their willingness to buy just about anything. I was no exception, most notably when I eventually purchased a Vera Wang dress. Wedding profiteers shrewdly took advantage of my vulnerability, insecurity, and my impossible pursuit of bridal "perfection" to pick my pockets . . . and my parents' pockets, and Andrew's pockets, and his parents' pockets, and our guests' pockets, and so on.

Again, a parallel exists between the bride and the adolescent girl. Teenage girls are the only group that marketers salivate over with equal avarice, because teenage girls are also caught in a state of intense insecurity and crisis. Inculcated with the faux-empowerment mantra that doing (and buying!) what they "want"—no matter what it is and without bothering to wonder how they came to want it—is an exercision of their rights, and rejecting all judgment or reproach of their choices as attacks on their freedom, teen girls buy almost as much stuff as brides do. The purveyors of every kind of product relish this stance of acquisitive defiance, particularly when it masquerades as female liberation and power. They invented it. And they are not shy about hammering it into the heads of modern brides, many of whom, like me, find it hard to resist.

One of the most enlightening moments in the course of writing this book came when a very old friend of mine, who happens to be a lesbian, told me she'd always wanted to get married in a white wedding dress, and that she didn't see the harm in it.

"But why *white*?" I asked her.

"I just always saw myself doing that," she said. "It's *my* idea, it's not like I want to do it because of the culture or something. It's just something I've imagined since I was a little girl. Nobody put the idea in my head," she continued to insist off my incredulous, skeptical stare. "And if I wear white at my wedding, it will be because *I* want to!"

It took me nearly twenty minutes to make her see that it was not only inaccurate but preposterous to believe that if she chooses to wear a white wedding dress someday, it will be a choice made completely independent of social pressures or expectations. She should be given credit, however, for seeing this in just twenty minutes, considering it took me nearly four years to write this book, and I was one of those brides who made a big deal about her dress being *ivory*. At the time, however, that was about as deep as I could go. It isn't easy to be analytical when you're supposed to be romantic, thoughtful when you're supposed to be dreamy, an anthropologist when you're supposed to be a princess. As bell hooks wrote in her foreword to the collection *Young Wives' Tales*, "It is easier to stand before a public world and demand justice (equal pay for equal work, reproductive freedom and more) than it is to stand in the space of our private longings for love and connection and call for a change in how we make love, how we create partnerships." But it is in our private relationships that change begins, and thinking about the way we wed—and changing it—may not only impact our marriages but our world.

"THE identity crisis in men and women cannot be solved by one generation for the next," wrote Betty Friedan in 1963; "in our rapidly changing society, it must be faced continually, solved only to be faced again in the span of a single lifetime." When I began writing about my wedding, I had an inkling that examining the way we marry would provide a window onto this ongoing identity crisis, but I had no idea it would shed light on so many aspects of a woman's life, from body image to housekeeping to work to sex, and I really had no idea it would shed so much light on the roles and rules for *men*, too.

I may have felt shoved into the role of pretty, professional party planner, but as the groom, Andrew was shoved into the role of hard-working, hard-earning career man, expected to react with sarcastic indifference to anything having to do with wedding planning—too busy for florists and too manly for china. Andrew resisted and rewrote this role as he went along, as many men do. He loved choosing the flowers. But writing this book made it clear to me that the world told Andrew just what it valued in him when it told him how to be a groom, too. There's a reason, for example, that men are expected to put up thousands of dollars to buy a ring when they want to get married. Brides must have beauty, but grooms must have bucks. Taking a closer look at the stereotypical role of Groom helped me to see the definition of manhood Andrew grapples with every day. We've both become amateur anthropologists as I've reexamined our wedding, and the process has made our marriage—the whole point of the wedding, right?—better.

I'm often asked if I'm writing a book about marriage. The easy answer is no: it's a book about weddings! The real answer, however, is yes. If there is one thing I learned from going back through my wedding experience and from interviewing other women about theirs, it is that *the way we marry matters*. The way we wed establishes and solidifies patterns in our private relationships that affect our marriages forever— though perhaps it would be more accurate to say "for as long as they last." As we all know, modern marriage has become an almost quixotic endeavor, with a fifth of first marriages ending after five years, and a third after ten. Doing the hard work of challenging stereotypes before and during an engagement, setting a premium on authenticity and communication rather than on conformity and chic gift bags, could help strengthen marriages-to-be. It might also give couples a chance to see more clearly when marriage isn't right for them.

I probably would have rebuffed anyone who asked me to second-guess my big, fat American wedding by saying a wedding is the last place, or time, to wonder why women wear Wonderbras. But since I married I've come to believe that my wedding was the moment when examining my situation was most important. It was not enough to thank my mother's generation for doing all the work, and pull my veil over my eyes. It was not enough to say *Andrew and I know what we mean by this*, and write my twelve-year-old bridal-self off to *all brides are like that*. It may be a little late to make up for it now, but with this book, I'm hoping to cheat—to tell my wedding story and, in the process, try to figure out why it happened the way it did, and how it could have happened differently.

one

The Proposal, Part One
The "I'm-So-Independent" Tap Dance

I was determined not to think about it. To think about it, or to obsess about it, really, would have made me one of *those* women—the ones who insistently inquire about the love lives of people they have just met because they are keeping score, the ones who want a ring on their finger (the bigger the better) to show the world that they are wanted, they are wife, that they are more powerful than the single women still looking— or so they smugly assume—for what they've got. You know who I'm talking about. The Bridezillas. The Others. The ones who want a wedding so they can be the center of attention for a year and a star for a day.

But that was not me! In 1999, the summer I turned twenty-seven, my boyfriend Andrew turned thirty, and our relationship turned three, I could say without hesitation that I had my priorities straight. I knew that the partnership we had built together, which had taken more determination and fortitude than I had ever understood it would, was what mattered. So I was not obsessing about when Andrew might officially propose marriage to me, because to fixate on when and where we dressed up in fancy clothes and made our love legal would have been to reduce my feelings to tawdry marriage-lust.

At least that was what I kept telling myself as Andrew and I approached the Napa Valley that June in our rental car, headed for a romantic, vineyard-adjacent B&B for a three-day, three-year-anniversary weekend that my man had planned all by himself. This was notable since Andrew is generally reluctant to plan things on a Thursday for a Friday, his usual excuse being that his job in private equity—definitely my stiffest competition for his time, since with work he appeared to have no commitment-issues—might require his last-minute attention. My mother had certainly noted this advance planning and was sure a proposal was in the works. She was maddeningly free of conflicted feelings or shame when it came to admitting that she thought I ought to have a ring and a wedding, and soon. While I spent hours defending Andrew and our mature, mutually understood intention to marry when the time was right, my mother said things like, "Didn't you always tell me that you wouldn't date someone for more than three years if you weren't engaged yet?"

"Mother! I said I wouldn't date someone for more than three years if I knew that I was *never* going to marry that person! And Andrew and I are going to get married!"

My mother, ignoring this, had then added with flinty high-noon panache befitting a Texas mother on the hunt for her eldest daughter's wedding, "*The three years are up.*"

The three years are up?! This from the woman who—in suburban San Antonio, Texas, no less—tried to convince me not to start shaving my legs in the seventh grade because it would mean a lifetime of enslavement to a sexist convention?

Perhaps I should have reminded myself that my mother had always shaved *her* legs. And in the car on the way to Napa I had to admit that she had gotten to me. Something had. Because I had bet all my girlfriends fifty dollars at poker night two days before that he was going to propose that weekend. My friend Jessica, a coworker of mine at the television news show I produced for and, at the time, my only married friend, had immediately jumped in with a concerned look and counseled caution. "Don't go into it like that," she'd said. If she were Andrew, she would wait until we were both settled in together in New York to propose. I'd tried to conceal my startled dismay. She was talking about an event more than seven months away. Andrew and I were both living in LA then, but I had recently been accepted to a graduate writing program in New York to begin that fall, and in perhaps the biggest commitment-statement of our relationship thus far Andrew had agreed to follow me there in January. He wasn't going to propose until *January?* Was Jessica serious? I was not sure she understood my situation. Her husband had proposed to her after they'd only been together a year— and he was ten years older than she was, and had probably never said to her, as Andrew liked to say to me, *What's the rush? We have time, sweetie! We have all the time in the world!*

I'd attempted to keep up my "I'm not one of *those* women" front that night, but I had the disconcerting feeling that everybody found it difficult to believe. Did I believe it? I was trying to. But I had to admit that I'd been ready to get engaged for many months by then, while Andrew seemed incredibly happy with things just the way they were. After all, he was getting free milk. I, the proverbial cow, had moved into his house that March, and while it was only "temporary," since I had stowed my emergency-flotation-device (also known as the contents of my own apartment) in a storage locker in Culver City for safe-keeping until I moved to New York that fall on my own, in my mind this symbolic abandonment of my single, independent life meant that we were going to be together forever. I assumed that it meant the same thing to him. I realized, however, not without some distress, that I hadn't been able to have a very direct conversation with him about this. But it seemed to me that some things could be safely left unsaid, things that had been understood between us from the beginning.

We both knew, for example, that for us, forever meant marriage. We'd begun our relationship knowing that at some point we would either marry or break up. We were two people who believed in marriage, and while it helped that our parents were still together after nearly thirty years, according to The National Marriage Project the vast majority of Americans our age still believe in marriage despite the fact that half of them grew up seeing it wrecked by divorce. Interestingly, a gay woman recently captured the essence of my feelings on the subject. "Why do I want to marry?" Donna Minkowitz wrote for *The Nation*. "For love. I believe that, in this world where all we have is our own mind, groping toward something good, two minds together—committed to each other's happiness and passionate about wanting to continue their relation—add up to something holy.... Why make it legal? ... If I take the risk and marry, I need and want recognition by society that this person is part of my family, in fact the closest part." Leave it to those excluded by marriage to make such a thoughtful case for it. Leave it to those entitled to marry to make a rule like this: two people who believe in marriage can't get married until the one with the penis officially proposes to the one with the boobs.

I didn't really want to think about why this was. But that was another thing that went without saying: Andrew wanted to propose, and I wanted to be proposed to. In this I was not alone: I have polled legions of women on this question and have only rarely heard otherwise. "I believe a woman *should* be able to propose marriage," Dana, a thirty-year-old historian from Texas told me, "but something in me would find it very hard to go against such an established tradition." Amanda, a twenty-eight-year-old writer from New York, put it this way: "I wanted a speech. I wanted one knee. I wanted to be surprised. Given the examples of TV, movies, and books, this seemed what I 'deserved,' or what a great, sensitive guy was 'supposed to do.'" My friend Marlo simply said, "I wouldn't need to propose if I found the right person." Truth be told, I felt the same way. If I proposed it would be because I'd "had" to. If I proposed it would be coercion, entrapment, desperation. If he proposed? Romance.

I would never have said, however, that the *decision* to marry was under Andrew's control just because he was the man. It was simply that the timing was at his discretion. In my mind the proposal was strictly a formality—a moment we both anticipated and valued that would clearly be diminished if it came in response to pressure from me. I was determined not to be one of *those* nagging, passive-aggressive women, either! After all, when I realized he was The One and was visited by the full weight of that messianic term—which for me primarily consisted of the realization that Andrew might be the last man I was ever going to sleep with—I'd had a complete meltdown! Women aren't supposed to have meltdowns about lifelong monogamy. Women are supposed to knock each other flat on dance floors trying to catch bridal bouquets, while men react with indifference to the garter-throwing portion of the evening, arms folded amusedly.

I knew, however, that I had not reached my girls-with-Barbies, happily-ever-after ending to the story by betraying the girl in me who had always ripped the heads off Barbies. My goal had never been to "get married." My hope had been to find a man I loved, and I had. The fact that I wanted to marry him did not mean I was a marriage-obsessed wedaholic. (An entire article in *Mademoiselle* was dedicated to the "phenomenon" of wedaholics: women who don't need "a silly thing like a man" to spend all their time wedding planning. "This is about being proactive, girls," the author, a self-confessed wedaholic, avers in a shameless perversion of feminism, "not about romance.") For me, it *was* about romance. This comforted me. It also made me feel kind of bad ass.

In the car on the way to Napa, however—as I found myself slipping into reveries about calling my family with the happy news and jerking myself out of them chidingly—it was clear: my bad ass was starting to go numb. And because I did not want to propose but to be proposed to, only Andrew had the power to wake it up again. And that wasn't very bad ass at all.

Lately this "ritual," this "formality," this bit about his being the proposer and my being the proposee, had begun to seem like a lot more than a formality. It had begun to seem like real substantial power that had been placed squarely into Andrew's manly hands. And lately it had begun to seem that for all my bluster and despite all my efforts, the gap between *those women* and me was closing fast.

I REMEMBER, during that time in my life, feeling very alone. And very crazy. I alternated between denial (I don't care about getting engaged!), frustration with Andrew (shouldn't the man I want to marry want to marry me so much he'd ask before I had to act this way?), exasperation with my mother (you're the one who always told me that in this brave new world marriage would *not* be the most important thing I did!), rescue-fantasies (Andrew will ask any minute, and then I will feel guilty for doubting him), and self-loathing (any woman with a shred of dignity, a fulfilling career, and a love like mine would not be pining for a proposal like a dolled-up, scheming little *Rules* girl!). Every time I tried to talk about what I was feeling I would quickly stop myself short because each emotion, alone, felt untrue to the whole. Worse, each emotion felt like a betrayal—either of Andrew, of me, or of us.

Countless other friends have felt this way too, and on this subject even my closest confidants—women with whom I can usually talk about anything, the kind of women rarely at a loss for words—stumble, blurt, retract, and withhold. My friend Robin, an interior designer who dated her boyfriend Chris for six years before he finally asked her to marry him, spent many hours exhausting herself as she attempted to justify, apologize for, and express her desire to get married, while at the same time trying to understand, criticize, and defend her boyfriend's continued stalling. It was hard. Eventually our conversations about the matter were few and far between, and having been in the same place myself, she didn't have to tell me why.

Like me, Robin felt split in two. Part of her cared so much about getting married she could easily have hailed from the 1950s. Part of her cared so much about resisting the tyrannical pressures put on women to marry she could easily have burned *Brides*. Neither side of herself told the whole story, but finding a comfortable place that was true to both sides proved practically impossible. Another friend of mine, a thirty-year-old screenwriter who has been dating her boyfriend, a thirty-one-year-old PR executive, for four years, attempted to talk to me about how she was feeling and found herself caught in the same trap—and all over the map.

"I can't see clearly," April started by saying. "I don't know how I feel. But I do know that it's embarrassing! I'm embarrassed by wanting to be married. I don't want to be the nag!" At the same time, she quickly pointed out, it was very difficult to accept that her boyfriend could see the situation *so* differently than she did, and refuse to propose while also insisting he loved her. "I never thought men and women were that different before," she said. "But they are. But then it isn't like Jon is some big selfish jerk! He is so amazing and sweet. I hate even having this conversation with you because I feel like I'm betraying him, but on the other hand I want him to be courageous for me, to do a brave thing. He gets the cow and the milk and I don't even get a little cheese. Isn't that a disgusting expression! The cow and the milk! My parents say that!"

"Wasn't he *dying* to marry me?" Amanda, the writer, remembers thinking. "We would talk about it a little, but it was frustrating. I hated bringing it up—or the fact that it was always me who brought it up. I couldn't believe that he'd turned me into 'that girl'—that girl who's pressuring her guy to marry her; that pathetic, desperate girl. I felt frustrated and powerless, and I hated it. I hated that in order for my life—and our relationship—to take the next step, he had to make the move. I was playing this passive role in my own life. I think it may be the only time in my life that that was the case. If I wanted something done, I could do it myself; if I wanted a change, I could change it. But when it came to marriage, suddenly this enormous life decision was out of my hands."

No wonder April, Robin, Amanda, and I, and so many women like us, felt so crazy. The daughters of baby-boomers, we had come of age in a crazy in-between time, the feminism-saved-us/feminists-are-man-hating-harpies 1980s. We were members of what my friend Alexandra once dubbed "the true sandwich generation": the generation of women sandwiched between the feminist revolutions of the 1960s and 1970s (which had largely subsided from view by the time I reached adolescence in the 1980s), movements that had given us a sense of freedom, entitlement, and power we mostly took for granted, and the reality that women—particularly when it comes to marriage and relationships—still find their freedom, entitlement, and power curtailed considerably.

The modern rules of engagement are a veritable thicket of the contradictions "sandwiched" women are expected to handle. Women who have learned to demonstrate their strength by taking responsibility for major life decisions are told that when it comes to *this* major life decision, they can best demonstrate their strength by not "forcing the issue" themselves. (A *Glamour* article from 1999, the year of my engagement-discontent, addressed this contradiction by saying, "Welcome to the passenger seat, ladies." and cautioning Ms. Can-Do to accept the fact that, "Strength, assertiveness and independence won't win this race.") Women who have been taught that they don't need marriage any more than men do find that the men they're involved with are mind-bogglingly, maddeningly free of anything but the vaguest desire to marry "someday," which makes it difficult to believe that men and women begin from remotely equal positions when it comes to getting wed. (Does anyone doubt that the teary, hysterical female hopefuls on *The Bachelor* felt far more desperation about marriage than the cocky, mostly-dry-eyed male contestants of *The Bachelorette?*) Women who were taught that romantic, traditional proposals are harmless in a post-feminist world find that in fact the proposal still has powerful, significant meaning as part of a system where men have remained the choosers, and women have remained the chosen— roles that undermine a couple's equality and give men a power that women simply don't have.

I was straining under the weight of these contradictions. But I really didn't want to think about them. Because more than anything I wanted to believe I could have it both ways: that I could have my romantic, traditional, surprise-me proposal, *and* hold on to my dignity, equality, and strength. I felt it was my right to have both of these things, in fact, an assertion also characteristic of a woman of my generation. Ally McBeal–style, I wanted to stamp my foot and say, "I want it all and don't you dare tell me I can't have it!" I wanted to use feminist rhetoric, in other words, as a way to demand my right to pre-feminist pleasures—and to justify my need for them.

And what about Andrew? Did he have any idea what I was going through? Did he feel like a sandwiched man, too? He had certainly proved capable of doing the same thing I was doing: using feminist rhetoric when it suited him, and falling back on tradition when it suited him, too. Whenever I screwed up my righteous, this *only-the-man-can-ask*-thing-is-totally-unfair anger and made a comment to him along those lines, Andrew would quickly appeal to the very source of my outburst: my sense of post-feminist, independent-woman pride. "Kamy!" he would cry, his dimpled cheeks feigning amused shock, "What's happening to you? Are you really so worried about what everybody else thinks? Aren't you confident enough in *us* (code: in yourself) to let things happen at *our* (code: my) pace?" It was hard to argue with this. Hadn't I learned that a truly strong woman was strong enough to let her man be a man? And his genuine, ardent belief in my self-confidence and strength meant a lot to me. Never mind that Andrew had no intention whatsoever of parting with his male privilege as proposer; to be perfectly traditional in *that* way suited him very well.

Both of us, then, were guilty of using feminism and traditionalism for our own purposes in a mix that was often hypocritical. But I couldn't help feeling that, as a woman, I was bearing a disproportionate burden for the contradictions between old and new, while Andrew, as a man, had conserved a disproportionate amount of the power. We both wanted our romantic proposal and our equality too, but we had failed to consider that as the party the tradition was traditionally intended to disempower, it would fall mostly to *me* to make our participation in it graceful for both of us. It did not contradict Andrew's sense of himself to propose marriage, but it contradicted my sense of myself to wait around for his proposal . . . but then again it fit in perfectly with my sense of myself . . . but then again it was insulting . . . and oh there I was, sandwiched again.

As the sociologist Arlie Russell Hochschild has argued, modern American marriage unites people who've changed less (men) with people who've changed more (women), and as such it is not always a haven from the pressures of the larger world but instead "a major shock absorber" for the tensions of the society, which bear unevenly on men and women—and, in my humble opinion, make women feel more crazy.

Of course there was a way—which I could see very clearly—for Andrew to make our participation in the proposal-tradition graceful and smooth. He could *ask* before I lost my mind. Couldn't he see, I wondered as I struggled to keep my head above water in a sea of contradictions, that all he had to do was step up, put on his romantic-hero suit, and throw me the diamond life-ring that would get both of us out of this mess?

I didn't know. But I hoped so. I was getting tired of swimming.

THE hotel in Napa was beautiful. I had ordered champagne and roses to be waiting for us there, so as soon as we arrived, Andrew, the one in our relationship who does the flower-arranging, carefully rearranged them and expertly popped open the champagne, too. I watched him as he changed into a clean black T-shirt and jeans, his muscular, compact runner's body as tan as a born redhead's can be. Andrew's close-cropped hair only turned dark brown after he graduated from college, and the last remaining red still flecks his trim beard. I slipped my arms around his waist as he studied the collection of CDs we'd brought along for the trip. My mouth was in his ear since, at five-foot-four, Andrew is an inch shorter than I am.

"I wrote you a poem," I said. I could feel him smile.

It was the first official poem I'd ever written for him. I used to write poems for my boyfriends all the time until I realized I was using them to invent emotions I wished I felt but didn't. I'd stopped because they confused me—not to mention the guys I gave them to. It was called "Thirteen Ways of Looking at Andrew," after "Thirteen Ways of Looking at a Blackbird," by Wallace Stevens. The twelfth stanza read:

12
A man and a woman walking.
Paths that diverge and converge,
Like riverbanks
Bounding one river.

My mother, still married to my father after thirty-five years, always told me that in a true partnership each partner walks his or her own path alone, independent and intact (my father also warned me against lovers who do not tolerate solitude), but that those paths must be heading in the same direction, share a similar goal, and be close enough in mind and spirit that the two walkers can always reach out and touch the other's hand—even if, at times, they are only able to brush the tips of each other's fingers.

That was the kind of conversation about love I used to have with my mother before one subject crowded out all others. Lately it had seemed to me that feminism had given me and my female peers ten years, from eighteen to twenty-eight (give or take, depending on what part of the country you're from) to be free and on our own, to pretend that in the new world we were not ultimately going to be judged by our success or failure in obtaining our MRS. degree. But at twenty-eight, the new Cinderella's midnight, rather than being congratulated on having a career, great friends, and being liberated and witty and admired for your accomplishments, *poof*, all anybody cares about is whether you are, or have any prospect of being, married.

Andrew, a thirty-year-old man, did indeed have all the time in the world, both reproductively and socially. But at twenty-seven I had plenty of time reproductively, too! Socially, however, I felt time was running out. At the ripe old age of twenty-seven, I actually felt my honeymoon was soon to be over—until I went on a honeymoon.

I was thinking about the south of France.

When I finished reading the poem, Andrew's nose scrunched up and his clear blue eyes crinkled and he did all the little things he does when he gets misty. I got in his lap and kissed his round, wet, lightly freckled cheeks. He patted my butt, a classic Andrew gesture intended to relieve the sappiness of the moment while savoring it at the same time. When Andrew and I first met he wouldn't even hold my hand in public, he was so private and reserved. "Thank you," he kissed into my ear.

I had no idea what was going through his mind. But I knew what was on mine.

We showered and dressed for dinner. When we were ready, Andrew told me there was something he wanted to do before we left. The sun was setting over the vineyards. I grinned. Then I tried to act as cool as possible. I didn't want to ruin it by acting like I wasn't surprised! I knew Andrew, who likes to think he is unpredictable, might have been discouraged by the impossibility of "popping" the question at that point. We both knew by then that he would deliver it to a ready and waiting recipient. So I did my best not to appear ready or waiting. But of course I was both.

"Close your eyes," he said, leading me over to the bed. I sat down. I heard the sound of the zipper on Andrew's bag, and then felt him sit down next to me. "Are they closed?" he asked. I nodded. He took my hands, and into them placed a small, cloth-covered box. My breath quickened. My stomach tightened. I could not stop smiling.

"Open it," he told me.

It was a jewelry box. Undoubtedly a jewelry box! Bright blue, velvety, the size of a paperweight. My mind registered this—it was a little oversized to be a ring box—but rejected the thought and sprung the box open carefully, holding my breath, to find . . .

Earrings.

Earrings???!!!

It could have been worse. My friend Terry's boyfriend, at a similarly perfect and obvious moment in the wintry English countryside, presented her with a Filofax. Still, I had to think fast, because suddenly I felt exactly like a twelve-year-old girl at the seventh-grade dance. I had gotten all dressed up, put on my fruit-flavored lip gloss and my V-neck sweater; I had made every effort to seem beautiful and perfect and *marriageable* and had stood against the wall for months doing nothing, thumping with desire but dutifully playing by the rules, and just at the moment I thought the boy I liked was finally going to ask . . . he hadn't.

I could not let Andrew see me like that. I was twenty-seven, not twelve. I had some pride. Not to mention the fact that the earrings were beautiful, and matched an equally beautiful necklace he'd given me for Valentine's Day, and to do anything less than love them and hug and kiss and thank him would have been revolting.

"Here," he added, "I brought your necklace so you could wear them together, to dinner tonight." He reached his arms around me and slid his fingers underneath my hair to fasten the necklace around my neck. While he did that our noses were touching, and he was searching my eyes, and I tried to eliminate all traces of disappointment from them but in a way (because I was no less possessed by my desire to Get Engaged due to this setback—if anything it had made my maniacal concentration complete), I wanted him to know. I wanted him to know without making it seem like I wanted him to know, so that my behavior would be irreproachable and his reproachable indeed. The truth was that I was incensed that he could be so clueless, and even more incensed that I could say nothing, nothing at all, because I'd officially become one of *those women*, a passive, hint-hint, manipulative little girl who couldn't ask for herself.

We went to dinner. I acted just the tiniest bit wistful and "far-away," but for the most part we were having a very nice evening. And gradually, with the help of the excellent Napa wine, the tension began to ease its way out of my forehead. We were somewhere between our first and second courses when the couple sitting right next to us got their dessert. With its arrival, a showy flurry of activity ensued. The restaurant's wandering violinist strode up to the table and broke into a romantic serenade. The maitre d' materialized with an unmanageable armful of roses. And this guy got up, got down on one knee, pulled out a ring box (definitely a ring box!), and just did it.

"Will you marry me?" he asked his tearful date. Lips quivering, she said yes. Yes! The entire restaurant broke into applause.

Andrew later told me that it was not until that moment, when he saw the stricken, disbelieving look on my face, that he realized what I thought was going to be inside that blue, paperweight-sized box.

"Wow," he said, looking at me wryly, but a bit sheepishly. "Did you see what that guy just did? That took some serious balls." He immediately studied his bread plate.

"Sweetie," I said, my lips quivering now, "Do you think *you* might ever do that?"

Somehow we made it through the main course. But as soon as we got back to the room, all hell broke loose.

"I had no idea you were expecting me to do that!" he cried.

"You had no idea!? That is the stupidest thing I've ever heard!"

"Fine, believe what you want! And if you were so set on it, maybe you should have let me know. Maybe you should have given me a script ahead of time."

"Excuse me?"

"Sorry," he spat, not sounding very sorry at all. He refused to make eye contact, as he always did when we fought. He was looking (glowering) everywhere but at me.

"Haven't you even *thought* about doing it?" I asked.

"No. I haven't really thought about it. Not in a specific way."

"*You haven't really thought about it?* At all? After three years?" I had broken out my trademark martyred whine. "Were you just going to let me fly off to New York, un-engaged?"

"What, you can't go to New York if you aren't engaged? What's that supposed to mean? You can't leave without having a ring on your finger?"

"*'A ring on my finger?'* Do you really think that's what this is about?"

"What is it about then? We're so happy! Everything is so great!" We paused. He eyed me suspiciously. "Have you been talking to your mother again?"

Every time I made a "comment" or a hint or an outright reference to getting engaged, Andrew inevitably asked me this question. I was sick of it. "Why are you always asking me that? Don't you think I know what *I* feel?"

I was on the brink of tears, and Andrew was raising his voice. Andrew never raises his voice. It made me angry that he was angry. I was the one that should have been angry. Wasn't I?

"Do you know what this is like for me?" I cried. "I *hate* it that I have to sit around and wait for you to do this. It makes me feel so helpless and stupid! It makes me feel like I have to be judged by you, that I have to be approved by you. If I asked you, you would hate it. You would probably say *no!*" I found this so tragic that I started crying in earnest. But at the "you would probably say no" line, Andrew shook his head, gave me his "no-win situation" look, and walked into the bathroom, slamming the door. This is a *win* situation, I wanted to yell. All you have to do is *ask!*

Why should I have to push him into this? I thought, sobbing on the bed. *What is wrong with us? Why should I even have to have this conversation?* It wounded my pride, yes. But it also wounded my pride in us. It damaged my idea of who we were together. Suddenly, faced with the biggest decision of our lives, we were not proceeding as a couple, but instead had permitted ourselves to be thrown into separate, opposing camps, as Man and Woman. How could Andrew allow this? How could I?

IT was so easy.

Like many couples, Andrew and I had "talked" about marriage without ever really, directly talking about marriage, hinting and alluding and telling ourselves and others that we'd "agreed" to marry "someday." But for Andrew this meant asking when he was ready, and for me this meant not being totally sure he was going to ask, even when I told myself, my mother, and anyone else who would listen that I *was* sure—but how could I really be sure until he asked? This imbalance was one reason why, that night, our carefully choreographed handling of the subject fell apart, and we had the no-holds-barred showdown that many couples also have in some form before they get engaged—even if they later erase the incident (or incidents) from their romantic histories (and minds). Terry, the recipient of the Filofax, was so distraught she attempted to leave the Devon country inn where she and her boyfriend were staying, forcing him to reveal his plan to propose a month later at New Year's. My friend Karen took her boyfriend of four years on an all-day boat cruise for his birthday thinking maybe, just maybe, he'd take the opportunity to propose, but two bottles of white wine and a day of boating later she couldn't take it anymore, and confronted him.

"I just don't think you're *ever* going to do this!" she shouted in response to his usual reassurances. "I don't believe you any more!" He insisted that he had every intention of proposing, saying he even had a ring. At that she stopped short, embarrassed but hopeful. He produced a green plastic ring he'd bought at Venice beach. "Are you serious?" she said, because Karen is the kind of woman who would have found a ring like that perfectly charming. "Well," he said, "I haven't asked your folks yet." She put the ring on and wore it for four days. During this time, however, he never acknowledged the ring's presence, much less his intention of proposing marriage to her or her parents. Humiliated, not to mention confused, she took it off and put it in a drawer. A year later they were engaged, and Karen felt guilty about having even told people that story.

True, not all couples have the "are you going to ask me or what?" blow-out. I've talked to women who were pressured about commitment rather than the other way around; to a few women who were proposed to before they were ready; and to one woman (only one) who proposed herself. But the fact is that only 5 percent of American women propose marriage to men, and this would suggest that for a marriage to begin with a man's proposal and a woman's acceptance is not the observance of a tradition based on the way things used to be between men and women but aren't anymore. Instead it is a logical expression of the way things are between men and women *right now*, and that is precisely what makes it so hard to shake and so important to understand—whether you are married, engaged, dating, single, or anything in-between.

The ways in which the proposal tradition reflects the modern state of the sexes also reflect, as might be expected, a mix of traditional and modern ideas. The current mix is better than what came before it—for men and for women—and anybody who suggests going back to grandma's rules is no friend of women, in particular. But a power imbalance between men and women has been preserved, and, more troublingly, modern ideas are often used to mask and gird it.

The first power imbalance women my age are saddled with when it comes to marriage? The nearly universally accepted notion that women want marriage more than men do. Peruse the shelves of the self-help section of any bookstore and you will find innumerable titles aimed at women in search of the ever-elusive "commitment" from a man. No such titles exist for men, though a few, like James Douglas Barron's *She*

Wants a Ring—and I Don't Wanna Change a Thing, attempt to help commitment-phobic men conquer their marriage fears. A search for "commitment" on the women's website ivillage.com produced innumerable articles ranging from "10 Things a Man Fears Most about Marriage" to "Seal the Deal and Make Him Commit" to "Marry Me, or Else?" to "Why Does He Freak Out at Any Reference to Marriage?" A search for "commitment" on the *Men's Health* website yielded, in one attempt, nothing. "Relationships," however, led to articles like "Unleash Her Inner Beast," "How to Date Out of Your League," "Secrets of the Sexperts," "Invade my Bed," and "Pickup Tricks." On *Esquire's* list "175 Things a Man Should Do Before He Dies," "Get Married" is number seventy-two.

Very often in the world according to self-help books and magazines, the battle between the sexes is clear: women want monogamy and marriage, while men want to have sex with as many women as possible for as long as they can get away with it.

True? Very few men or women I polled on the matter agreed with this "truism." This was unsurprising, partly because it's a generalization that clearly fails to consider individual personalities, histories, etc. At the same time, however, most agreed that these stereotypes affect relationships between men and women, which would suggest that they either have some basis in truth, or that they are so prevalent they interfere with the truth, or both. Women certainly talked about combating the stereotype in their dating lives, often feeling "guilty until proven innocent" of marriage-hunting from the get-go. (This doesn't only affect thirty-somethings; even as a freewheeling twenty-two-year-old in LA I had guys patronizingly tell me they weren't ready for anything serious before we'd even had a second date.) Augustine, a nonprofit director from San Francisco, told me that as she's gotten older "more and more men assume that if you want to go out a second time it is to discuss wedding plans." As for men being "guilty until proven innocent" of being only after sex, most women said they didn't believe this was true, but at the same time repeated, again and again, that men propose because "it's harder for men to commit."

It is this belief that has made men, when it comes to marriage, the chased sex. (Think Chris O'Donnell in the movie *The Bachelor*, running down the street being chased by thousands of women in white.) In the not-so-distant past, women countered men's commitment-aversion by being the *chaste* sex: they withheld sex until men offered marriage. (Historically men have demanded chastity of marriageable women, too, of course—largely, as Samuel Johnson famously observed, because "the chastity of women is of all importance, as all property depends on it," meaning that men needed to know that their sons, a.k.a. the inheritors of their property, were really theirs.) My mother certainly never gave up her milk for free. And in a sense, she worried I'd done just that.

I confess. After three years, Andrew and I were having sex! So was that it? Was that why, as two people who had kind-of sort-of agreed to marry eventually and who had always had a very equal relationship, we had sunk into *marry-me-or-else* cliché? Because Andrew was "naturally" averse to marriage and I should have been luring him into a game of hunter and gathered-up? The fact is that there is truth to the stereotypes, but dismissing them completely or stating them as incontrovertible facts is the worst kind of cop out. Instead they ought to be a jumping-off point, the beginning of a deeper, more interesting discussion that takes us *forward* instead of backward. To call for a return to our grandmothers' ways is to call for a return to a time when women were forced to trade sex (service and childbearing) for marriage (providing and protection), a trade that was always grossly unequal, aimed at controlling and commodifying women's sexuality, and sustainable only as long as women could not provide for or protect themselves.

So no, I did not screw up by screwing too soon. The cow is a red herring. It was not about what Andrew was getting for free. It was about what I didn't have, what feminism still hadn't been able to give me: marriage itself.

I will never forget the feeling that Andrew *had* marriage. That he was walking around with it in his pocket, confident and content (with all the time in the world), while I had to get it from him because my pockets were empty. And while feminism may have taught me that as a woman I didn't need marriage, I was never taught that it was mine to bestow upon a man. Girls are still taught to believe that men possess love, commitment, and ultimately marriage like a birthright: that even when a man isn't giving it out (when he's alone), he has it to give. Boys are still taught to believe that women are constantly in need of love, commitment, and ultimately marriage: so if a woman isn't getting it (when she's alone), she is looking for a man to give it to her with the voraciousness of a creature born hungry. (They are also taught that a woman who says she isn't looking for commitment is lying and most likely setting a trap.) Yes, boys and girls are still told that women walk around with sex in their pockets, while men hunger for it eternally. But at least the possibility that women want sex as much as men do has been acknowledged—why hasn't the thinking changed about men and commitment, too?

Because the partner who controls commitment (a.k.a. marriage and money) is much more powerful than the partner who controls sex, especially when women can be raped—a violent repudiation of her control by a man. And only a fool or a saint parts with power willingly. Men still hold the powerful commitment card, and while lots of women point to a woman's power to say "no"—to a date, to a proposal, to sex— real power doesn't have to wait for invitations to be exercised. For all my liberation I still lived in a world where men choose, women are chosen; men bestow marriage and commitment, women pursue it; men love (propose), while women love back (say yes). If relationships are a negotiation, this inequity makes it hard for women to sit down at the bargaining table as equals. I wanted/needed Andrew to choose me. That was nothing new. But as a sandwiched baby-boomer daughter I was grappling with a few new twists.

Among the contradictory messages with which I had to contend? I grew up being told that feminism had freed women to take charge of courtship, to choose boys and ask them out—while the boys of my generation were still being raised to believe *they* were in charge of courtship, and all that had really changed was that they could now expect nice girls to have premarital sex. I was also told that since all the rules had been abolished—even though they hadn't been—if I "chose" to play by the old rules, waiting around for men to take the initiative, I had only myself to blame. Unsurprisingly, this led to some serious confusion, resentment, and self-flogging when it came to dating and relationships.

My mom, for example, told me that in the new world, I was free to ask boys out. When I was twelve, in a loving, optimistic, but disastrous attempt to stoke my grrrl power, she convinced me to ask Trace Olson to the Valentine's dance. I asked. He was awkwardly silent, then said he wasn't going. Apparently, Trace Olson's mother had not given him the girls-can-ask-guys-out memo. As it turned out, nobody had given the boys I knew that memo, and I knew I'd made a mistake. I never forgot that experience, and from it I absorbed two messages: I should be able to ask boys out, but I can't. And in a typical sandwiched-woman contradiction, I have always felt just as strongly about my right to ask guys out as I have felt about wanting them to ask me out instead.

Anne, a lawyer in Seattle, Washington, absorbed this lesson over time: "When I was younger, I used to be much more aggressive about men and asking men out on dates. I stopped doing that. In my experience, if a man does not ask you out there is a reason, and I have experienced needless heartache by finding out why they did not ask me out in the first place." Guys, of course, experience this needless heartache all the time when they ask women out. The difference is that when a man asks a woman out, he is showing his interest, not his desperation; when a woman asks a man out, she is signaling her weakness, not her desire. A man who asks a woman out does not concede power in a relationship that hasn't even started; rather, he exercises it; a woman who asks a man out concedes power the minute she opens her mouth, and may never get it back.

I resented and resisted these "rules," and it was I who asked Andrew out for our first date. He had no problem with this (as many men don't), but as the stakes got higher, Andrew's insistence on determining the pace of our courtship grew. He liked it that I asked him out, but I knew he would view my saying "I love you" before he did as pressure—so I waited for him. And I knew that if I proposed marriage he'd feel I was taking something away from him, or worse, emasculating him, and that was a factor in my belief that he should propose, too. (The website theknot.com counsels women who are considering proposing to "be sensitive to his ego"—clearly not a worry when men propose to women.) But it was not just his feelings I considered as I let him take the lead on commitment. My resistance to making the first move grew at each stage, too. I didn't mind asking Andrew out, but it upset me a great deal to think that I would "have" to say "I love you" first. And a marriage proposal? Out of the question. Again, as the stakes got higher, my need to be chosen—publicly, clearly, and traditionally—increased.

An article in *Glamour* titled "No Guts, No Guy" neatly illustrated the chooser/chosen contradiction women my age espouse. The article begins by rousing women (*it's 2004, girls!*) to act: "Why is it that you can march into your boss's office and ask for a promotion without giving up your 'girlness,' but when it comes to taking the initiative with someone you want to date, you turn into a pale, trembly Victorian? Not only is this attitude self-defeating (and lonely!), it also limits you to just *reacting* instead of acting." It then goes on, however, to assure them that this action will be the only action they have to take:

> I'm not telling you to walk up to the next cute guy you see and say, "Hey, want to buy me a diamond ring?" I'm simply saying that making the first move doesn't make you the guy. . . . Yes, you can still let him pay for dinner; yes, you can still let him initiate that first kiss; yes, you can let him open doors and throw his coat over puddles and eventually get down on one knee in front of God, country and 25 fellow diners in a really expensive Italian restaurant, even though *you* asked *him* out first.

In other words, feminist ideas are great! . . . as long as they are abandoned precisely at the moment they might *really* challenge men and women to change the way they think about themselves as actors, or re-actors, in love.

Is it possible to be feminist and feminine, to be a new woman and a chosen woman, too? Every woman I know would like to think so. And one group who has cynically played on baby-boomer daughters' fervent desire to do both is the relationship gurus—authors of books like *The Rules*. (Or *Marry Me: Three Professional Men Reveal How to Get Mr. Right to Pop the Question* or *Find a Husband After 35* or *The Surrendered Fiancée*—the list goes on.) On the one hand, books like these exploit the disillusionment, suspicion, and sense of betrayal with which many women my age regard feminism, saying, "Feminists don't understand the obvious: men like to pursue, not to be pursued, men like to be *men!* And if you like men you better accept that or you'll end up like a feminist—dateless and alone." On the other hand, they expertly use feminist rhetoric to appeal to baby-boomer daughters' sense of self-reliance: "Don't passively wait around for marriage to just happen! You are a strong woman who deserves a loving, successful husband, and you should do everything in your power (including lying, manipulating, trickery, and, of course, buying my book) to get what you want." It is ironic that in this universe, feminists get duped and used by men because they give them too much credit, while anti-feminists don't trust men one bit, which is why they succeed in marrying them.

Women buy these books in staggering quantities, because they expertly tap into the fears baby-boomer daughters have about feminism, particularly when it comes to romantic relationships: that it is unrealistic, that it recklessly gave up the power women *did* have over men without giving them new power to replace it, that it meant being unattractive and un-chosen. These are genuine fears, particularly because social change happens slowly, and women who behave as though the world has caught up with them are bound to have some head-on collisions with it. The problem (thank god) is that most women I talked with were unwilling to part with the crucial advances feminism gave them even if it meant tough times. They believe that women are equal to men, that they should not have to depend on men for financial support, and that they have the right to make their own life decisions and to be honest in their intimate relationships.

So what to do?

Not *The Rules*. Nobody I know followed its pathetic program literally, especially once they were in a relationship. Who wants to play mind games with the man you love? I cringed at the thought of being passive-aggressive; I recoiled at the notion of being manipulative or conniving. So I did the only thing I could. I came up with my own mix of traditionalism and feminism. I did the "I'm-so-independent" tap dance.

A woman wants to get married. Her man complains of pressure. He makes it clear that under such circumstances he can't act (delivering, by the way, the male version of the ultimatum: stop pressuring me or I'll never propose), but he also makes it clear that the kind of woman he wants to marry is the kind of woman who is not "hung up" on marriage, who is "confident enough" to let her man propose when he's ready. He congratulates himself on expecting so much of her—and then asks her to get on stage and do the "I'm-so-independent" tap dance. The woman in question is then supposed to cease all marriage-related pressure, dedicate herself to work, assume an attitude of cheerful busyness, and generally shut up. If she does, she'll get the ring. This woman is being asked to prove her independence, in other words, by participating—head held high and without complaint—in a tradition that utterly undermines it.

Laurie, a dance teacher from Denver, Colorado, was ready for marriage in a past relationship, but when she talked to her boyfriend about it, "he implied that I was clingy, over-sensitive, and overreacting, and that if I really loved him I would be supportive by not making demands." Feeling ashamed, "I tried to change myself and 'need' less. This made me miserable and sick." As the sociologist Arlie Russell Hochschild observed in her analysis of advice books written for women in relationships, often a woman is advised to shift from "manipulating her husband [or boyfriend] to manipulating herself." The slave, Hochschild notes, always acts more than the master. Andrew and I both put *his* need to be completely genuine before mine, and as a result I worked up a sweat performing my act before and after Napa (a major stumble) because I accepted the idea that while manipulating Andrew was demeaning, manipulating myself was somehow a demonstration of independence and self-respect.

But what could be needier than making a display of your real, genuine, hard-earned independence—performing it for approval—in order to convince a man to marry you? In books like *The Rules* and *Marry Me!* a woman's independence is denigrated to the status of a tactic, or, worse, an artifice, another feather to add to carefully constructed feminine plumage. A career is good, *The Rules* implies, because it makes a woman appear "happy and busy" during courtship, but after marriage it should never challenge her man's. (*Marry Me:* "Ugly Truth Number Two: He's the star of the career show—like it or not.") *The Rules* summed it all up with a two-word oxymoronic instruction: "Act independent." Advice like this isn't just pathetic, it's immoral. It undermines women's integrity. The books aimed at women my age trumpeting the use of feminine wiles in the pursuit of marriage cultivate the retro and wrong-headed assumption that women are partial, dependent beings who *do* need marriage so much that as an end, it justifies any means—including pretending they don't need it.

There is one other aspect to this—perhaps more insidious, and certainly more insulting: the thinly veiled notion that a modern woman is guilty until proven innocent of having gotten uppity, of having forgotten her proper place. Sometimes I felt I was being asked to prove that my independent, go-get-'em, take-control self would never assert itself so much that it would interfere with *Andrew's* independent, go-get-'em, take-control self; sometimes I felt that my "I'm-so-independent" tap dance was really an "I'm-so-deferent" tap dance in disguise, designed to mollify and reassure the masculine ego. "Don't worry!" these books coo, "yes, we are modern women—but not so modern that as wives, we won't know when to back down!" Seen this way, a woman's willingness to respect the male "right" to propose no matter what is a crucial test of her viability as wife material—and of her acceptance of male dominance in the marriage to come.

Deep down, I suspect that this was what made me really angry. But I put my tap shoes on anyway. It's easy to dismiss books like *The Rules*, to fling them away in anger, as I did. But then you miss seeing all they have to teach you about yourself. The prescriptions are wrong, but as a primer for the disease they reveal a lot. If Andrew and I had been willing to admit how much certain ideas we assumed ourselves to be above had sunk into our bones, we might have stopped blaming each other for failing to play the roles tradition dictated and questioned the roles instead.

In Napa, however, lying on a hotel bed on my stomach sobbing, yanking Kleenex by the fistful out of a box on the floor so that my nose didn't run all over the sheets, I did not have the energy or the inclination to engage in heavy-duty analysis. I was even less inclined to do so because, like Andrew, I thought I knew exactly what had happened. It was simple: Andrew had taken so long to propose that he had forced me to obsess over his proposal like one of *those* women, and he was a jerk because he should have helped me avoid this at such a momentous time. He also thought it was simple: he hadn't asked because he wasn't ready yet, and I was pushing him to act mostly because the multibillion dollar wedding industry, my friends, and my family had gone to my head.

He had a point.

Another thing that makes it very hard for women to sit down at the relationship-negotiating table as equals? The fact that even now, marital status is the primary yardstick by which women are judged, and for single women a marriage proposal is akin to redemption. "Marriage confers status on a woman in a way no other social institution can," Laura Miller observed in *Salon.* "To get the most out of being single, a woman has to develop a skill that is seemingly harder to come by these days than a good man: the ability to be happy even when other people are convinced you can't be." It's not just that men are choosers, and women are chosen, it's that unchosen (i.e., unmarried) women are treated like defectives, while men—at least until they hit forty—are not. (As Barbara Ehrenreich described it in *The Hearts of Men*, it wasn't always this way: in the 1950s unmarried men rightly feared being labeled homosexuals. But the sexual revolution presented a third way: as long as a man made such a brazen display of chasing tail that his hetero-ness was unassailable, he could dodge marriage as long as he liked.) Women chant, "It's okay to be single!" on *Oprah*; it's tough to imagine men doing the same.

"People assume a single guy is making a choice," my friend Devon, who is single and living in Dallas, Texas, said to me. "People assume a single woman can't possibly have made a choice. Instead they assume that she is being made a choice about."

I never experienced the worst of this treatment because when I met Andrew I was twenty-four, a veritable baby compared with most women I know. But the stories my single women friends tell me are both appalling and unremarkable. ("Appallingly unremarkable" is more like it.) A thirty-three-year-old lawyer standing on a street corner in New York is approached by a teenage boy who looks at her hand and asks, "Why ain't you married yet?" A thirty-two-year-old woman tells her mother she's going on vacation with her best friend and her mother groans, asking: "Aren't there any *men* going this time?"—then repeats her conviction that her daughter and her unmarried, thirty-four-year-old best friend must be lesbians. A woman in her early thirties who has just earned her Ph.D. from Yale calls a friend's mother only to hear: "I heard your good news!"—not about earning her Ph.D. but about going on two dates with *someone special*.

"I've heard a friend describe being single in your thirties as something akin to missing a limb," Marie, an unmarried artist, noted dryly. "It's an overly dramatic description but sometimes it feels accurate." A single man in his thirties is not missing a limb—he's missing a ball and chain. Even the hip, self-sufficient ladies of *Sex and the City* complained constantly of the stigma attached to the unmarried woman. (Catherine Orenstein described this aspect of the show—the preoccupation with "snagging a man"—as retro, but I'm afraid it's perfectly up-to-date.) Their complaints were all the more remarkable considering that these women barely interacted with the principle applicants of "why aren't you married yet?" pressure: mothers.

I may have convinced myself before leaving for Napa that I was "focusing on my feelings," not waiting for Andrew to do anything.

But my mother was waiting. In fact, as soon as Andrew and I had finished chasing each other around the table, a process she respectfully recognized as being our own affair, and I reassured her that Andrew and I would someday sit down at it together for the rest of our lives, my mother took this as an invitation and pulled up a chair. Apparently she planned to sit there until we provided an occasion for her to get up and dance—preferably to "Brick House," played by a cheesy cover band.

I had never expected this from my mom. A baby-boomer who'd left her 1950s, how-to-be-a-housewife upbringing behind in the 1970s to embrace feminism, she'd encouraged her two daughters (by the time feminism made it to Texas she already had two children and, by 1976, three) to conquer the world with unbridled hubris. I remember her spinning the globe in our family room saying: *Anywhere you want to go, Kamy! Anywhere!!* And while she'd always told me that marriage and motherhood were wonderful things, she'd never said anything to suggest that a wedding mattered much to her, or that marrying the man I wanted to spend my life with would be as important to her (more important?) as finding the man I wanted to spend my life with in the first place. Later I came to understand her better, but at the time I couldn't understand her at all, and the conversation I had with her right before I left for Napa perfectly illustrated the divide.

"Sooo . . ." my mother said, in a tone I'd never heard from her prior to the last few months, "it sounds to me like Andrew has planned a very *spe-cial* weekend for the two of you to celebrate your anniversary. It sounds like he went to a *lot* of trouble!"

"What is that supposed to mean, Mom?" I countered. It was amazing how instantly her tone, her expectation, her demand, could immediately erase all memory I had of my own expectations. If Andrew's delay in proposing was making me feel like I was standing around on a doorstep waiting to be let in, my mother's expectation made me feel like she was sitting in an idling car by the curb watching me wait, and like an embarrassed teenager I wanted to turn around and violently wave her off.

"Oh, nuuuuh-thing," she answered, making a little hmm-mmm sound, as if she were "tickled," as if I were a child and she knew what I was going to get for Christmas.

"He's not going to do it, Mom!" I preempted.

"And why not?"

"Because I don't want him to!" That was a new one.

"What do you mean you don't want him to? You want to marry him, don't you?"

"Yes! Yes, I want to marry him. And he wants to marry me. But not right now! I'm about to start graduate school, and the chance to write full-time is so precious to me. How could I waste one minute of it on caterer-florist-bridesmaids-dress-wedding-cake *crap*?"

My mother, as usual, did not miss a beat. "Kamy!" she said, sucking in her breath with a scandalized, incredulous laugh, "you don't mean that you want to wait until *after* you've finished graduate school?"

Yes! I wanted to scream, because during that speech I had concluded that the last thing I wanted was for Andrew to ask me to marry him, because a proposal would mean a wedding. This was something I had managed to forget completely. I did not want to squander my newly minted writing life picking out napkin rings and a tiara to put on my head like I was the final item to thunk down on top of a Martha Stewart wedding cake! This realization made me feel very independent, restoratively *bad ass*.

"If you wait until you've finished graduate school," my mother continued, hardly concealing her horror at this thought, "you won't be engaged until you're twenty-nine, and then you won't be married until you're thirty, and then you'll want to start having children. And you've said you want to be married for a few years before you do that, even though it seems to me you've already had your child-free, coupledom fun-phase, but after the age of thirty the chances of complications with a pregnancy begin to go up. . . ."

Whoa. The biological clock! This threat seemed especially absurd and premature. My mom was pushing me harder than usual. I decided to push back.

"Mom. Listen to me. Andrew and I are really, really in love. Do you know how amazing that is? I know you do! I found what you always wanted me to find! What does it matter, all this engagement stuff? Why does it even matter to you at all when I'm telling you I'm loved, I'm in love, I'm happy I'm happy I'm *happy!*"

I should have said that a long time ago, I thought. The heart of the matter.

"Of course I'm glad you're happy, Kamy," my mother answered levelly, in a tone that was not in the ballpark of sing-songy. "And I don't appreciate the implication that I'm not. But when two adult people love each other, and have told each other and their families that they plan to spend the rest of their lives together, they get engaged."

And on and on like that we went, neither of us giving an inch, my tone becoming more and more frantic, like someone desperately in love who is being broken up with and who believes that if they can just make the point about why they should stay together *one* more time, the conversation would make sense again because the two of you used to agree about everything and it is impossible that such a misunderstanding could be irreparable. Meanwhile my mother's tone remained unsettlingly calm, like the firm, implacable partner who is bringing the hammer down, who can no longer be reached through the old reliable channels.

Her invitation to pull up a chair and insert herself into our relationship had read, apparently:

In honor of **KAMY'S** stated commitment to **ANDREW**, you're invited to hassle, hint, meaningfully allude, and otherwise relentlessly badger **KAMY** about if and when **ANDREW** is ever going to ask her to marry him, with the aim of exerting so much pressure on her that she finally issues **ANDREW** a version of the ultimatum you would like to issue yourself: *If you loved her as much as I do (i.e., as much as you should), you would have asked her to marry you the day you met her! So shit or get off my daughter's pot!*

Andrew was aware of this invitation. I think he thought I was partially responsible for sending it. I guess I was; undoubtedly I was using my mother as a way to tell him what I wanted. Andrew's parents, on the other hand, had never received such a thing. (Or if they had they'd declined to open it.) Andrew took pride, in fact, that his parents had not been on a similar, parents-with-sons-in-long-term-relationships mailing list. They had not even brought up the subject of marriage with him yet. This was partly because Andrew's family is not like that. But Andrew's pressure-free environment had less to do with Andrew's family than with the fact that he was the man.

It would have emasculated Andrew for his mother to lay into him about proposing the way my mother was laying into me. (Emasculation here referring to treating an adult person like a child—in which case women can be emasculated, too, and are.) There was also no reason for Andrew's mother to believe that he was being treated badly, or that he was unappreciated, or with the wrong woman because she hadn't proposed yet. She did not have to tell him to stand up for himself *because he was in charge.* People don't fret over the fate of a guy who has been dating a woman for a long time and isn't engaged. They might think he's getting away with something, and try to push him for that reason; they might think he's taking advantage of his position, and try to push him in his girlfriend's defense. But they don't pity him, and they don't think he's being humiliated, diminished, or embarrassed by the wait, because unless he's proposed and been rejected, he's *not.*

In other words, women get more pressure from their mothers to marry than men do partly because their mothers are trying to protect them. This is a traditional behavior that has been bolstered by modern times. My mother, for one, felt that the new system, which frees women to give up everything (namely sex, but also financial independence in the case of moving in together) without clinching a definite commitment in return, puts them at a dangerous disadvantage when it comes to negotiating relationships. Friends of mine have told me that their mothers also expressed concern about their daughters being at the mercy of men who no longer feel duty-bound in any way when it comes to their dealings with women, and sometimes this has the paradoxical result of causing them to urge their daughters to work even harder to please "the good ones." Robin, the interior decorator, was actually instructed by her career mother to cook more.

Many mothers also pressure daughters about marriage, of course, because in another mix of the traditional and the modern, they believe that feminism has made it possible for their daughters to enjoy a lifelong, loving partnership with a man without sacrificing themselves, which means they can be unrestrained in their advocacy of it. As Marie put it, the pressure also comes from "the hope/fantasy/reality/wish/belief that being married might actually bring something nice into my life." This hopeful fantasy about marriage comes even from mothers whose experiences with the institution have been less than great, though a few women I talked to did say that their mothers, far from pressuring their daughters to marry, actively discouraged them. Mia, the literary agent, said her mother told her, "even if it's just before you're about to walk down the aisle, it's never too late to change your mind." In a more questionable mix of the traditional and the modern, however, baby-boomer parents who have married and divorced multiple times still feel compelled (entitled?) to pressure their progeny to marry. As Larissa Phillips wryly noted in *Salon*, "everyone in my family and my boyfriend's family, grandparents included, [broke] their marriage vows," and yet all pressure her to marry her long-time boyfriend anyway, "shocked and befuddled that someone would choose to avoid the whole swampy mess of broken vows and failed traditions that they've left in their wake."

The pressure on women to marry, then, seems to override any sensible discussion of marriage itself, and in this climate it is little surprise that women become fixated on earning male attention, love, and desire; another reason that *being chosen*, whether a woman then chooses to choose back or not, takes on immense importance. "We see ourselves through that lens," Mia said. "'Are we desirable enough to marry, to go public with?' Often the reason we wait for his proposal with bated breath is because we don't know the answer to that question for ourselves. We don't know because it's always been about his choice." (The wild popularity of Greg Behrendt's and Liz Tuccillo's book *He's Just Not That Into You* underscores this—when will there be a book for women titled *You're Just Not That Into Him?*) Insofar as Andrew was asking me to question and resist the immense pressure put on women to marry, his insistence that I perform the "I'm-so-independent" tap dance wasn't all bad. But insofar as Andrew (and I!) treated my desire to marry with sexist skepticism—because when it comes to wanting to get married women can't be trusted—we did a disservice to my status as a thoughtful, mature adult.

We also did a disservice, believe it or not, to "other people's opinions." More than any other issue, Andrew raised "other people's opinions" as anathema to the decision to propose, and seemed to be seeking a place where he could behave totally "authentically" and individually, thereby assuring himself (and me) that he was doing the right thing. One of the most consistent things I've heard from women is that a man's proposal should be made "freely" because otherwise one can't be sure it is sincere. One friend, who waited years for a proposal she would have welcomed years before, put it this way: "In retrospect I wouldn't change a thing, because having a man who is absolutely ready to give everything is worth far more than a man who's doing what he thinks is probably the right thing, because the time is right, because I say so, because others say so. Seeing that he knows it unequivocally for himself—priceless."

I knew what she meant. Andrew and I both coveted his ability to act as a totally free being—agency women have long been deprived of, which they deeply admire in men. But by doing this Andrew and I both employed a very male point of view: valuing actions that were individual, not communal; admiring decisions that were independent, not interdependent; viewing the impact of "other people's opinions" with scorn rather than seeing that marriage is *about* other people's opinions—other people also being known as family and community; opinions also being known as social norms. Women should not be made to feel like amputees because they aren't married. That kind of pressure I condemn. However, when a man is the marrying kind, he should not get away with pretending that his proposal is a totally, unequivocally private matter between himself and nobody else. Marriage is a public institution, intended to compel individuals to take responsibility for each other. It is a civil pact and a social system, and individuals who choose to partake in it are not expressing rugged individualism, they are acknowledging the ties that bind. Women know this intuitively, and in my opinion it is a good thing.

I think Andrew was the kind of man who was ready and willing to see this point of view. He believes in the rightness of male-female equality on principle, as many men do. But I think the ready-made privilege he got as the man in the proposal tradition made it very tempting—and far too easy—for him to stall, scowl, and withhold instead, like one of *those men*, the kind of men who can't commit, the kind of men who care more about proving their independence than about showing their love. And the ready-made position of passive paralysis I got as the woman in the proposal tradition made it very tempting—and far too easy—for me to pout, cry, and bully like the kind of woman who needs a rock and a registry to show how much she's loved, the kind of woman who wants a wedding so she can be the center of attention for a year and a star for a day. And I was not that woman! And Andrew was not that man.

We should have done better.

ANDREW did eventually emerge from the bathroom that night, calmer, and I did eventually rein in my most violent sobs. (Maybe I reined them in first, and Andrew took that as his cue to come out of the bathroom.) And then Andrew came over to the bed and put his arms around me. He stroked my hair while I cried a little more. I grabbed his hand and held onto it tightly. He picked up the box of Kleenex and put it on the bed.

"Listen to me," he said. "I am not judging you." I immediately started to speak, but he shhed me. "We judged each other already," he said quietly. "To get here. But we're through judging each other. Because we *love* each other. I want to spend the rest of my life with you. I think we've known that, or at least I have, for a long time. Probably from the day we met."

Andrew was reassuring me again. *What would it be like to be the one reassuring him?* No matter. I rested my head on his lap, looked up at him and smiled. He smiled back. Laughing, I said, "So then why don't you just ask!?"

"Because I don't have my act together yet! This kind of thing requires the acquisition of certain items, a certain amount of planning!" I hadn't considered this. All I had to bring to our engagement-moment was my "yes." Andrew was expected to show up with a costly item of wedding-related jewelry.

I squeezed his hand. We both knew it was lame. But we wanted our romantic proposal too much to care. That night in bed, Andrew and I lay on our sides in our favorite position, with him behind me. He touched the tops of his feet to the bottoms of my feet, snuggled his hairy shins against my smooth, shaved calves, pressed his quadriceps into my hamstrings, and his pelvis into my butt, and cleaved himself to me right up to my neck and hair, which he brushed his lips against. It felt very, very nice.

"You are not waiting for something to happen," he whispered in my ear. "The thing we were waiting for, what we always wanted to happen— *it happened already.*"

It happened already, I repeated to myself as I drifted off to sleep. And in a way, I felt like I had just asked him, and he had just asked me, and that we had given each other our answer. But of course we hadn't—and we both knew it.

two

~∞~

The Proposal, Part Two
The Real Thing

Six months later, Andrew and I still weren't engaged. But things between us were great! (*Great!*) I had moved to New York to start
graduate school. Andrew was still in LA but he was due to join me in
January. In the meantime I was loving my classes! I was loving writing!
And I was loving Andrew!

Best of all, I was no longer possessed by a maniacal desire to Get
Engaged!

I had come to my senses, I thought, I had come to my *self*—focusing
on my work, I was doing my "I'm-so-independent" tap dance with
style. This was what I told my friend Franny over dinner one night in
late October. Franny had been with her boyfriend Joe since college.
They had been dating (with some breaks) for nine years.

"It was such a relief to just let it go," I told her. "To get perspective
and relax."

"Yeah," she said. Then she smiled. "Although you know, at some
point you're gonna freak out again. And then you'll get over it, and then
you'll go right back to freakin' out. Except then it will be even worse."

At this, the casual smile on my face crumpled into a grimace. I think I actually blushed, I felt so totally busted.

Of course I was going to freak out again. But I was undoubtedly in a strong non-freaking-out period. It helped that my mother and I, by mutual agreement, were no longer discussing the subject. I had no idea how long we could pull that off, but I think both of us were happy to give it a try. Andrew has annoyingly suggested that my memory of this period is selective—saying that during these six months I was frequently unable to restrain myself from occasional barbs, teary moments, and questions like, "Would you want a band or a DJ at your wedding?" diplomatically using the term "your" rather than "our" but employing a jokey/martyred/threatening tone just in case he'd forgotten that the white wedding elephant was *still in the room.* This is a highly credible suggestion but I choose to ignore it, just as I chose to ignore it then. Acknowledging it would have called attention to the fact that Andrew and I were in post-ultimatum limbo.

Yes, I said *ultimatum.* Because the fact was, I had issued one. At the time I would have been greatly offended by the very idea. Clearly I had done no such thing! Did I say, "Marry me or else"? Never! Had I said, "I want to get married and I need to know that you are going to ask me!"? Yes. What's the difference? Not much. But it is a difference many women cling to because it is the difference between feeling that the proposal, when it comes, bears the precious imprimatur of male independence, and the feeling that it has been tarnished by female neediness. One woman neatly illustrated this contradiction when she told me that she "set guidelines in my mind that at certain stages in a relationship . . . if my boyfriend wouldn't talk about our future I would move on [because] I can't stand deadbeats and I would never want to be with one," then responded to my question about issuing ultimatums by saying, "I would never deliver an ultimatum. It would cheapen the entire experience."

When discussing ultimatums women use terms like entrapment and coercion, and question whether a proposal delivered under duress could be trusted or would even be welcome. Many suggest that women who deliver ultimatums essentially propose marriage themselves—yet another reason a woman who fervently wants to be proposed to will deny ever having given one. What's the point of getting what you want, these women ask, if it isn't what you want? But when what you want is to get what you want without ever having to say what you want, getting what you want can be very tricky indeed. And the fact is that most women say "marry me or else" in one way or another.

In light of this unstated state of affairs, can the modern-day proposal live up to the hype? Can it be authentic, romantic, and surprising—enough to make all the tension, hurt, and anger of the preceding months (or years!) melt away—and can it appear, at least, to be completely untainted by pre-engagement haggling? That was what *I* wanted. And that's what Andrew wanted too. After all, the proposal is the one part of the wedding process that belongs exclusively to the man. It is his Heroic Romantic Moment, and—as everyone knows—heroics are not for girls.

THAT Thanksgiving, Andrew and I decided to meet in Boulder, Colorado, Andrew's hometown. We always had Thanksgiving there with his family so this was no surprise . . . except that this year, Andrew's family wasn't going to be there. They were all going to Florida, where Andrew's grandparents lived half the year. Whoops!

Andrew told me he wanted to go to Boulder anyway, just the two of us. I said, "Are you *sure* you don't want to go to Florida?" then booked my ticket to Denver—nonrefundable. It seemed like a naughty, special holiday, just Andrew and me for Thanksgiving. Since I'd started at Columbia we'd been seeing each other every two weeks at the most, so I jumped at the chance for a long weekend to ourselves. I didn't think much about his insistence that we go to Boulder without his family. I figured it was because of the mountains. The real mountains, not the LA kind but the big Colorado kind that Andrew needs to run around in periodically in order to survive.

Boulder has been Andrew's family's home base for more than thirty years. His father, David, is a professor at the university (with a Ph.D. in aeronautical engineering and a specialization in detonations, he is literally a rocket scientist) and the family moved there when Andrew was six weeks old. Andrew's mother, Caryl, was a full-time mom who also taught piano lessons (a New Yorker like David, she was a student in the preparatory division at Julliard), led the Colorado Music Festival, and coordinated the family's sabbatical stints to various places in Europe. Boulder, however, was always home, and Andrew is fond of walking along the mall downtown in his Patagonia fleece, arms spread wide, breathing in the mountain air and saying, "It is good to be with my people."

Best, however, to be with the mountains, and if you walk up the street from Andrew's house on Kohler Drive, heading west and uphill, you will run out of pavement after about five minutes. The neat suburban front yards give way to open space, and trailheads wind their way up to the base of the Flatirons—the place where the eponymous dark-brown rock formations that dominate Boulder's skyline thrust up out of the sloping foothills to form leaning monoliths that point with their peaks to the north, like massive iron filings anchored to the earth pulled northward by the pole.

Andrew began running on Boulder's mountain trails—Skunk Creek, Royal Arch, Mesa—when he was in junior high, and spent hours on them in the rain, the snow, and the hard-baked summertime, training for cross-country meets, bounding over their steeps like a red-headed mountain goat. Andrew sees running as an act of physical clarity. He also uses it as a time to think. (When I'm running I think: "How many more minutes do I have to do this?" and "Why is that speed-walker passing me right now?") Andrew's thoughts attach themselves so specifically to the landscape that he can sometimes reconstruct an entire thought process by re-running the same route. Thus certain ideas, over time, affixed themselves to specific places. Like the vision he'd had, since he was a boy, each time he flew by the big flat rocks just below the Enchanted Mesa Trail. Every time he passed those rocks he thought, *This*

*is the spot where I will ask her to marry me. Someday I will ask her—who-
ever she is—and when I do, I'm going do it right here.*

That was one secret, in our life together, that he had always kept to
himself.

I ARRIVED in Denver from New York on the Tuesday morning before Thanksgiving. Andrew was driving his convertible out from Los
Angeles—his parents were going to keep it for us in Boulder for as long
as we lived in New York. He was due to arrive Wednesday evening. I
was working at David's desk in the basement when Andrew called Tuesday afternoon—twenty-four hours before his estimated arrival.

"Sweetie!" he said. "I am making great time! I drove all the way to
southern Utah with the top down! I'm freezing my ass off but it feels
amazing!"

"Where are you?" I asked.

"How should I know? Utah! I just bought some Oreos, naturally.
And three Cokes. Oh! And some sunflower seeds." He sounded hyper.
I laughed. "I'm going to keep driving and see how far I can get," he said
breathlessly. "I'm in the zone!"

I was beginning to worry about Andrew's ability to drive the additional
five hundred miles to Boulder. The road over Vail Pass is narrow and full
of precipitous, non-rail-protected curves. Andrew promised to call and
check in with me later, and also promised he wouldn't drive if he wasn't
100 percent awake, or at least so pumped full of Coca-Cola Classic that
you couldn't have put him to sleep in a sensory-deprivation chamber.

At midnight the phone rang. "I'm in Grand Junction!" he practically
shouted.

"Are you insane?" I asked

"This isn't really a two-day drive," he said. "It's only a two-day drive
for losers."

And at four o'clock in the morning, there he was. Flipping on the
lights. Flipping them off again. Climbing into his slightly lower version
of the two twin beds his mother shoved together for us whenever I came
to visit. Grinning madly.

"I cannot believe you did that," I said, extremely pleased, traversing the crack to snuggle up against his still cool, wind-whipped body. Outside, it was beginning to snow.

"I can do a lot of things," he said. "You just watch me."

THANKSGIVING morning the sun came out. The city was carpeted with a thick blanket of snow. Andrew woke up first and wrapped himself around me tightly, his long-john bottoms warm and soft as he nuzzled and squirmed until we were both awake and he leapt out of bed, saying we ought to go upstairs and start cooking.

"Wait a minute!" I cried, bouncing up on the bed like a kid. "It's Thanksgiving! You owe me a poem! Where's my poem?"

Every year at my birthday, more or less (because Andrew always got extensions, as he did on fifty-nine of the sixty papers he wrote in college), Andrew wrote me a birthday poem. That past July 5, for my twenty-seventh birthday, Andrew had requested an extension (as usual), but this time he had deferred longer than ever, finally announcing that I would not see his handiwork until Thanksgiving, which was ridiculous.

"Kamy," Andrew said, in an aggrieved tone, "I can't believe you would demand something so delicate of me as though it were a, a, *product*. I am an artist. I will give you your poem when your poem is ready." Obviously, he had the poem.

Upstairs, the house was filled with the bright crisp warmth of sunlight bouncing off new-fallen snow. We spent hours together in the kitchen, preparing our rack of lamb (having chosen, thank god, to skip doing a whole turkey), chopping mushrooms for the soup, and making Stovetop stuffing. By noon we were done prep-cooking, and had only to bake, boil, and sauté things to be ready to eat.

I was exhausted. I wandered into the family room and turned on the TV, hoping to catch some football. Andrew poked his head in and suggested we go for a walk. I told him I was too tired. He disappeared. After a few minutes I got up and walked to the stairwell. Andrew was standing at the bottom, completely bundled up and ready to go, wearing a bright red backpack. He was smiling at me with such delight, and was bouncing with so much nervous energy, that I couldn't help but laugh.

"Why are you looking at me like that?" I asked.

"I dunno," he said, smiling and bouncing on his toes.

"What's in the backpack?"

"Maybe some champagne. Maybe champagne and a glass for me, and maybe a glass for you, if you'll get down here so we can go." I walked down the stairs, summoning calm. *Maybe he's going to ask,* I thought without thinking it, *but if he reads me a poem and we drink champagne in the mountains, that is going to be amazing and perfect. I am not going to be Evil-Ungrateful-Engagement-Obsessed-Chick!*

I looked in the mirror and saw the puffy, pale visage of a person experiencing serious allergies. I smoothed my hair back into an unwashed, slightly oily ponytail. I reached into my pocket and pulled out some Chapstick.

"Are you coming!?" Andrew called, backpack clanking impatiently.

"Hold it together man!" I said. "I'm coming! Calm down!" Then I slipped the Chapstick back into my pocket and put on a little lipstick instead.

WE held hands walking up Kohler Drive. Andrew stopped to take his right glove off, and my left glove off, so we could hold hands properly. We walked for twenty minutes or so, talking and being silent, too. As we made our way up we stopped several times to look back at the valley, made new by the fresh, unbroken snow. The sky was clear and blue and the sound of snow melt, trickling down the muddy veins of the trails, accompanied us.

We reached the Mesa Trail. After going another hundred yards or so, Andrew motioned for me to follow and began to pick his way down a gentle slope, off the trail, until he reached a clearing and a broad, flat rock. "Here," he said.

The rock sat in full sunlight, so we shed our outer layers and used our jackets as seat cushions to set up camp. Andrew took out the champagne and sprung the cork free. We'd made a practice of having champagne at all kinds of occasions to facilitate a mood of perpetual celebration, so this was not so unusual. We raised our glasses for a toast.

"To the mountains," I said.

"To us," he replied. We sipped. I looked at him, and he beamed at me. I smiled back, trying to let him see all the way down to my toes.

Andrew put his hand between my neck and my collar and rubbed his thumb along the base of my skull, quiet. Then he set down his glass.

"So, I *might* have a poem for you," he said, turning towards the backpack and pulling out a small, cream-colored envelope with gold trim. I laughed. It was the stationery I'd presented him with when I moved to New York, soliciting love letters. This was the first time it had been put to use. He extracted three folded stationery sheets, each lined with his careful cramped print. Andrew writes his poems over time, on scratch pieces of paper, crossing things out and making a mess, and in the end copies them neatly onto his delivery method of choice. Every other time he'd written me a birthday poem he'd handed it to me to read. This time he held onto it. His hand was trembling.

"I'm going to read it to you," he said. And then he reached his arm out towards me, wrapping his fingers around my shoulder to pull me in. I took his cue and dug my head into the concave cradle where his shoulder met his chest. I was giving him, and me, some privacy. My heart was pounding in my chest. So was his. I could hear it.

"Dear Kamy," he began. "First of all, I love you. And I always will." I smiled and snuggled, laughing. A quote from the infamous "love letter" he'd written me on his sixteen-day trip to Peru a year after we began dating, which had begun exactly that way and had then turned into a decidedly unromantic *National Geographic* travel article.

"A poem for you," he continued. And then he began. In stanza after stanza, in a strong steady voice, only faltering occasionally, he recounted our life together. Trips we had taken, places we had been, moments of intimacy and trust and tenderness, references to things secret and shared that only we two could decipher. In the beginning his refrain was, *all I need*; in the end it was, *and we were seeking ourselves, and each other . . . and we were seeking ourselves, and each other.*

I began to cry. Over and over, in the poem, he used my name. I wasn't sure if he was asking me, but it didn't matter. He had put us into words.

"Kamy," he said, looking down at me then, so I looked up at him. "I once said I was not the type to stand on a table and declare my love for you." I laughed—a quick, nervous blast—and he shot me a smile. "But now I stand on more hallowed ground. Where I was formed, scraped my knees, understood beauty. Here I stand, gazing into your eyes, and touching your cheeks"—he touched them, his voice breaking—"and covenant to you my love."

I drew my breath in sharply, laughing and crying by then. He *was* asking me. I clasped his hand tightly atop my shoulder, to tell him yes, to steady him, because, somehow, it seemed to me we were doing this thing together.

"As the ancients of these lands said: As long as the grass grows, the wind blows, and the river flows. I will love you. Kamy," he managed, pulling away from me to look directly into my eyes. "Will you marry me?"

By that time I was bawling. We both were. My nose was running, my cheeks were slick with tears, our two faces were so close together that I could hardly see him (he appeared to have three or four squinty, tear-filled eyes), and with the wind blowing and my hair wrapping around my face all was a jumbled, fuzzy, spectacular mess, so I just closed my eyes and kissed him and said "yes" kiss "yes" kiss "yes!" He laughed and cupped my face in his hands and we kissed some more, and then he said, simply, "Good."

And then he reached into his jacket and pulled out a diamond ring. It was a perfect fit. I laughed again and asked him if he had known what size to get, by any chance, because months ago over dinner he had shown a keen interest in one of my six-dollar rings from Venice Beach, even going so far as to try it on his own finger.

"Oh please," he said. "You had no idea." Once the ring was in place he let out a deep, satisfied sigh. "Wait!" I said, practically jumping up and consequently knocking my champagne glass right off of the rock and into the snow.

"Don't worry about that," he said, retrieving it and placing it back on the rock. "It's only my mother's crystal."

"No it's not!" I protested. (It wasn't.) We laughed, a little wildly. We both felt some relief that the most dramatic, ceremonious moment had passed—it had been a strange new dynamic for us, our relationship's first foray into the realm of ritual.

"Listen," I said, as Andrew retrieved the glass and made a to-do out of wiping it clean of pine needles and snow. "This is important."

"What is it?"

"I want to ask you!"

"Okay," he said, pleased, sitting down and drawing himself up to be asked.

"I realize this lacks suspense."

"Why? I could still say no."

"Exactly! So. Andrew," I said, clasping his hands tightly, and locking his eyes with mine, because I wanted my mini-moment to be taken somewhat seriously, at least. "Will you marry me?" I asked, trying not to grin like an idiot.

"Yes," he said, as solemnly as he could through his matching idiot-grin. "I will marry you."

"Yes?" I shouted. "Yes!" I put up my arms in the "V" for victory sign, knocking my champagne glass right off of the rock and into the snow again, but somehow it survived both blows. The wind was picking up, and we had to put our jackets back on. As we huddled together Andrew lifted my left hand and looked at the ring again.

"This thing was burning a hole in my pocket all the way here!" he said.

"How long have you been planning this?" I asked, delighted.

"Why do you think I flew to San Antonio last week?"

This stopped me in my tracks. "Because you had a business trip?"

"Kamy," he said, very proud of himself just then because he could tell that this, at least, was coming to me as a complete and total shock. "I did not have a business trip in San Antonio. I went there to talk to your parents. Not to ask their permission," he added quickly, "just to tell them that I was going to ask, sometime soon, and get their blessing."

I was stunned. Once again, my eyes filled with tears. I had never expected him to do that. It was not the kind of thing, in my mind, that Andrew would do. For half a second it seemed like a weird thing to do, but then I reminded myself that he had done it for me, because I am so close to them, and probably because he knew they'd been beginning to wonder about him. It was another gift. I hugged him again.

The sun was dipping behind the tips of the Flatirons. Our fingers grew stiff and red but we sat quietly on, memorizing things. Eventually Andrew picked up the bottle of champagne and poured the rest into both of our glasses. He put the empty bottle into the backpack and said, "Let's walk down the mountain. I'm starving." So we carried our glasses with us and began to pick our way down the slope together, hand in hand.

It was perfect.

PERFECT. Andrew pulled it off, indeed! It did live up to the hype. It was more amazing than I had imagined. Everything was all better now. We could finally move on.

Except.

Except what? I was thrilled, yes, content, yes, but at the same time a thrum of adrenaline was rising into my ears. A ticking excitement to do . . . what? I was bouncy, punchy, markedly more so than Andrew, who looked like he'd just had sex. I, on the other hand, was itching for action. And I was dying to call my mom.

Which led, within an hour of our becoming engaged, to our first wedding-related disagreement. (If you don't count the preceding six months of unspoken disagreement about the proposal.) He wanted to keep the news to ourselves for as long as possible. I started thinking about calling my mother as soon as we walked in the front door.

"Don't you think it would be better to wait before we tell every-body?" Andrew asked as we commenced cooking dinner. "Wouldn't it be nice to have this just for us, just for one day? We could call everyone tomorrow. They won't mind."

"But I have to call my family to say Happy Thanksgiving," I said. "And I mean, isn't that a big part of this whole thing? To tell your family? To share it?"

Andrew shrugged. Unsurprisingly, considering the totally different journeys the two of us had taken to get to that point, our perspectives were different. To begin with, Andrew had not been the seller who had not yet sold, standing on marriage's front porch waiting to be let in, dying to turn around and tell his mother, waiting impatiently in the idling car, that she could finally go home. (Though he had been the man standing in the doorway feeling increasingly self-conscious about keeping a perfectly nice woman standing on his porch while her mother gave him the evil eye.) More importantly, however, Andrew was not itching for action because he had just pulled off the caper of his life. He'd been planning for months, working painstakingly on the poem, darting in and out of high-security jewel-dens in the diamond district every time he visited New York. (My friend Franny later sug-gested that this is a modern-day "hunting and gathering" ritual, an op-portunity to show off manly skill in the treacherous capitalist jungle.) He had just crossed the finish line of a long race, whereas I, after months of being stuck in impotent, embarrassing limbo, had finally heard the sound of the starting gun.

I was not the type to hear it and take off in the direction of wedding magazines and caterers. But the oft-repeated cliché "the proposal is all about the man; the wedding is all about the woman" underscores the fact that the moment a man and a woman decide to get engaged has tra-ditionally been the moment when a man takes action and a woman does . . . nothing. (Hence many women cope with their desire to do something, finally, by grabbing the baton and plunging into wedding planning.) Andrew had pulled off his Heroic Romantic Moment, yes, but where was mine? I wouldn't have changed Andrew's for anything—

I still wouldn't. It was a beautiful gift. But for all my love and desire to have nothing to do but say "yes" left me feeling like a girl who also had a gift to give, but had to keep it inside.

Very few women have fantasized about proposing, it's true. But many women have fantasized about being proposed to, and I think there is more to these fantasies than dreaming of the day a man shows he loves them "just that much," though lots of women say this is what they crave. In fantasizing about how a man will propose, a woman also fantasizes about how she would propose if she had the chance. *If I were him I would . . .* gives women a way to pleasurably indulge their own romantic feelings, to give life to *their* romantic heroism, to give all the things they want to say to the man they want to marry a voice. But in the end, the voice has to be his.

Women of my mother's generation were supposed to smile and accept being silenced. Women of my sandwiched generation, however, often seem to have trouble restraining themselves from elbowing in on the action. The more subtle drop hints beforehand about what they'd like; the least end up stage-managing their boyfriends' proposals as they are happening. The website theknot.com's feature "Proposals: He Finally Asked! How You Reacted" included several examples of this: one woman described her boyfriend going "on and on" until she interrupted with "Have you asked me yet?" at which point the embarrassed boyfriend did; several women asked their boyfriends to ask again because they weren't ready or weren't satisfied with the proceedings (one made the guy ask three times!); another woman orchestrated a second proposal in front of her family because the first proposal (over breakfast) hadn't convinced people that they were "serious"—and perhaps hadn't convinced her, either. Most women, of course, describe their men's proposals in glowing terms, and even those who might have felt disappointed don't let on. (Worse than a lame proposal is the ungrateful woman who says a proposal is lame.) But is it any wonder that when two people who want to declare their desire to marry are allotted only one proposal between them, men often feel that women are holding them to the oh-so-hard-to-live-up-to *If I were him I would* standard?

It would seem obvious, then, that women would be happier if they had their own proposals to orchestrate, leaving men to plan in peace. But over and over, women tell me proposing wouldn't make them happy at all. I believe there are lots of reasons for this, some of which I've discussed: the way women are raised to think of themselves as objects of love, not as lovers; the way a woman's desire to marry is belittled and devalued as a coercive, untrustworthy desire while a man's desire to marry is valued as a heroic decision that must be made "alone." But there is another reason women want men to propose, a reason that makes reciprocity impossible. Women want men to propose because men are supposed to prove that they are, at long last, grown up. And women don't propose because everyone knows that women are grown up already.

Think about it. Is the proposal the mutual moment when a man and a woman pledge to spend their lives together, or the one-sided moment when a man cries uncle and finally submits to a woman's authority? Too many relationships bear out this sitcom cliché: husbands are reluctant, silly, unruly boys, kept in line (and kept adult) by their wiser, more mature wives. Most women I know would bristle at this and insist it has nothing to do with them, but the notion that women are responsible for making men assume "adult" responsibilities is deeply ingrained in our culture, and it affects all of us. As Barbara Ehrenreich argues in *The Hearts of Men: American Dreams and the Flight from Commitment*, men who resist marriage have always been labeled "immature" (also code for "failing to conform") and women have always been tasked with bringing these men into line by making husbands out of them.

Growing up, I often heard my mother and her friends talk about "training" their husbands, and my father and his friends saying things like "I just do as I'm told," and "she's the boss!" when referring to their wives. Incredibly, in yet another sandwich-generation contradiction, women my age have actually dressed this old-school dynamic up in feminist clothing. A recent *Glamour* article titled "Is *This* Girl Power?" mentions the popularity of T-shirts with "down-with-men" slogans like "Boys are stupid: throw rocks at them," along with the book *Down,*

Boy! A Girl's Guide to Housebreaking a Man as disheartening examples of what the author calls "Bad-Dog Feminism"—an attitude increasingly embraced by baby-boomer daughters, which says not that men and women are equal, but that men and women are *so* different (and women are so superior) that men must be treated like "a bunch of snuffly, leg-humping, loud, messy creatures in need of a good smack on the nose with a newspaper." In other words, women know best, while men are hopeless adolescents who must be brought to heel—or down on one knee.

Men buy into this idea, too, using it both as an excuse for bad behavior *and* as a reason to marry. One man told me he married in large part because he felt like it was time for him to "settle down" and become an adult; his wife agreed and plays the role of disciplinarian in their relationship. One reason I believe Andrew was so adamant about excluding my mother from our deliberations was his angry rejection of the idea that he was a boy who had to be told (by women) what to do. I, on the other hand, resented the implication that I had any such designs on his autonomy. But when so many women treat men like boys (one woman on theknot.com tells of accepting her boyfriend's proposal, then instructing him to get up before his "nice suit pants" got dirty), and so many men seem desirous of a kick in the pants from women (men say they hate ultimatums, but so many depend on their issuance, waiting impishly to be scolded into eating their broccoli/buying a ring), it is little wonder that tension over the proposal is so often characterized in terms of tension between the individual (man) and the society (women)—between grownups (women) and adolescents (men).

This both belittles men's adulthood and encourages their worst impulses. It also suppresses the anxieties *women* have about becoming grownups. I remember thinking that I was going to be a subpar wife because I was not the sort to get Andrew to come home early, eat right, dress properly, and take his vitamins—the kind of wife described in *The Case for Marriage*, where authors Linda J. Waite and Maggie Gallagher argue convincingly that men benefit from marriage largely because their wives make them behave. The truth was that Andrew was more likely to make me behave than the other way around, but this narrative was so strong we played our parts anyway: I cast aspersions on Andrew's maturity, muttering about Peter Pan, and he groused about getting old and becoming the Tamed Husband James Douglas Barron ominously describes in *She Wants a Ring*. The truth was that we both were grownups and we both were afraid of taking such a grown-up step. But Andrew was the one who was supposed to show that he was ready, and I was the one who was supposed to be ready even if I wasn't.

There's one more reason that proposals are not reciprocal, however. They also symbolize a transfer of power. I'm not sure that this was true of Andrew and me, but if I'm honest I'll admit that I was tired of his having all the power, and my having none, and I welcomed the proposal as "goodbye to all that." Many women take this to another level by *physically grabbing* the ring out of their boyfriends' hands before it can be civilly handed to them. Why? It's a power grab, and these women have been itching to make it for years—some of them since childhood, when they first experienced "power envy," as Simone de Beauvoir once put it (as opposed to the overly literal idea of "penis envy") in relation to boys. These are the same women who demand that their men get down on one knee—not just to show that at long last, he is the humble supplicant while she sits in the seat of power, but to show that she has finally acquired the larger public power that is only possessed, in our society, by women who are wives.

Again, this is an inequity that used to be more pronounced. Only a generation ago, women had no power at all outside of marriage. Gloria Steinem, Betty Friedan, and others believed this state of affairs was bad for women and for men: as Steinem wrote for *Time* in 1970, she believed liberating women would mean "No more dominating wives, emasculating women, and 'Jewish mothers,' all of whom are simply human beings with all their normal ambition confined to the home." Has this come to pass?

To an extent, yes. Women my age have been freed to take their ambition public, and men are expected to be "ambitious" at home in a new way, too. But change takes a long time, and it has only just begun. Not only that, but many women my age, sandwiched between feminist rhetoric and reality, are angrier than *ever* at the freedom men enjoy outside of marriage—freedom they still find themselves denied, but to which they now feel entitled, too. Little wonder that women, expected to be mature, mini-grownups even when they actually are adolescents, mightily resent the fact that male adolescence only seems to be getting longer in a post-feminist world. (The editor of *Maxim* pronounced that for American men, it now extends to forty.) Little wonder they feel a sense of vindication or even triumph upon extracting a marriage proposal. Little wonder that they would like, if only for one moment, for that man to get down on his knee.

One woman I interviewed told me men should propose because as things stand, "the balance of power in relationships is so utterly fucked—women have to bear the brunt of the shit in a marriage—child birth, child-rearing, twice the work, often a back-seat career, healthcare for the family, and on and on and on . . . and as a result the marriage proposal fulfills an unbelievably pleasurable romantic fantasy for me. Perhaps that sounds a tad cynical, but I don't think there's a person alive that doesn't feel that in his or her bones when they think about that exchange." I'd say it's a bit more than a tad cynical; I also have to admit I see exactly where she's coming from. But a proposal should not be a moment to codify, reinforce or—as this woman, for all her outrage, suggests in the end—resign oneself to that kind of marriage, or that kind of power imbalance between women and men. Instead it should be the moment when a man and a woman agree to attempt something human beings probably can't ever do, but should never cease trying to do: love one another in a way that leaves power games behind.

OUR first wedding-related disagreement finally resulted, fittingly, in a compromise. I could see where Andrew was coming from: he understood that the second we told everyone our news of our engagement it was going to transform into an event, and the precious, delicate contentment we felt at that moment would be hard to find again. He could see where I was coming from: unlike him, I had not already told my parents the good news, and, being a lifelong people-pleaser, I couldn't wait to share news that would please everyone so much. So we agreed: no family phone calls for a good five or six hours, until evening.

The rest of the cooking took about an hour. We kept bumping into each other in the kitchen, meeting each other's eyes. After dinner we walked into the room with the large window that faces east, where we could see the city lights flickering in the black of the clear, cold night. We lay down together on the woven carpet; I rested my head on top of his chest. We lay there together for a long time in silence, drifting in and out of sleep, in and out of dreams. Something was different between Andrew and me. Deeply so.

I had convinced myself that it wouldn't be. This was one way I'd made myself feel better about not being engaged when I wanted to be. I'd told myself it was all an outward display, a formal, public thing for other people, because what really mattered was the private bond between us, a bond that wouldn't change just because Andrew proposed. But it had. I realized that, even though we would have denied it, the question we'd begun our relationship with: *Are we going to stay together?* had still been with us until that afternoon. Perhaps it was just that the whole exercise of asking and answering it, even if in the affirmative, left us completely for the very first time. (As one long-married friend pointed out, it comes back later.) Perhaps I'd underestimated the power of an "outward display," as though Andrew's and my willingness to announce our commitment to everyone was no different than our willingness to aver it to each other. But we were about to make ourselves accountable in a way we hadn't before. And we each had made a leap of faith that was extremely meaningful and comforting to the other.

I also felt different that afternoon, of course, because the white, two-ton, *are-you-going-to-get-engaged-or-what* wedding elephant had finally stepped off my chest and left the room! It felt like we were alone again, and it was so nice. What I didn't understand was that I was also feeling restored to myself, able to hold my head high after having bent into such forced, convoluted shapes in order to survive the whole proposal thing. I believed that the worst was over. Nothing about getting married, I thought, would put us into such stereotypical, tricky roles again! We had walked through our towering *man* and *woman* doors to join hands on the other side; our interests were aligned once more.

In other words I had no idea what I was getting into, and it was bliss. It lasted for about an hour. At seven o'clock, my eyes snapped open and I sat up. I nudged Andrew teasingly. He attempted to pull me back into my prone position, but I was having none of it. My mother was waiting. It was time to make the call.

My dad answered the phone when I called home. I could hear the clink and clank of Thanksgiving cleanup and many voices in the background (at least thirteen people were there, having driven in from all over the state of Texas) and then the hush as my dad walked into the master bedroom and closed the door behind him.

"Hi Dad," I said, smiling in the goofy, reflexive way you do when you are walking off an airplane and know that family members will be standing in baggage claim waiting for you.

"Hello sweetheart," he said, "and a Happy Thanksgiving to you."

"You too. Did you have a nice dinner?"

"I convinced your mother to let me make jalepeño cornbread but everybody ate potato rolls. But that's all right. This is not a real experimental crowd."

I laughed and said something pointless.

"Uh huh. So. How was *your* dinner?"

"Very nice," I said. "Pretty amazing, actually. I've got some good news."

"Well," my dad said, his voice edged with playful impatience. *"What is it?"*

"We're engaged!" I blurted. "Andrew asked me to marry him!"

There was a brief moment of silence. "Well," my father said, his voice breaking. "Well. I am *very* happy. I'm happy for you. For both of you. He's a very fine man. He came to see us, you know. He flew all the way here to sit down with your mother and me and tell us just how much he loves you. That really meant a lot."

I started to tell my dad the way Andrew had proposed, but he cut me off. "Kamy," he said. "Remember, Andrew was here a week ago and swore your mother to secrecy for *six months*." Six months! I had no idea Andrew had subjected my mother to that degree of torture. "So I ought to put her on the phone *now*!" I wanted to tell him all about it, but apparently mothers must be called in immediately for such occasions.

After a minute she picked up the line. "Hello?" she said.

"Mom," I said. "Guess what."

"Oh Kamy," she said. "My firstborn." And we both started to cry.

AFTER an hour or so on the phone, the feeling of satisfaction from that afternoon was solidified . . . though a little dented. For one thing, my family was already asking about a date! As though the proposal had been a *proposal*, submitted in PowerPoint, as though the presentation of the ring had been accompanied by the production of a calendar, or, better yet, as though Andrew had said: "Kamy, will you marry me . . . on August 12th at five o'clock, and would you like the beef or the salmon?" Still it was one of the happiest hours of my life, and we hadn't even told Andrew's parents yet.

When Andrew called his family in Florida, however, he did not tell them the news right away. He played with the phone cord and chatted amiably for awhile. They talked about the weather, about the convertible and how to get the registration taken care of in Colorado. This drove me crazy, but it perfectly suited his family's style. I sat nearby reading the paper, which he and I both knew I wasn't reading at all.

"So," he finally said to his parents. "I have some news." And then he told them the story. Naturally I listened in. When he got to the "Will you marry me?" part I thought, next comes the part where I asked him to marry me. But it didn't. He left it out.

How could he leave that out?

I waited a minute. Still no mention. Finally I couldn't resist saying, out loud, "And then I asked you to marry me," as though I were just fondly reminiscing, harboring no expectation that my amendment would be passed along to his parents.

Andrew nodded towards me with eyes twinkling. "Kamy asked me to marry her, too," he said, grabbing my hand and squeezing it. "I said yes, by the way."

I smiled at him, feeling sheepish for making such a big deal out of my "Will you marry me, too?" It was silly to insist that it get equal treatment, as though Andrew and I had proposed to each other. I hadn't proposed. I hadn't made Andrew feel the way he had made me feel. I hadn't made myself feel the way Andrew had felt, engineering his proposal to me. My proposal had been an afterthought. So right then, I made up my mind. *I'm going to propose to him,* I thought. And that will fix everything.

LATER I did propose to Andrew, and it was a very good thing. But it was too little, too late, and it did not fix everything. We should have seen that the *way* we got engaged mattered a lot—ironically, in light of all the surrounding drama, we failed to take it seriously enough. At the time, however, we saw only two, flawed alternatives to getting engaged the way everybody else did: I could have proposed to Andrew when I was ready, and he wasn't yet, thereby depriving him of his much-anticipated Heroic Romantic Moment, or we could have decided to marry over a series of sensible conversations, tacitly agreeing to skip Heroic Romantic Moments altogether. But I loved Andrew's proposal. It was a very good thing. It was so good, in fact, that the only bad thing about it was its being so ridiculously one-way, and the fact that for months beforehand we both knew it would be. This was a very bad thing, and couples shouldn't put up with it.

If I had to do it over again, I would not have cried into my Kleenex in Napa while Andrew locked himself in the bathroom, or exchanged veiled ultimatums (me: you better propose soon or else; Andrew: you better stop pressuring me or I'll never propose at all), or blamed myself and Andrew for the frustration and awkwardness we felt around the whole proposal thing. Instead I would have made a bold, third-way proposal of my own. I would have proposed . . . *Proposal Month!* Woo-hoo!

It sounds like a corny homecoming-theme week, but really, Proposal Month could work, and anything is better than the current system that unnecessarily strains couples who love and respect each other, while also reinforcing negative dynamics they may have already been working to change. The idea is simple: when a couple is ready to get married they agree on a month during which each will propose to the other. During Proposal Month, both partners have the chance to propose *and* be proposed to. (A friend and her boyfriend decided "Proposal Weekend" would better suit them, and plan to take a long special weekend somewhere with the intention of proposing to each other then.)

Many people I've talked to about this have objected that the element of surprise would be lost. Wouldn't it have been kind of lame, they ask, if when you saw Andrew standing at the bottom of the stairs, red backpack clanking with anticipation, you'd known exactly what he was about to do because it was Proposal Month? If Andrew and I had designated a Proposal Month, however, I can guarantee you he would have gotten a big kick out of throwing some red herrings my way. (How fun would *that* month be?) More importantly—do you seriously think I didn't know what Andrew was up to?

Of course I did. At the very least I knew it was coming, and this did not diminish his proposal at all. Almost nobody "pops" the question anymore without having reached some tacit agreement about marriage first, which means that when couples talk rapturously of "surprise," very few of them mean literal, "I had no idea he wanted to get married!" surprise. Instead they are referring to the proposal's method and timing. And this kind would mostly be preserved in Proposal Month. What would be lost is the thing that "surprise" really stands for: male initiative and its counterpart, feminine passivity. A proposal shows that a man has gone to great lengths and expense to declare his willingness to commit, that he arrived at his decision on his own and is acting on it freely. It imbues the proposal with the aura of his independence—the ultimate male romantic stance. To say "I surprised her" is to say "I did it because *I* wanted to."

Surprise is also impossible unless one partner does nothing, and in 95 percent of proposals that partner is the woman. A woman's *response* to a proposal—she is "shocked," she cries, she's thrilled, impressed, this has just "happened" to her, she never sought it or pushed for it—shows that she never had any thought of imposing her desires on her man, and would never have dreamed of acting until he did. Her inaction from the time she makes it clear she would accept an offer of marriage to the time the offer is made stamps her acceptance with the imprimatur of her passivity—the ultimate female romantic stance. To say, "He surprised me" is to say, "I had nothing to do with it!" This kind of surprise—not the kind of surprise you would preserve by secretly planning your own proposal—would be lost with Proposal Month, and good riddance.

How would this have worked for Andrew and me? When I was ready, I could have said to Andrew: I love you, we both want to get married, what do you say to proposing to each other a few months from now, are you free in August? And he might have said: I love you, I want to marry you, you want to marry me too . . . how about November? This might have pissed me off. But if I'd known I had to save up my money and buy a gift and fly out to see his parents to announce *my* intentions (I would have liked to have done that, by the way—the idea of recognizing his parents for creating the amazing human being I wanted to marry, and formally telling them so, is a beautiful one, and the letter I later wrote to them was not enough), I might not have thought November was such a bad idea. I might have used the time to think. Or freak-out.

Another major problem with only-the-man-proposes? Too many women do not go through what James Douglas Barron (in *She Wants a Ring*) calls The Great Preoccupation. Women are so focused on being chosen they often don't think hard enough about marriage itself. As one woman put it to me, "I don't know if I'll really know if I want to be married until I'm proposed to. It's like not knowing what to order until the waiter arrives." My friend Suzy described a past relationship in which she was so intent on getting her guy to commit she didn't take the time to deeply ponder her own feelings. "We moved into a house and started a real life together," she said, "and that was when I finally realized he wasn't the one. I was so busy pushing for commitment I never took the time to think: is he the right one for me?"

I had fallen victim to this too, but earlier in my relationship with Andrew, when I became obsessed with if and when Andrew was going to say "I love you." I learned my lesson when, after eight months, he finally said those three little words, and I opened my mouth to answer him . . . and nothing came out! It was very embarrassing after all the complaining I'd done—and eye-opening. I'd had no idea how much my focus on *Andrew's* feelings had been interfering with my contemplation of my own. But at that moment I knew I needed to say "I love you" to Andrew, not just "I love you too."

What's the difference between "I love you" and "I love you too?" Andrew put it to me this way, when I asked: "I love you for who you are in the world," he said, "for who you are even if I didn't exist, for who you are when I'm not in the room."

He loved me, in other words, not for how I treated him, or how I made him feel, or what I did for him, but for who I was. This was beautiful, and it was what I needed to hear. Because while the way someone feels for you and the way you feel for him are inextricably linked—it's not like Andrew sat around nobly loving me from his observation post in another room, he wasn't invisible, for Pete's sakes, this wasn't *Ghost*—at that moment I realized how different it would have been if I'd begun my relationship with Andrew building to my "I love you" rather than to his. Instead I had been building toward the moment when I could say "I love you *too*"—a lot like building to "yes" instead of "marry me."

Over the course of the following year—armed with his "I love you," it must be said—I did experience The Great Preoccupation, putting myself through the soul-searching, panic, and pondering that many men go through as they prepare to propose. (I questioned the sanity of lifelong monogamy, I looked up old boyfriends, I became obsessed with death, I imagined gray hairs growing out of Andrew's ears someday, etc.) Many women, however, find themselves doing this *after* they get engaged; something I believe goes some way towards explaining why there are Bridezillas and not Groomzillas, why there are wedding therapists for brides and not for grooms, why more women initiate divorce in this country and why many men fear their girlfriends are so hung up on getting engaged that they haven't really thought about whether or not they want to be married. "The enormity of the situation tends to hit women in the early stage of engagement," Michael Cunningham, a psychology professor, observed in *Cosmo's Engagement Survival Guide*. "Men have usually thought it out *before they got down* on one knee . . . [while women] haven't done the emotional homework to prepare themselves for the commitment they are about to make."

"There was definitely a point," my friend Amanda told me, "when I caught myself feeling so wrapped up in wanting a proposal that my mind wasn't on 'what would it be like to be with this person forever' but rather 'why isn't he asking me?' A few weeks before the proposal came my head definitely started to swim." A friend of mine's boyfriend once told me that he feared that his girlfriend was so marriage-obsessed that she hadn't really thought about whether or not she wanted to be married, and he was afraid if he asked he'd get something like my "I love you" freeze-up in response. "We talk about *getting* married all the time," he said, "but we never really talk about *being* married."

Jaclyn Geller, in her book *Here Comes the Bride: Women, Weddings, and the Marriage Mystique*, suggests that men are freer to express doubts about marriage than women. She also thinks, however, that marriage in general is a bad idea. I don't. I do think cultural pressures exaggerate men's doubts about marriage just as they exaggerate women's zeal. Women should be freer to express their doubts. Men should be freer to express their zeal. Or, perhaps—if you believe that men and women naturally tend one way or the other—women should be encouraged, maybe even pressured, to explore their doubts and question their zeal, and men should be encouraged, even pressured, to do the reverse. (Maybe men should chant on *Oprah*: "It's okay to want to get married!")

My mother always told me that feminism was about liberating men and women to embrace the best in each other to create a more total, whole way of being. She made this point most memorably when I called her from a pay phone outside my Feminist Studies 101 classroom to ask her if women should learn to separate sex and love, as all men supposedly do (having just heard a lively debate on the subject), and she said, "Do you think feminism is about women being 'liberated' to imitate stereotypical male behaviors no matter how depressingly bereft of compassion or dignity they are? The idea of attaching love and sex is a good one, and if people are so desperate for orgasms they should just masturbate! Buy a vibrator for Pete's sakes!" Betty Friedan dedicated *The Feminine Mystique* to "all the new women *and the new men.*" You can't have one without the other. But being a new woman (or a new man) is hard.

It is, however, the right thing to do. The most common objection I hear to Proposal Month? *Sometimes I just need to be the woman, and I need him to be the man!* I understand. I felt, and feel, that need. But shouldn't we at least *try* to take the very best things about being the woman, and the very best things about being the man, and combine them to make the very best grown-up people, capable of seeing past that need?

Women are absolutely right to value the feminine role of proposee. But what's valuable about being the woman in a proposal is not being dependent, or being paid worshipful tribute as an object of love, or passively relying on another person to make major life decisions for you. It is the ability to embrace being loved and cared for, to derive comfort from receiving love openly without equating that sensation with weakness. It is the acknowledgment that a love-partnership is about letting the beloved take the lead at times. It's being able to say, "I love to hear you tell me how you feel about me; I *need* to hear you tell me how you feel about me" without embarrassment.

It is hard for Andrew to embrace being loved and cared for, to tell me he needs to hear the way I feel about him, to let me take the lead at times. As a man he has been consistently, harshly socialized to avoid admissions of dependence or vulnerability, and he avoids them not just because they might diminish the power that is his birthright as a man but because he has been trained to survive in a world that forces men to deny and repress that part of themselves, often at great expense to their emotional lives. Marriage, of all places, should be a refuge; women should look for ways to help their partners learn to say "yes" to being objects of love, rather than pining away for "marry me."

At the same time, saying "Marry me" instead of "yes" would have forced me to push myself to be masculine in ways that I would like to be. What's valuable about being the man in the proposal is not being in control, or regarding your lover with predatory ownership, or taking charge when it comes to making major life decisions. It is risking loving first, and feeling entitled to do so. It is the ability to proclaim your feelings openly without worrying that it will diminish their worth; it is acknowledging that it is your responsibility to take the lead in a love relationship at times. It's about saying, "This is the way I feel about you" without embarrassment. It was hard for me to detach my love from being loved, to buy Andrew cards and flowers as I romanced *him*, to see my love as an expression of my independence and not as existing at odds with it. But Andrew needed to help me learn to say "marry me"—not just insist upon my "yes."

One final concern overshadows Proposal Month. If I'd had a chance to say "marry me," would I have said it too soon? Many women I know assumed so when imagining what would happen if women were given the "right" to ask. "It would be a disaster if women were in charge of proposing marriage," Marie, a twenty-six-year-old from California, told me. "Man, I know girls who would ask after just one date." (Their counterparts, of course, being men who are so arrogant, that they assume women *do* want to marry them after just one date.)

But this assumption is based on things staying exactly the way they are. Thinking about proposals differently ought to make men and women think about themselves and their relationships differently from the get-go. (And imagine our daughters, if they were raised from girlhood to fantasize not just about being proposed to, but about proposing!) As the sociologist Arlie Russell Hochschild has observed, men and women are given different sets of "feeling rules" as they learn to manage their emotions in socially appropriate ways. When an individual has feelings that are appropriate to his or her gender, they are encouraged and developed. When they aren't, they're ridiculed and squashed. One woman I talked to did propose to her boyfriend, who smiled, demurred, and then pretended it never happened. "I do resent," she said, "that my proposal to my boyfriend seems to count for shit." So she should. When a woman *does* go through the painstaking emotional work to get to the point where she is ready to marry, this process should not be devalued and ridiculed just because she is a woman. "My boyfriend has stated that he thinks I would marry the next person who asked," Sophia, a twenty-nine-year-old doctor in San Diego, told me. "Which I find horribly insulting." Many men think this way, however, because they are all too aware of the "feeling rules" for women—and suspicious that their partners are incapable of thinking (or feeling) outside of them.

True, changing the rules would cause some discomfort, confusion, and pain. But too many women feel caught between being true to themselves and taking part in a ritual that asks them to repress their true selves. Feminism helped psychologists to see that all healthy adults were androgynous—meaning they possessed the best of both stereotypically "male" and "female" qualities (which Virginia Woolf rightly argued should not be labeled "masculine" and "feminine" but simply *good*)—and women should not, when faced with making such a momentous decision as the choice to marry, be asked to regress from behaving like healthy adults. If it is so natural and satisfying for women to passively wait for men to propose, why do so many women feel ashamed, frustrated, embarrassed, and angry as they try to do what comes "naturally"? Why not be "fearlessly sincere," as Simone de Beauvoir once enjoined, and by doing so be more moral, more honest, and more responsible for oneself? And while you're at it, have *fun*?

"I spent thirteen years in an all-girls school," Laura, a thirty-five-year-old venture capitalist from Pennsylvania, told me, "and when prom time came, we had to do the asking. I liked it because it made me really look around and think about who the ultimate date would be." Maddy, a twenty-six-year-old from San Francisco, put it this way: "If women [knew they were going to propose] it would really force women to look inside themselves and wonder if they were ready or not. . . . I also think that if we were traditionally in the role of the 'chooser' we'd have a lot more confidence in ourselves and our choices." More than anything, women ought to *have* choices—real ones. Betty Friedan once wrote about the mistaken choice: the choice women in the 1950s felt they had to make between work and family. Women my age, mouthing feminist rhetoric, make the mistake of choice: using the word "choice" to defend their desire to accept traditional roles even when these roles don't fit. Choice can only exist when real, socially acceptable alternatives exist. When it comes to proposals, they don't.

Andrew and I wanted to believe we could have it both ways—to enjoy the immense emotional satisfaction of enacting our romantic childhood fantasies and remain true to the principles of our grown-up partnership. I don't think this is possible. But even if it were it would still be a failure, because getting engaged is not just about two individuals. It is a public act, with public meaning. And reinventing it has a significance that extends beyond the self. The breathtaking, joyful moment you decide to spend your life with the person you love may seem like the worst moment for picking a fight with your culture. But when you marry, your culture picks a fight with *you*. In the case of the rituals and traditions of weddings, the culture picks a fight with women in particular. And it would be better for women—and for their relationships—to fight back.

three

⌒∞⌒

The Ring

My Baptism by Bling-Bling

So there you had it. We were engaged! Andrew and I had agreed to join forces, to spend our lives together, to have sex a few times a month (as many times as the majority of married Americans muster, according to the Kinsey Institute) until we just couldn't do it anymore, with or without the assistance of prescription drugs. This was the heart of the matter. But it was of no small importance to me that being engaged would bring an end to all the things that had made being a not-yet-engaged woman so irksome. No longer would I feel just a little embarrassed as my boyfriend reserved his option to buy while leaving me on the "for-sale" shelf with my expiration date showing—or feel pathetic for being embarrassed about it. No longer would I have to be reminded that unmarried women—even now that *everything has changed!*—are still treated as objects of pity, or worse, with alarm. No longer would I have to feel that it was my job to be passive and patient (and do my "I'm-so-independent" tap dance, too), because Andrew possessed a power off-limits to me.

In other words I believed, in my fantasy-land version of engaged life, that things would return to normal. Reality check number one? The ring.

It is likely that the diamond ring (with the possible exception of the wedding dress, which is only worn once, not for *life*) is the most emotionally, socially, fiscally, and psychologically packed symbol associated with weddings. Incredibly, I had not considered this. Incredibly, I had not given it a second thought. But that was about to change. One of us walked away from that teary, momentous moment with a ring finger still as naked as the day he was born. One of us, however, walked away with a ring finger conspicuously living up to its name. My re-entry into the world (without Andrew at my side, since he was headed off to Tokyo while I was flying back to New York) was to be my baptism, baby. Not by fire but by ice: my baptism by bling-bling.

I had only been on my own and ringed in public for about twenty minutes when, riding the tram through the Denver airport to my gate, it came to my attention that two women standing next to me were staring fixedly at a point somewhere in the vicinity of my head, but not at my head exactly. I was still feeling serene and a little high, with Andrew's smell lingering on my skin (we'd ridden together to the airport), so it took a moment for this to sink in. But as the tram swung from side to side, these women kept reflexively flicking their eyes to this point, as though staring at the horizon to avoid getting seasick. Curious, I followed their gaze to find . . . my left hand, gripping the metal pole in the middle of the tram. Suddenly all three of us were looking at my left hand. And then, after an instant of incomprehension, I realized that all three of us were looking at my ring. The two women—who already knew this—quickly averted their eyes.

I averted my eyes too. Far worse than their looking at it, it seemed to me, was my standing around staring at it. There is a scene at the end of *The Secret of My Success*, that 1980s Michael J. Fox classic, where in order to communicate that Michael has popped the question we see the lucky woman in evening clothes on a New York balcony, holding her left hand up to the light, turning it this way and that. She is ogling her diamond with such rapt engrossment it looks like she's been lobotomized, and the diamond has done it. I was not going to stand around staring at a diamond engagement ring! Not in public, anyway. I didn't want anybody else to either. So after waiting a few minutes, in order to avoid appearing to rebuke the ladies on the tram, I took my left hand off the pole and slipped it into my pocket. I felt like I had just zipped my fly.

Wearing the ring, apparently, had caused me to attract the attention of women who wouldn't have seen me before. For some people this attention is undoubtedly part of the appeal. For other women, however, a ring that solicits this kind of attention is crass, like wearing a low-cut shirt and a push-up bra. I don't think my ring was crass, but I did later come to call the phenomenon I experienced on the tram Ring Cleavage, because the only thing I'd experienced that even came close was having men stare fixedly, plainly at my breasts. Plenty of women did not stare, however, because they liked my ring—something I generally assume when a man stares at my rack, not my rock. Plenty of women stared because they wanted me to know I couldn't expect to wear a two-carat-plus diamond ring and *not* be stared at.

A few minutes later, the tram slowed to a stop. The moment had passed. But as the women disembarked ahead of me, a funny thing happened. I suddenly found my eyes—and I swear the impulse, at first, was totally unconscious—I suddenly found my eyes darting in the direction of their left hands! Or, I should say, in the direction of their hands in general, because I have never been able to tell my left from my right without holding up my hands to see which one makes the "L." It did not occur to me to use my newly ringed hand as a point of reference in this calculation.

Needless to say I was too slow. Hands gripped roller bags and little kids and people blocked my view, and as soon as I realized I wasn't going to get a look I realized what I'd been trying to get a look at, and I felt icky and looked down at the ground.

"I can't believe I was just trying to check out those women's rings," I thought. "I've never done that in my life! Why did I want to see their rings? To see if they had rings? Yes. To see if they were married? Yes. To see if their rings were as nice as mine? Oh no. Oh yes. I was. I was? Just a little bit, just for a second. Oh my god!"

Wearing the ring, apparently, had also caused other women to catch *my* attention in a new way—or their rings, which suddenly flew into view after having been practically invisible to me before. Lots of women I know have described this spike of awareness around the time of their engagement. My friend Jessica, however, who wears a 3/4-carat ring, resisted it for obvious reasons. "When I do notice them," she said, "inevitably they're bigger then mine. I'm the same way about boobs—I don't notice other women's unless they're pointed out to me, then I realize they're bigger than mine." But I was noticing. That afternoon, having never noticed one that I could remember, I saw diamonds everywhere. And I could tell that my ring was on the big side.

Andrew and I never had a single conversation about the ring. I now realize this put me in the minority of women, but I had only two close ringed friends at the time, and had managed to avoid workplaces where women showed up with fancy rings and all were expected to gather round. (My friend Sarah, an OB-GYN resident in Pittsburgh, laughed out loud when she saw my ring—I'd told her over the phone that I was afraid it was too big—telling me that some of her fellow OBs wore rocks so big newborns risked having brilliant-cut indentations pressed into their heads at delivery.) I was not a jewelry person—or a handbag or shoe person, which are in the same fashion food group—and my mother was not well-versed, either. I was clueless when it came to rings, and that meant I was also totally unprepared for what happened to me next.

I had boarded the plane and was sitting in my seat—a middle seat—minding my own business, when suddenly it jerked violently forward. And the next thing I knew the young woman seated behind me was actually making physical contact with my left hand.

She was holding it, to be exact. I turned to see her face craning over the back of my chair—her arm shoved between my seat and the one next to it—and was met with a look I can only describe as gushy, but also, off my startled stare, somewhat apologetic. I hardly remember what she looked like (the angle was not ideal) but I guessed she was four or five years younger than I was. Her hair was short and dyed blonde, her sweatshirt was pale pink, her earrings were gold, and while these details may seem sketchy I guarantee they are more than she observed of me. She only had eyes for my left hand, and specifically, for my newly acquired symbol of eternal love.

I pulled my hand away instinctively, but she continued staring. For a moment I felt some confusion about whether I ought to hold my hand up for better viewing or stick it into my coat pocket as I'd done earlier. Now I wondered if I'd been a Grinch. *Are diamond engagement rings like babies, or dogs?* I wondered. *Are they meant to invite conversation from strangers, to allow people to share a little joy with you for a moment, to give them a chance to gush and be happy vicariously, even if just for a little while?*

This was a nice idea. With some effort I decided not to put my hand in my pocket, although I didn't hold it up for better viewing, either. I smiled instead.

"Oh my god," she said, "I am so sorry. But that is such a beautiful ring! I just had to get a better look at it. It's *exactly* what I want! Emerald cut, 1/4-inch platinum band, slightly raised setting, but I think I want baguettes, two on each side, half-carat ones, you know?" The accuracy of her knowledge, expressed so handily in diamond jargon, startled me. It shouldn't have. In a world where design-your-own-engagement-ring websites like adiamondisforever.com get 480,000 hits a day and women play fantasy diamond the way men play fantasy baseball, bandying about the stats of the 4 Cs the way my brother and my dad talk ERAs and RBIs, her acumen was really no surprise. Were diamonds the ultimate female competitive sport? I wondered.

"Did you design it?" she asked.

"No," I said, "my boyfriend picked it out."

"Did you just get engaged?"

"Yeah," I said. Then, curious, "Why do you ask?"

"You called him your boyfriend."

"Oh, right. I'm supposed to say fiancé." My delivery of the word "fiancé" seemed to squash our brief camaraderie. But I did not like the word fiancé. I did not like the idea of suddenly saying "When my fiancé arrives . . . " or "Have you met Andrew, my fiancé?" Andrew and I had agreed to get married and now I was supposed to refer to him in French? Fiancé isn't even French, it's Franch. It's like "chaise" instead of "plastic lawn chair." I realized I couldn't imagine using the word "husband," either. Somehow a lot of women who say "husband" sound like they're name-dropping, as though saying, "I was just talking with *my husband*" was the equivalent of saying, "I was just talking with *the president*." And when some men say, "I was just talking with *my wife*," it sounds as though they are saying, "I *am* the president." Andrew was not the president.

"How many carats is it?" she asked, without batting an eye.

This question startled me so much I recoiled, blushing and stammering. I felt like she had just asked me how much money Andrew made—which of course she had.

"I don't know," I lied. Just then, the pilot announced that the plane was about to depart. The young woman retreated. "I'm sorry," she said, "for jumping over you like that." As she sat down I heard her say softly: "He must love you very much."

He must love you very much. This was heart-achingly sweet. I felt like a jerk. But with that comment lingering in my head, I looked at my diamond anew.

He must love you very much. The size or quality of this ring have nothing to do with how much Andrew loves me! I thought. That was ridiculous, although the flight attendant later repeated the comment, and others frequently said the same thing—undoubtedly influenced by ads like those recently run by Cartier, featuring big rocks with the tagline "*What extraordinary love looks like.*" (Sometimes people said: "You must love *him* very much," as though I could not help but love any man who would give me such a honking hunk of jewelry—a concept I found even more disturbing.) If Andrew had followed another career path—pursued a career in public policy, for instance, as he almost did after graduation, and hadn't been able to afford something so expensive, would that have meant that he loved me any less? Or that I loved him any less? Of course not!

On the other hand, *wasn't* it a sign of love? Andrew had put considerable effort and significant resources into giving me this ring. It showed his commitment was serious and real. ("The ring is the proof," as one woman put it.) When I'd showed it to my Aunt Patsy in Colorado, part of what had caused us to smile at each other with unabashed delight was precisely the idea that Andrew loved me very much. Andrew had certainly meant to show me that—and my family, too. I'd felt wonderful about it, proud. Valued.

Valued? As in, appraised? As in, feted for what I was worth?

It was hard not to think that way, as absurd as it was. It was hard not to feel that I had just been anointed as a very worthy woman indeed; "worth" being the key word. Devon, a thirty-three-year-old PR executive in Dallas, told a man she was dating that her friend was spending $12,000 on a ring for his girlfriend. "Oh, you're worth much more than a $12,000 ring!" he'd said, and she'd felt flattered. Another woman's mother, when she saw the modest ring she and her fiancé had chosen because both of them were broke, said, "Oh darling, you're worth much more than that!" They felt *shamed*, and saved up for another. Still another friend got a two carat cubic zirconia "stand-in" ring because she was pregnant when she got engaged, and things were in a rush. "When the 'real' diamond arrived from Europe about six months later," she said, "it was a perfect round one carat. And even though I knew it was stupid, I felt demoted somehow."

Even though I knew it was stupid, I felt awarded somehow. But for what?

I have heard some women say, "Don't let any man come at me with less than a carat." I suppose they mean that a man who offers less than a carat is either cheap or doesn't sufficiently value the relationship. That could be the case. But it is hard to imagine a man saying to his friends: "Don't let any woman come at me with less than a carat!" Not just because it doesn't work that way, but because it would humiliate a man to imply that his girlfriend had the power to value him that way at all. Ringed, I wondered, was I back to that? I the loved, Andrew the lover; I the recipient of the prize, Andrew the awarding judge? Was it possible that rather than shedding that dynamic post-proposal imbalance, I was now wearing it on my left hand?

As soon as that thought formulated itself in my head, I banished it. I did not want to think about my ring that way! For the first of many times to come, I put my bling-bling blinders on. *This ring only means what Andrew and I say it means!* I said to myself. *And when I propose to Andrew and give him a present, it will be all right.*

Just then, as I remember it anyway, the plane banked to the left, and sharp rays of sunlight swept in through the window nearest me, striking my ring. I was instantly surrounded by tiny rainbows, each the size of a dainty tile in a mosaic, quivering with my slightest move. They were everywhere, on the wall, on the curved white airplane ceiling, on the back of the tray table in front of me. I looked around sheepishly to see if anyone had noticed. They hadn't. The young woman behind me was asleep, *People* slumped against her food tray. So I gave in to a deeply pleasurable, private feeling of joy. I thought of him. I thought of that moment. I remembered the first dream I'd had about the ring, the night Andrew gave it to me, in which a male assailant tried to attack me and I vanquished him by punching emerald cut–shaped holes into his face with my left hand. The ring made me feel protected somehow. It definitely made me feel loved.

It was beautiful, this ring. It was a symbol, I told myself, a meaningful, time-honored symbol in the history of marriage—the diamond symbolizing the strength, beauty, resilience, and invincibility of the marital bond, the band symbolizing a joining of two souls so complete that they form a circle without beginning or end. And it only meant what Andrew and I said it meant.

How could it mean anything more unless we let it?

NUMEROUS women have responded to me with almost identical arguments when I've raised questions about diamond engagement rings. First they cite tradition and what the ring symbolizes, often sounding, as I did during my engagement, exactly like an ad written by the De Beers diamond cartel. Then, when confronted by the almost universally acknowledged fact that diamond engagement rings also symbolize many things (too many) that have little to do with pure and enduring love, they pronounce these nastier, far-from-romantic meanings irrelevant because their diamond ring only means what they and their beloved mean by it.

How can an object have traditional, universal meaning and at the same time have only the meaning two individuals give it? The answer is simple: it can't.

Believe me, I know. I tried very, very hard to ignore the universal meanings made perfectly obvious to me as other people grabbed my hand, or stared at my hand, or commented on the ring on my hand in ways I couldn't believe. My experience, of course, was shaped by my ring: just big, clear, and white enough that people's responses to it were exaggerated above the normal levels. This exaggerated response forced me to see a whole bunch of stuff I didn't want to see—like for instance that diamond rings are as much about money and status as they are about love. As with Andrew's proposal and my yes, I wanted to enjoy my diamond engagement ring so much—and felt so entitled to this enjoyment—that I ignored the discomfort my ring caused me and others, namely other women. Engaged women with small rings or no rings are commanded to thrust their left hand forward, but often they are not left feeling "valued."

"Most women glance at my ring and then avert their eyes like I have a scar or something," a good friend told me. (She and her husband affectionately—but with some chagrin—call her ring "the chip.") A woman who chose a nontraditional ring said, "Many people have looked at my ring with surprise and disdain."

I would hesitate to tell a close friend of mine that it was wrong for her to want or wear a diamond engagement ring. I wanted and wore mine. I would say, however, that every woman (single, divorced, married, or dating) could benefit from a reckoning with the rock. Like the proposal tradition, the ritual of the diamond ring repays close attention. Because like the proposal tradition, it tells us what men and women are supposed to be about, and more importantly, what they are supposed to be *for*.

THE first little hole in the diamond-ring defense that says diamond rings are pure symbols of undying love? Men don't wear them. Men buy

them, and women wear them—not because women are biologically disposed to baubles and men are biologically disposed to buying stuff, but
for a lot of other reasons, reasons I intuitively understood as soon as I
stepped out, newly ringed, in public.

I understood, for instance, that many women (à la Charlotte in *Sex
and the City*) view marriage as the sorority they most desperately hope
to pledge, and indeed my enthusiastic neighbor on the airplane had
treated me with the fawning admiration of a freshman during rush—
my ring the evidence that I was *in*, and in good. (One woman told me
her ring made her feel like she was part of a club, "like I should give the
special head nod any time I see another woman with an engagement
ring on.") Marriage is not a fraternity men are climbing over each other
to join, nor do they eagerly brand themselves the instant they've joined
it. Immediately after engagement, the spotlight shone on me, not Andrew, because in the eyes of our society marriage was more important
for me than it was for him. As Jaclyn Geller put it in *Here Comes the
Bride*, the ring is a tangible symbol of *the* critical social victory for a
woman. And unlike the wedding band, which often matches the
groom's in cost and style, the diamond engagement ring, like the proposal, is antithetical to reciprocity between a woman and a man.

My friend Alexandra, who has three beautiful children and a really
big rock, said: "I see other women looking at (my ring) all the time. I
am uncomfortable about this 90 percent of the time because I sense
envy from them. Perhaps because I was single for so long and held so
little hope of having one—the ultimate symbol of belonging, to a club,
to a man—I feel for anyone who either doesn't have one or doesn't have
one as great as mine. It is a 'There but for the grace of God—and my
husband—go I' kind of thing."

Geller also quotes Suzanne Finnamore's novel *Otherwise Engaged*, in
which the narrator describes, post-engagement, "a sense of triumph. It's
primal, furtive, my ovaries cracking cheap champagne. I win." Many
women I talked to said one of the diamond ring's primary functions was
to make other women jealous, "either because you have one and they
don't, or because you have a nicer one than they do." Tia, a graduate

student living in Virginia, described a marriage-panic among the women in her first-year class: "The main cause of this hysteria? In one of our classes the seats were arranged in a 'U' and along one of the sides of the 'U' there were about six women all with *big* rings. So all night, these girls would look at these rings. One of my friends in particular had a freaked-out conversation with her boyfriend every night after that class." A powerful social pressure: a row of women saying (without having to come out and say it): *I win.*

If proposals reiterate the painful truth that men choose, while women are chosen, the ring publicly stamps a woman as chosen for the world to see. It is the desirable woman's prize, and everywhere we see it represented that way: sparkling on the cover of books like *Closing the Deal: Two Married Guys Take You From Single Miss to Wedded Bliss*, featured in ads like the Saks Fifth Avenue spot depicting a delighted woman panting on top of her boyfriend in the park with the big diamond ring she's just fetched gripped between her teeth (*good girl!*), and blown-up in celebrity magazines like *US Weekly*, where the cover story "Hollywood's Twenty-Five Most Romantic Proposals" was accompanied by a full-page "Twinkle, Twinkle" feature with photos of sixteen engaged and married stars' diamonds, topped off by Catherine Zeta Jones' ten-carat whopper.

"It's a symbol that you've found the man you want to spend the rest of your life with," Anne, a lawyer from Seattle, told me. "On a more antiquated score, [it says] you've 'arrived' because a man wants to marry you." In another sandwiched generation contradiction, women my age, purportedly freer from fretting over marriage than any previous generation, may actually have made diamond rings a bigger deal than ever (and bigger than ever—according to a study conducted by the Fairchild Bridal Group, engagement rings were the "top growth category" between 1999 and 2005, leaping from an average price of $2,982 to an average price of $4,146, a 39 percent increase), not just because they are marrying later and, via their boyfriends, can afford bigger rings, but because they are more pessimistic than any previous generation about marriage and perhaps seek to compensate for this insecurity partially by requesting, and receiving, pricier pledges of it. For these women, the sense of triumph and relief upon "landing" a ring can be acute in a whole new way.

I felt this. A man wanted to marry me and I was wearing his desire around town. It was thrilling. (Alexandra also described the ring as a woman's "ultimate life accessory.") The symbol of his commitment to me was worth so much. Worth more than mine to him (making it more important to proudly display) because he was a man, and men have more trouble committing. Worth more because he was a man, and men choose. Worth more because he was a man, and men are, well . . . *worth* more.

As in, worth more cash.

The second hole I found in the "diamonds-are-pure-symbols-of-undying-love" defense? Love is not the first thing that springs to most people's minds (or out of their mouths) when they see a two-carat-plus rock. J-Lo's love may not have cost Ben a thing, but everybody knew her six carat pink diamond cost him a fortune. Lots of women don't get big rings, or even rings they like—and lots of men can't yet afford the rings they'd like to give, either. But as time passes and fortunes accumulate, couples may upgrade. *Upgrade.* A perfectly logical term when you consider that the diamond ring symbolizes something else, something made clear by the series of questions Andrew was asked by almost every diamond seller he met: "How much money do you make? How old are you? What do you do? How old is your wife? Who do you socialize with? Who does she socialize with?" and finally: "How much money do you make again?"

I wasn't just wearing Andrew's commitment on my left hand. I was wearing a couple of his paychecks. (The De Beers salary calculator, featured on practically every page of adiamondisforever.com, rigorously enforces *this* universal meaning of the ring.) Men may not be climbing over each other to join the fraternity of marriage, but they have been known to step directly onto each other's heads in their quest to join the fraternity of the successful male. A diamond engagement ring is a neat way of letting one's newly appointed spokeswoman advertise one's success very clearly (in our case, as clearly as a VVS_2), and while this is a cynical way to talk about a gift that brought tears to my man's eyes, burned a hole in his pocket as he plotted its perfect presentation, and filled him with love and pride as he slipped it onto my hand, it was hard for me to hold on to those meanings when one meaning seemed to talk the loudest.

I CALLED Andrew the night before I was due to go to Columbia for my first post-engagement graduate school class.

"I'm kind of nervous about going in there with my ring," I said. I was sitting in my studio apartment on my couch, the first couch I'd bought with my own money. My job as a television producer had just begun to earn me some when I'd decided to stop doing it. Now I was living in an apartment the size of Andrew's bedroom in LA, furnished with my teenage bedroom set, assorted stuff donated by my family when I'd graduated from college, and the few things I'd bought myself. Andrew had owned his own home for four years by then and had furnished it like a grown-up. When we moved in together officially, most of my things were going to go. How I was going to feel when I moved in with Andrew in January carrying little besides my books, my clothes, my knickknacks, and some Body Shop products in my arms—a modern day trousseau?

Suddenly Andrew's conspicuous success, and my lack of success thus far, seemed very worrisome.

"Nervous?" he repeated, curious. I hadn't said anything like that to him yet. I hadn't expressed any ambivalence about my ring at all. "Why would you be nervous?"

"I just don't know anyone very well there yet," I said half-heartedly.

"Okay," he said cautiously, after a minute of silence from me. "So . . . ?"

"I don't know!" I said. We both started laughing. I dropped it.

But the next day, as I walked out of my apartment and up the hill on 116th Street to the Columbia campus, it was my stomach that was dropping. I knew why I was nervous. I felt like I was out of control of my identity. The past few days had provided me with ample evidence that my ring was going to talk without my permission. An ad by the jeweler A. Jaffe in *Brides* reads, "Some jewelry speaks louder than words." They got that right. And in that environment more than any other, I wanted my ring to shut up.

What was I afraid it might say? Most women I've asked initially aver (as I did) that they don't judge a woman based on her ring—you don't know whether she or her husband picked it out, you don't know whether it's a family ring or whether it's new, etc. But when pressed, most agree on one simple thing: a woman's ring instantly tells you whether or not she has money. As Mary Peacock succinctly put it on women.com:

> Etiquette decrees that a man present his intended with the biggest and best rock he can afford, putting the couple's wealth and status on permanent display on her left hand. If she prefers antique garnets, they must endure the assumption that he can't afford more. If a diamond is petite, it's pitied (just try saying it suits your casual lifestyle). If it's reminiscent of a small swimming pool, it invites equally unwelcome speculation about your fiancé's finances and your joint taste for conspicuous consumption.

"Happily," Peacock quickly adds, "most people don't dwell for too long on the financial signals emitted by engagement rings." Right. Which is why you chose to begin your article by talking about it. "My immediate reaction is to say that the diamond engagement ring represents commitment," my friend Devon, a thirty-two-year-old PR executive in Dallas, said. Comforting. "My immediate reaction as to what others may think, though, if you have a big ring, is not, 'Oh, she's engaged' but 'Wow, the guy she's marrying must have a lot of money.'" Not so good. Corrie, a food writer in San Francisco, expressed what I was really afraid my ring was saying: "I assume anyone with a huge rock is a socialite with a boob job." Oh no.

I had only been in school with the other MFA students for about twelve weeks by then. But as I approached campus, my image of my fellow students—struggling writers, twenty-something artists sacrificing for their art—took on increasingly romantic proportions. I edited out the students I knew were being supported by wealthy parents, as well as the few students I knew of who were married. Instead I grouped everyone together into one big bar-tending, bohemian, chain-smoking, whiskey-drinking, cold-water-flat-living, struggling-artist mass. And I knew with absolute certainty that this mass could not contain, without some measure of disdain and distrust, a twenty-seven-year-old fiancée with highlights and a rock.

"This doesn't mean anything, this doesn't mean anything," I thought to myself as I walked into class, smiling lightly when in fact I felt light-headed with defensiveness, anticipation, and guilt. "This ring only means what Andrew and I say it means, this ring only means what Andrew and I say it means. . . . "

I sat down. About two seconds later I burst. "How was your Thanksgiving?" one of the two women I'd sat down next to asked me. "Andrew and I got engaged!" I said, flushing but suddenly determined that nothing about this was bothering me at all. This was happy. People would be happy!

"Let us see the ring!" they said. I showed it to them. And they said, almost in unison, "Damn. What does Andrew do again?"

By then I knew that many women (at least one of these women, I was sure) were capable of assessing the approximate worth of a ring at a glance. As I withdrew my hand from inspection I remembered this, and felt that I had just been seen naked. Except, horribly, it wasn't me naked. It was somebody else naked, somebody else's body! Because *I* couldn't afford this ring, it had nothing to do with me or who I was or what my priorities were, I was a grad student living off savings and government loans in a studio apartment, wearing a hand-me-down coat. But then there was this ring. It was invading my privacy, talking about me loudly in the third person while standing right next to me, saying: *This chick isn't going to have to wear hand-me-down coats for long! (She won!)*

No one in that building was paying anything close to the kind of attention to me that I was paying to me, of course, but my ring did not go unnoticed. After class a woman I did not know so well approached and asked to see it. In her eyes was a kind of cold malevolence, belying her broad smile. (One woman I interviewed said several women "angrily" praised her three-carat ring.) "Very niiiice," she said. And I realized, this woman felt like I was stepping to her! The ring didn't just symbolize my prize in the land-a-man sweepstakes, or Andrew's money and the fact I'd gotten my hands on it, or that I had "sold." By wearing it I also appeared to be *purposely* saying those things to other women. My ring was talking smack. My friend's husband John has described certain women as wielding "attack rings," and at that moment I knew why.

I walked out feeling shell-shocked. I looked at my ring, which I loved so much. Just what *was* this all about? I wondered. Again, my experience was exaggerated—not only because I had a big ring, but because of the disparity between Andrew's and my incomes. Most twenty-something couples I know are not in this situation, or not so starkly; a poll conducted by Match.com showed that 48 percent of respondents date people with roughly equal incomes, and in fact 20 percent of men dated women who earned more. Many women have also established themselves more firmly in a career by the time they marry than I had. The ring, however, anticipates (and helps to enforce) a reality that overtakes most couples *after* marriage: while many dating couples earn roughly equal salaries, most married couples don't, particularly after they have children. (The loss of income women suffer with each child they bear has been well documented.) It is especially rare for a woman to be the primary breadwinner in her family. Only 17 percent of married women earn $5,000 or more than their husbands do, while 60 percent of married men earn at least that much more than their wives.

In other words, as time goes by, men make, and control, more money. A man's primary function in our society is to earn—it is also his primary qualification to marry. According to a study cited by *Mother Jones*' article "For Richer or Poorer," an increase of one dollar per hour in a man's wages increases the odds he will marry by 5 percent.

It isn't hard to see why some men resent their default provider position. The likelihood, for example, that any of the male poets and writers in my class at Columbia would marry a female version of Andrew was low. But if these men did find provider wives? It's hard to imagine any of them accepting a flashy diamond as a symbol of their agreement to marry, much less consenting to show off such a symbol in public. It would be humiliating. Yet somehow this was not supposed to humiliate me.

Why do men, not women, propose? Because men are seen to be offering something, while women are seen to be accepting it; because men are seen to be assuming a burden, while women are seen as being relieved of one. This prejudice ignores the fact that most wives work outside the home, and it completely discounts the burden women assume as wives and mothers—labor to which society still assigns paltry monetary value (and therefore little value, period). In this light, many things about the pre-proposal dance take on a different cast. The accusation that all women are "guilty until proven innocent" of hunting for commitment is revealed to be an accusation of treasure hunting: women are guilty until proven innocent of trying to get their hands on a man's patronage. This also underlies the element of surprise in a proposal—a woman's passivity is also her best defense against this thinly veiled questioning of her character. As Edward Jay Epstein reported in his *Atlantic* article "Have You Ever Tried to Sell a Diamond?", "the element of surprise, even if it is feigned, plays the same role of accommodating dissonance in accepting a diamond gift as it does in prime sexual seductions: it permits the woman to pretend that she has not actively participated in the decision. She thus retains both her innocence—and the diamond."

The implication, of course, is that the woman doesn't just retain, she gains. "Landing a man" means "landing a man's money"—and the chance to live off it. Marie, an artist in New York, said, "Women get the good ride at this one point. It works for me."

What, exactly, is "the good ride"? If Marie was referring to being so wealthy one can afford to play tennis all day while hired staff care for one's home and children, very few women get it, married or not. Very few *people* are that wealthy, but it remains a fact that while boys are taught to aspire to wealth by earning it, girls are taught to aspire to wealth by marrying it, and statistically, this advice is sound. Yes, feminism has made a tremendous difference by upping women's ability to earn, but it isn't hard to improve on practically nothing, and one only has to skim U.S. Census data to see how firmly wealth remains in male hands. In 2000, only 3.8 percent of full-time women with a bachelor's degree earned over $100,000 a year, compared with 16.1 percent of men. The overall income disparity between these two groups was nearly $16,000 a year. The more money you're talking about, the more pronounced the gap. On *Fortune* magazine's 2001 list of the country's 400 wealthiest individuals, 358 were men and forty-two were women. Of the forty-two women, thirty-three had inherited their wealth (as had twenty-seven of the men). But married to most of those 358 men? Very wealthy women indeed.

This state of affairs among the country's elite has a huge impact on the "success narrative" boys and girls internalize and later bring with them to their relationship negotiations as they approach marriage. As Linda, a married twenty-nine-year-old illustrator from New Jersey, put it to me, "both men and women are after a sense of security when they leave home, [but] men are brought up to believe that they provide this security for themselves and their families while women are nudged to think that they will only be completely secure when they find a husband."

Why do men propose? In the basest terms, because men are hiring, and women are applying; because men are buying, and women are selling. The diamond ring perfectly embodies this transaction—and advertises its price. Talk about crude.

Again, it is a gross oversimplification to apply this wholesale to most individual relationships. I certainly repudiated it when it came to mine! But when I ask women, "Assuming there is such a thing as a marriage market, who are the buyers, and who are the sellers?" almost every single one instantly replies that men buy, and women sell. Rather than feeling angered and indignant at this state of affairs, however, and resolving to continue the battle to even the playing field, an unfortunate number of sandwiched women again prove themselves adept at combining feminist rhetoric and traditional thinking in a ludicrous way, actually attempting to present high-end husband hunting as an empowering pursuit. This gives rise to articles like *Marie Claire*'s 2003, *go-get-'em, girl!* article titled "Wanted: $mart, $uccessful, $ingle Men," which dressed up a fifties sentiment in twenty-first-century clothing. Pronouncing: "Feminism freed me . . . to sell myself *only* to really rich guys!" isn't empowering, it's gross.

Many sandwiched men are no better. They too tend to embrace feminism only as far as it suits them, claiming to want a woman who is financially independent, who won't be a "drain" on their resources (the "I'm-so-independent" tap dance is very much the "I'm-financially-independent" tap dance when it comes right down to it) and who will "contribute" within the marriage. But while men my age do indeed want a woman who works, they are less likely to be comfortable with a woman who earns considerably more than they do. On the reality show *The Bachelor*, the male prize's prize-worthiness is generally put in terms of his ambition and success—but the yummy bachelorettes' vocations (from the first show) included "event planner" (the winner), "Miami Heat Dancer/Physical Therapist" (the runner-up), and "Hooters/Insurance." ("Hooters/Insurance" made it to the second round, unlike the one doctor, one lawyer, and one neuropsychologist.) Yes, almost all the women had jobs (only one "college senior!"), but not the kind of careers that put women in the position of competing *with* men rather than *for* them. "Don't be a mooch," these men warn women, "but don't be a man, either."

As it stands, the diamond ring tradition tells couples, just as they are about to begin their lives together, that the ultimate romantic act is for a man to spend money on a woman, and for a woman to be gratefully in his debt. Again, this does not accurately describe many couples' financial realities, but the narrative is so powerful it overwhelms the facts, and more importantly it informs couples' sense of themselves, each other, their partnership, and how to conform to the larger social norm—all of which makes it very difficult to resist. Buying something the couple can use together undermines the socially prescribed meaning; a woman spending thousands of dollars on a nonfunctional gift for a man undermines it; a couple pooling resources to buy the ring undermines it. But the very *idea* undermines equality between men and women.

I could not think in these terms that evening in New York, or at least not so clearly. I was reeling with mixed emotions as I walked back to my apartment. More than anything I felt hurt, like the competitive, status-driven, money-fixated goings-on around my ring were threatening to turn the most beautiful thing in my life into something ugly. Safely home and alone again, I started crying. I called Andrew.

I never said anything about the ring. I couldn't. But I did unload the emotions and fears I felt at the time—about becoming a dependent, about losing my sense of self as an individual, about becoming a wife. He reassured me. He told me how successful I was going to be someday. Andrew may have been attracted to my wish to write, thinking (as I had) that it would be a compatible career with motherhood. But he had always demonstrated a respect for my ambitions that was unflinching and real, and had always made it clear that my professional life, in our life together, would be a priority. That night, he helped me put my anxieties in perspective. I told him I was going to start calling him my finance instead of my fiancé. He actually thought this was funny. He was a good sport.

I never asked him the question that was really on my mind. What was he thinking when he decided to buy me this ring?! I told myself the answer was simple: "I'm in love, and this is the most beautiful diamond I've ever seen." That night I sat in bed and stared at my gift, smiling and repeating: *this only means what we say it means; this only means what we say it means; this only means what we say it means*, until I believed it again.

Almost.

Two weeks after Andrew and I got engaged, we met up in Cincinnati for my college roommate's wedding, in which I was to be a bridesmaid. In that short period of time I had managed to forget my ring issues almost entirely. I had discovered an upside to this whole ring/engagement thing, and I was milking it for all it was worth.

The epiphany came the week after I got engaged. I'd been having trouble with the movers (of a firm I had dubbed "Cheap and Macho") who were coming to move my couch, bed, and kitchen stuff downtown to Andrew's and my new place. (His things weren't going to arrive until later so we were moving mine, one last time, as a stopgap.) These guys were trying to add all kinds of extra fees. Suddenly, in the midst of another exasperating phone conversation, I said, "My fiancé is going to be helping me with this move." It was a small thing. I didn't say he was a corporate big willy. I didn't say he was threatening to hire a different moving company for my third-hand stuff. But it was as though I'd said, "I'm an adult," where before I'd been a girl. I sounded like my mother when she said, "This is Mrs. Wicoff" on the phone, using her wife-voice—as authoritative as my dad's doctor-voice. It worked. They backed off.

Later I broke out the f-word with American Airlines because they were giving me a hard time about using Andrew's frequent flier miles for a ticket. "I'm booking these for myself and my *fiancé*," I said, feeling shameless but inspired. That *really* worked.

Naturally, dropping (name-dropping) "fiancé" made me sound more adult. Marriage is, or ought to be, an adult activity, and when Andrew alluded to his marital status it would make him sound more adult, too. But it made me sound adult, period! Career success distinguishes the men from the boys; marriage and motherhood distinguish the women from the girls. In her book, Jaclyn Geller cites an article in *Brides* which read: "Even if you already own a condo, spend vacations in the great museums of Europe, and run the family business, in most societies that diamond on your left hand is a signal that you've really grown up." My friend Devon complains that when she goes home to visit, she is still treated like her parents' daughter, rather than like a grown-up, adult woman. She feels—rightly I think—that as soon as she marries this will change. A thirty-three-year-old man with a successful career as a PR vice president at one of the biggest firms in the country (like Devon) would not be treated like a boy until he proposed marriage to a woman.

There was another reason, however, for the power of "fiancé." The movers hadn't suddenly treated me with respect only because I was going to be married. They'd also changed their tune because by saying "fiancé," I had threatened them with a man.

The ring did not just symbolize money; it was also a sign that said, "Mess with me and you don't just mess with a woman, you mess with a man, too." (This reasoning drives single women to recruit male friends to accompany them to auto dealerships, even when they know exactly what kind of car they want to buy—the man's presence puts the other man "on notice.") I knew this intuitively, but it is worth pointing out that for most of American history coverture guided laws regarding the married: wives were "covered" by their husbands, who acted for them in all official respects, and women had no legal right to conduct their own business because business could *only* be transacted between men. Thanks to the advances of feminism, I had been conducting my own business for years before I teamed up with Andrew. Plenty of the men I dealt with did not give me my due, but I did my best to force them to contend with the reality that very often, the buck now stops with women, who have bucks of their own to spend and know how to manage them. Part of me cringed at the idea of copping out now by trotting Andrew out on my left hand. But part of me was happy for the help.

At the Embassy Suites in Cincinnati, for instance, I happily advertised my soon-to-be-married, grown-up status. "I'm checking in for myself and my *fiancé*," I said, having completely overcome my allergy to that word. When Andrew arrived he grabbed my left hand like a proud papa, having missed his baby, and I didn't mind one bit.

Then we left the hotel, and I got wakeup call number two.

It was a mid-sized wedding, unpretentious, warm, and full of Midwestern folks. Everyone was incredibly nice. But my ring . . . well, as my Aunt Patsy had prophesied when she saw it, it had grown three sizes as soon as I'd left Manhattan. ("Don't worry," she'd said when I'd expressed concern about its size. "It'll grow and shrink depending on what part of the country you're in, and you won't get a second look in New York.") In Cincinnati I attracted attention in a way I hadn't yet experienced. It wasn't just that every time I said I was engaged, people automatically said, "Let's see the ring!" (As if to say, *"Prove it!"*) I expected that by then. It was that even when I was minding my own business, perfect strangers would come flying toward my bling. It was on this trip that I nicknamed my ring The Deathstar for its tractor beam–like pull.

First it was my roommate Clarissa's three great-aunts. After an initial, avid inspection, they took to crying in unison, "Have you seen her *ring*?!" every time I walked into a room. At the church Friday night, the wedding consultant actually left Clarissa's side, in medias rehearsal, to cross the room and examine my hardware. "I saw that ring when you came in," she said teasingly, as though I'd been coyly keeping it from her. At dinner, three different people pointedly asked me what Andrew did for a living, and oh, how many carats? Then, at the reception, a woman I had not been introduced to sidled up to me on the dance floor, leaned in to my ear, and said, "I don't know how you keep from falling over, wearing that ring on your hand."

By Sunday brunch, I was in full freak-out mode again. Walking up the sidewalk to Clarissa's brother and sister-in-law's house, I said to Andrew, "I am feeling really weird about this ring." It was the first time I'd said it out loud. He gave me a quick, concerned look, at which point the holiday-wreathed, jingle-belled front door opened and the great-aunts spotted me from their perch on the couch. "Everybody!" they cried, and I am not kidding, there are witnesses, "Have you see her *ring*?!"

The only women left who had not seen it gathered around me dutifully. I weakly tried to act the part—in a sharp role reversal, after pressuring

Andrew to grow up and propose, I was now supposed to act like a delighted child showing off a present while Andrew stood off to one side, the mature and beneficent father, eating his frittata. He was the man, above it all, while I was surrounded by women who felt varying degrees of envy, boredom, admiration, apathy, and irk, but who all felt compelled to smile and compliment me. "It's a constant hand-grabbing, oohing and aahing fest with her girlfriends," John Mitchell, author of the snide manual *What the Hell Is a Groom and What's He Supposed to Do?* writes. "They will continue to grab each other's hands well after you're married to view this piece of compressed carbon."

Andrew was hardly sneering, but many men do. On the one hand, standing back smugly while women gather is not an expression of superiority but a defense—because the ring symbolizes a *woman's* power, too. ("The diamond ring is the 1950's female power totem," as Alexandra, stay-at-home mother of three, said.) I was definitely seen as empowered; after all, I had gotten Andrew to permanently, publicly renounce his freedom, to give me his marriage! Men may attempt to neutralize a woman's new power by patronizingly saying, "You know girls, they love to gather around silly jewelry," but as all the other guys know, this power can be formidable. Ask any man kicked out of the driver's seat the instant wedding planning starts.

Despite this, however, I *did* feel silly. And plenty of men are quick to say how silly they think it is to spend a small fortune on a diamond, suggesting they do it grudgingly or at least indulgingly. *Esquire's* "Things a Man Should Know About Marriage" makes this point by saying, "Some women believe expensive diamond rings are silly and expensive. We've not yet met one." (In other words, we've not yet met a sensible woman.) *Glamour's* "Ask Jake: A Man's Opinion" column was more forthright: theorizing what the world would be like "if it were all up to men." Jake suggests that, "All diamond mines would shut down . . . because instead of spending two months salary on a piece of ice, we'd spend it on the down payment for a modest beach house."

Lisa, a thirty-two-year-old freelancer in New York, said, "My husband thinks it's the worst tradition ever, just as bad as what Hallmark has done for Valentine's Day. He may think this because he had to buy the ring, but he offered me a plasma-screen TV instead and I almost took it." Amanda, a twenty-nine-year-old writer, was also offered an alternate engagement gift—a painting by her favorite artist. "[My fiancé] kept insisting that it's all marketing."

These men were genuinely prepared to skip the ring, but the truth is that Jake is full of shit because most men aren't and won't. Most men, in fact, are very attached to the idea of buying a diamond engagement ring, and for every woman who told me her husband resisted there were many more women who told me they tried to talk them out of it. "I wanted a ring, but not a diamond one," said Anna, a twenty-eight-year-old writer in New York. "But when we were looking, Greg kept encouraging me to look at diamonds. 'Don't you think this is nice?' 'Don't you think this looks so timeless and classy?' He was being completely genuine and sincere, and it was clear to me how much the tradition meant to him." Anna now wears a diamond, as do many other women I know who would have preferred a different kind of ring or no ring at all.

Men like Greg are often motivated purely by a sweet sense of romance, but many men also feel the ring directly reflects their manhood, and they don't want to go public with a half-carat hard-on. Because of the immense pressure on men to qualify as providers before proposing, some feel intense anxiety about proving themselves, and some spend absurd sums of money on rings they can't afford. "[My fiancé] became obsessed with size," Rachel, a property manager in Washington, D.C., told me, bringing to mind another male obsession of similar provenance.

"I've got a girlfriend with a *gigantic* ring," Leslie, a thirty-seven-year-old full-time mom in LA told me. "I know it's not her personal choice, but one that her husband picked out to show off his earnings." Interestingly, men who self-righteously insist on ignoring "other people's opinions" when it comes to proposing almost always cite "other people" when explaining their insistence on buying a diamond. Obviously the party whose sense of womanhood or manhood is most associated with a particular custom has the most at stake in publicly participating in it. Just as women are highly focused on getting engaged, men are highly focused on buying a ring that will make others take note. "I wanted to show I was serious," one friend's fiancé told me. (She'd wanted a Heavenly Bed instead.) "I didn't want people to think I was cheap," another man confessed.

Like many men, of course, Andrew had also been thinking, "I won!" (He frequently, teasingly tells me "I won!," in fact, sometimes when we go out at night and he thinks I look beautiful, or other times when he's feeling particularly happy and pleased.) And standing in that living room being admired—even though as a woman, trained to think of myself as an object, I sometimes found it quite enjoyable to be objectified that way rather than in some other ways I could mention—I couldn't help feeling that while the ring was my prize, I, *me*, myself, was Andrew's. He didn't have to wear a flashy diamond to show what he'd acquired. All he had to do was point to me and say, "Mine."

"Men like to have that sparkling carbon 'deed' that women like to show off," Alexandra said. "She says, 'I belong to somebody!' and he says, 'That one's mine, and from the size of that rock, you know I *mean* it!'"

To be honest, I usually get a huge grin on my face when Andrew looks at me and says "I won." I feel a thrill of pride. At the same time, I would hope—as with so many things—that this feeling of having hit the jackpot is reciprocal, and not a case of Andrew gesturing to me and saying, "I won!" meaning, "I own!", leaving me to gesture proudly to my ring and say "I won!" meaning, "I'm *owned*!" Standing by that post-wedding breakfast brunch table, however, I wasn't so sure. I wanted to take the ring off, take that group of women gathered around me, point them in the direction of Andrew, and say, "I won!" Because Andrew and I belonged to *each other*. I believed this, and I knew Andrew believed it, too. So in the rental car on the way to the airport, again filled with mixed emotions and an overriding sense of guilt for caring how those infamous "other people" reacted to my ring, I only managed to say, "How did you choose this ring?"

Andrew smiled and turned to me with a look of genuine concern coupled with, to my irritation, amusement. He seemed to think all my ring-related misadventures that weekend were kind of funny.

"Sweetie," he said, "come on. Everyone just thinks it's beautiful! There's nothing wrong with that." I felt like he'd just said, "Everyone just thinks you're hot!" after I'd complained about men making crude comments to me on the street. He wasn't wearing the goddamn thing! He wasn't wearing anything at all! I wanted to tattoo him at that moment; to haul him into a back room and brand him on the forehead. I wanted him to spend a minute in my shoes—or in my ring.

"Did you think about any of this when you picked it out?" I asked him. It was the closest I'd come to showing my frustration. I still delivered it with half a laugh.

"I just thought it was so elegant and simple," he said. "And I thought about you and your style, about getting something that suited you." He was driving. It was cloudy but he was still squinting, as he often does, only turning to look at me occasionally.

"It is my style. It is. But it's elegant and simple and kind of *big*," I answered.

"It's not that big!" he retorted. I know Andrew had hoped the ring would speak highly of him to my family and friends, but I'm certain he hadn't wanted it to speak too stridently—that was not his style. He is very competitive, but his style is to downplay it. "I almost got you something a lot smaller," he told me, the first I'd heard of that, "and I was just about to buy it when at the last minute they brought me this, and it was just so incredibly beautiful, I felt like I had to get it, like it would be crazy not to once I'd seen it. I just wanted to, you know, I just didn't think, I mean. . . . " He trailed off. Neither of us spoke. Without looking at me, he grabbed my left hand, the hand closest to him.

I got it. Spending more than he'd planned to, more than seemed rational, had seemed like the right thing to do. I squeezed his fingers. It seemed like that to me, too.

I felt incredibly lucky. As Jessica, proud wearer of the 3/4-carat ring, later told me: "Every time I look at it I think about how excited and nervous and crazy-in-love he was when he went all by himself to pick it out. It cost way more money than he should have spent at the time, which I find both romantic and ridiculous." Years later, having made it in the world, her husband worries that the ring makes people think he's either cheap or unsuccessful, and he hates the idea that other women have something to lord over his lady. (And him, let's be honest.) "If he could," she said, "he'd steal it off my finger in the middle of the night and replace it with some huge rock. But I've threatened him with everything from maiming to divorce if he does that, so he won't." Now that's romantic.

"It's disgusting of me," said Amanda, the writer from New York, "but for some reason I'm hard on the women with the big rings . . . [but] about the women with the small rings, I make all the nice assumptions. I imagine him working hard to earn it. I imagine them being poor but in love and trying to make it."

The thing is, not everyone is as fiercely loyal as Jessica, or as sentimental as Amanda. And women with small rings are subjected to plenty of humiliation and unkindness (not to mention respect and admiration) they don't deserve, while women with big rings are treated to respect and admiration (not to mention humiliation and unkindness) they don't deserve, either. A small ring from Andrew, who had succeeded so early and so well, would have been strange. A big ring from Jessica's husband, at the time they decided to marry, would have been impossible. But we are both judged by the rings we wear, and our husbands are judged by them, too. That's the way of the world, and, like it or not, it's the way of diamond rings.

THREE and a half years after I got married, I took my ring off and dropped it into our safety deposit box at the bank. I'd been wearing it more than four years. Andrew and I decided to leave the diamond in ring form, because it is so meaningful to both of us that way. I take it out to wear on special occasions. The last time was as a surprise to him on our anniversary, and seeing it on my finger made him all misty. It made me misty-eyed, too. Afterward I kept putting off returning the ring to the cold metal drawer it calls home, "forgetting" to go by before the bank closed, "having" to wear it over the weekend, and thinking a lot about why I took it off. Like the ring in *Lord of the Rings*, the power of the ring almost overpowered me. But when I finally took it off again, I instantly experienced the relief and peace I'd felt when I'd relinquished it the first time.

I still have a hard time explaining to some people in my life why I don't wear it. But Andrew understands completely, which helps a lot. He now sees, as I do, how far diamond rings have strayed from what the scholar Joseph Campbell described as the essence of the marriage vow: "I take you as my center, and you are my bliss, not the wealth that you might bring me, not the social prestige, but you."

There was another thing, however, that made parting with my ring much easier for Andrew and me: researching the roots of the diamond ring tradition. Very few people know exactly where the "tradition" comes from, but many of the women I interviewed speculated that the history of the diamond engagement ring was really the history of a company and a brilliant ad campaign, and one woman got it exactly right: "De Beers needed to sell diamonds, and they launched a vast marketing strategy during the early 1900s [it actually didn't get going until 1938], and it was totally swallowed by American culture." After more than sixty years, this marketing campaign is still going, with De Beers spending nearly two hundred million dollars a year ($33.5 million of it on magazine ads, a number surpassed only by Nike, Sara Lee, and The Gap) to reinforce the "tradition" it spawned for untold financial gain. To date, no other country has fallen so hard for De Beers' hard-sell, though Japan runs a close second. (According to Stefan Kanfer's *The Last Empire: De Beers, Diamonds and the World*, less than 1 percent of Japanese women wore diamond engagement rings in the 1940s; by the 1970s 75 percent of them did.) In Europe, only Britain has shown remotely the same susceptibility.

The historical roots of the "tradition," such as they are, do appear to be European, however. According to adiamondisforever.com, the De Beer's website devoted exclusively to marketing:

The tradition of giving a diamond engagement ring as a promise for marriage began in 1477 with Archduke Maximillian of Austria and Mary of Burgundy. . . . From this time forward, the royal tradition of giving a diamond engagement ring began to be embraced by people around the world, eventually becoming as much of a milestone in one's life as the engagement itself.

It's the bit about "from this time forward, the royal tradition of giving a diamond engagement ring began to be embraced by people around the world" that is a stretch, if not an outright lie. For one thing, from 1477 until the late nineteenth century, diamonds really *were* rare—so rare that prior to the late nineteenth century, when diamond mines discovered in South Africa proved capable of generating twenty million carats in fifteen years (nearly the number produced in two thousand years by India and Brazil combined—the only places, heretofore, that diamonds had been found), only royalty could afford them. And Americans did not embrace them as engagement rings until De Beers realized it was facing catastrophic overproduction (catastrophic for the price of diamonds) and set out to make diamonds the only legitimate symbol of engagement.

Prior to 1938, the year the advertising agency N. W. Ayer took over marketing diamond rings to Americans for De Beers, diamond rings were worn by some American women, but they were hardly considered an engagement requirement. By the end of the 1950s, however, as Edward Jay Epstein recounted in his *Atlantic Monthly* article about the history of diamond marketing, N. W. Ayer gleefully reported that "since 1939 an entirely new generation of young people has grown to marriageable age, [and] to this new generation a diamond ring is considered a necessity to engagements by virtually everyone." Half of all American brides received diamond engagement rings by 1950; just ten years later the number had risen to nearly 80 percent. In an astoundingly short period of time De Beers and its marketers made the diamond engagement ring, in their words, "a psychological necessity," successfully convincing young couples that if they couldn't afford a diamond they should wait, save, beg, or borrow rather than skip it.

"Eighty-five percent of American women own at least one piece of diamond jewelry," Matthew Hart reports in his book *Diamond: The History of a Cold-Blooded Love Affair.* This is good for De Beers because every day of the year, also according to Hart, 328,000 carats of diamonds come out of the ground. (Even more mines have been found in Russia and Canada over the years. "Eternity rings" were invented to cope with the glut of small diamonds from Russian mines that had to be marketed and sold.) "The ingeniousness of De Beers' marketers," Hart writes, "lies in having forged a link between something people do not need, diamonds, and something they do need, love." They've forged links with other human emotions, too, of course. As Nicky Oppenheimer, inheritor of the De Beers fortune, once said, "My grandfather used to say that in their dependence on gold and diamonds, the Oppenheimer fortunes were based on human stupidity and human vanity. I prefer to rely on human vanity." And so he does.

De Beers has also been incredibly effective at convincing women and men of diamonds' "eternal emotional value," thereby preventing them from selling and disastrously flooding the market. (In "Have You Ever Tried to Sell a Diamond?" Epstein made a clear case that turning around and selling a diamond, once purchased, is very hard, and others have made the same point since.) As Robert N. Proctor observes in his forthcoming book *Agate Eyes,* there is one flaw, however, in their creation of "the perfect consumer good": the fact that diamonds, barring divorce or remarriage, are needed only once. Like the wedding industry, De Beers finds ways around this, recently pushing "three-stone" anniversary rings, for example, sales of which grew 54 percent in 2003 after already growing 74 percent in 2002. In September 2003 (tied to the opening of *Cat Woman,* no less), it launched a "right-hand ring" marketing blitz. In a pitch-perfect perversion of feminist rhetoric targeted at sandwiched women, the "right-hand" ring campaign suggests that if women feel oppressed by the retro, sexist, maddeningly unshakeable importance people place on acquiring the approving "stamp" of a diamond engagement ring, they should rebel . . . by buying a diamond ring *themselves* and wearing it on their right hands! The ads flatly undercut any feminist message, of course, by alternating in emphasis between a woman's right hand and her left ("Your left hand purrs. Your right hand pounces. Your left hand asks you 'when.' Your right hand tells you 'now,'" etc.), aiming to inflame *all* sandwiched women's insecurities at once, rather than settling for just one. The ads barely disguise their real text: "Your left hand wants desperately to be married. Your right hand is embarrassed by this. Women of the world, forget trying to figure out why or how to change it. Just buy more diamonds!"

Recently, after years of prodding, the cartel agreed to join in preventing the trafficking of "conflict diamonds" used by rebel groups to fund horrific and bloody civil wars in Central Africa. This is laudable, but I became so cynical about the diamond trade during my research I would not be surprised if De Beers calculated that global outrage at the carnage could be used to their advantage in restricting, in yet another way, diamonds' supply—thereby increasing, in yet another way, their price. Stores like Saks Fifth Avenue now offer diamond "birth certificates" to keep purchaser's consciences clean, but in light of the difficulties of determining a diamond's provenance, and the havoc the trade has wreaked on millions of Africans, conflict diamonds are yet another reason to opt out.

It is not only a testament to the power of De Beers, however, that despite all this, rejecting the diamond ring as the symbol of engagement would *still* be hard. It is also a testament to our need to conform, our need to participate publicly in tradition (even in those manufactured by corporations), and our need to adhere to the gender roles that underlie the presentation of a diamond by a man, to a woman. I resisted parting with my ring for a long time, even though I was more acutely conscious of my discomfort with it than most women I know. Throughout the years I wore it, I coped by saying to myself, "I am not going to let (that awful person/De Beers/my insecurities/the worst of human vanity) take this beautiful tradition away from me!" But I should have been saying, "I am not going to let myself (be a billboard for De Beers/participate in something that makes women feel bad/wear a diamond price tag)—I am going to find something else to do instead."

Many couples already do something else. Requesting a totally different sort of gift, like a titanium bike (one woman I interviewed was thrilled to receive this as her engagement gift), is one possibility, though still flawed by being one-way; pooling resources to buy something both partners can use is another. I like this idea, though I'd probably opt for a painting over a plasma-screen TV—having something that lasts and can be passed down through the generations seems more in keeping with the spirit of the union being forged. When it comes down to it, I remain attached to the idea of rings ("Once you let go of a symbol, what will you use to replace it?" as one woman pointed out), because they are always with you, because rings (not diamonds) *are* objects of historical significance in the history of marriage, and because they constantly remind the wearer of his or her commitment. "It's the most expensive thing I've ever owned in my life," Amanda said. "It was so strange to me, carrying this precious thing everywhere I went. But then, I guess that's it—a marriage relationship, this person, is suddenly the most precious thing in the world, and it's like they're constantly there with you."

The ring, obviously, should not be as expensive as it often is. (According to an article in the *New York Times*, Jewelers of America reported that grooms spent $4.3 billion on diamond engagement rings in 2004.) But at the same time it also seems romantic and appropriate to invest in it—because the fact is that investing in something monetarily is one way to show, and, frankly, to test, commitment.

In Denmark, both members of the couple wear engagement rings. They wear them on their right hands until, at the wedding ceremony, the rings are transferred to the third finger of the left. If I had to do it over again, I think I'd do what the Danes do. Miss Manners sneered at the idea of engagement rings for men, saying, "Miss Manners is not listening to the cry of tradespeople who want to supply such items," but it is hard to imagine a more ridiculous objection, particularly as it suggests that engagement rings for women have nothing to do with tradespeople. The fact is that women could benefit from saving up for such an object too, as a demonstration of *their* seriousness—and it would be especially romantic if they chose to propose with it. I also might consider an entirely new option, created by friends of mine after reading the opening chapters of this book. The man in question, a very creative, resourceful, and romantic guy, found a jeweler in the city where he and his girlfriend had decided they wanted to marry, and together with his fiancée asked the jeweler to make two engagement rings for them, his in white gold, and hers in yellow gold. They then requested that the jeweler attend their wedding and, after the ceremony, melt the two rings down (something the guests can watch if they like) to create two entirely new rings, made from a hybrid of metals utterly unique to them.

This solution, so fresh and beautiful, is further evidence that if one is willing to jump out of the diamond-ring box and think differently, the possibilities are endless. I discovered this for myself when, about five months after I put my diamond engagement ring away for good, Andrew happened to lose his wedding band in my Aunt Patsy's pool. The loss stung and we looked everywhere for it, but it was gone. Eventually we saw that we had been given an opportunity. That fall we visited a jewelry designer who suggested we create two rings using our shared birthstone, the ruby. Both would be made of platinum, but mine would be studded with 1/4-carat rubies all the way around, while Andrew's would have ten matching rubies set into the band's inner ring. We got them just in time to wear them to my family's Christmas gathering that year. I wish we'd gotten them in time for our wedding.

four

Home

Weddings Are Women's Work

Within days of our engagement, Andrew and I made a pact. No wedding planning until after the New Year. This seemed like the right thing for so many reasons, reasons that multiplied as my ring-related experiences and other weird engaged-woman moments increased my unease about the whole wedding thing. There was only one problem. We were spending the Christmas holidays (in other words, the last remaining days of 1999) with my family in Texas, and my mother, naturally, wanted us to get married there. In fact, she'd raised the subject of visiting potential wedding sites in San Antonio over the holidays within minutes of my telling her the story of Andrew's proposal. Despite this, Andrew dispatched me to Texas (he was to follow me a few days later, since I was spending nearly two weeks at home and he couldn't take that much time off work) with this directive: "Remember, no wedding planning until the year 2000! *United front!*" I waved to him as the cab pulled away and thought, "Yeah, right."

This "yeah, right," however, had been solely directed at the notion that Andrew and I would get away with spending a week in San Antonio without looking at wedding sites. I had not been expressing any doubt that Andrew and I would be a united front when it came to planning our wedding. Whenever I had given any thought to wedding planning, before or after getting engaged, I had always assumed, if in a vague, general way, that Andrew and I *would* be a united front, operating as a wedding-planning team, fair and balanced to a fault, sharing the labor and the load without any of that *the-bride-does-this, the-groom-does-that* crap—particularly of the "the-groom-does-*nothing*" variety. I knew Andrew was not the kind of groom to say "just tell me where to show up," and I was not the kind of bride to say "just get out of my way." About that, I was right—Andrew was a very "involved" groom, and I was hardly a show-runner bride.

This did not mean, however, that in the end we shared the load equally. Instead, despite the fact that Andrew actually cared a lot more about many wedding details than I did, I still became the point person, the one with the things-to-do lists and three-ring binders, the wedding-workhorse and the hub. Why? Not because I was in graduate school and he was working full-time—though I told myself this was the reason. Plenty of women who work full-time assume primary responsibility for wedding planning, too. They do it because wedding planning is the first kind of labor a woman performs as a wife.

As such, it is a very significant thing because marriage—though men and women my age don't like to think of it this way—is not just about love but about labor, and how it gets divided. Ninety-four percent of the twenty-something never-married Americans surveyed by The National Marriage Project agreed with the statement "When you marry you want your spouse to be your soul mate, first and foremost," rejecting the idea that marriage is primarily a partnership devised to raise and rear children (only 16 percent agreed with that), and maintaining, as 82 percent of respondents did, that women should not rely on marriage for financial security. (A similar question was not asked about men, nor were respondents asked whether men should rely on marriage as a way to raise children.) The notion that marriage is solely about soul mates, driven by love and far above, or at least not about, children or financial entanglements, probably stems from my generation's fear of divorce (only love will keep us together!) but can eventually drive couples to divorce, too (if we aren't in love anymore, why stay married, what for?).

I, too, subscribed to the notion that the only reason to marry was because you'd found your soul mate, and it is a testament to the power of this idea that, despite having already struggled with issues of money, womanly dependence, and role-playing when it came to my relationship, I not only attempted to dismiss these issues after my engagement (we're in love, we'll work it out!) but *actively repressed thinking about them*, because they were, quite simply, unromantic—and romance is what engagements and weddings are all about.

Right? Right . . . except that engagements, as I'd already discovered, are also about codifying a very specific kind of relationship between a woman and a man, and wedding planning is about this, too. In fact, it is a form of training camp, putting brides and grooms through their wife-and-husband paces in preparation to assume these roles. And nothing could have been more effective in forcing me to contemplate this than going home for the holidays, where I could not help but be reminded of the way my parents have divvied up the work in their marriage . . . or wondering how Andrew and I would.

IF Andrew's house is best described as Modern Colorado Academic, my house is best described as Classic Texas Suburban. There's a basketball hoop and a grill out back, trimmed hedges in the front yard, dried flowers in the family room, cowboy art on the mantle, a big-screen TV in the living room (accompanied by about ten remote controls), and yellow wallpaper in the kitchen. There is always a grocery list going next to the telephone, and a case of bottled water in the fridge. My family moved there when I was eleven, and I think my parents will be there for a long time to come.

It felt good to be home. During the evenings I spent alone in my old bedroom, in the glow of the copious Christmas lights my dad puts up every year (which make our house look like an old-school Mexican restaurant crossed with a disco), I managed to ignore the *USA Today* article titled "Record Number of Couples to Wed in 2000," a.k.a. the "You

Better Find a Wedding Site *Now*" article, which had been left suggestively on my dresser drawer. I was beginning to feel fairly optimistic, in
fact, about upholding Andrew's and my no-wedding-planning-till-2000
pact. This optimism had been considerably abetted by an unforeseen
event—one that had instantly yanked my mother right out of the
Mother-of-the-Bride role she'd been planning to inhabit upon my arrival
(in the preceding weeks, she'd already begun teasingly signing her emails
to me as the "M.O.B.") and placed her directly into the mother-of-a-
sick-child role she'd inhabited dedicatedly for years. Just before coming
home, my younger sister Kimberly, in a drunken bar brawl (she might
contest that, but it sounds sexier than "I stepped on the curb wrong,"
which is what actually happened), had managed to break her foot.

This event, while annoying, embarrassing, and painful for my sister,
had not been so bad for me. Because from the moment my sister arrived, my mother had been completely focused on helping her heal, and
this had granted me an unexpected reprieve from any discussion of
wedding planning for the first few days of my trip. "You owe me one,"
Kimberly had whispered to me when I'd hugged her hello, managing a
grin. "With my crutches and my broken foot, I have completely drawn
her off the scent."

Three days in, however, my sister was on the mend, and my mother's
brow had begun to unknit. I failed to sufficiently note this on the third
evening of my stay, however, as I blithely wandered into the kitchen
where my parents were finishing up a casual dinner. My mother was
standing next to the wood block island, eating a yogurt and reading the
paper. My dad was at the kitchen table doing the crossword. I opened
the refrigerator. My mom put the paper down. Her eyes, clouded over
for days with concern for my sister, had a refreshed, enlivened aspect.
This aspect was trained on me.

"Soooo?" she began breezily. "Have you thought any more about
going to see some wedding sites while you're here?" As though the
thought had just occurred to her.

I flinched, and focused on the contents of the refrigerator. Then, as
calmly as I could, I turned around and smiled back. "Mom, didn't I al-

ready tell you? Andrew and I decided we'd rather not think about any wedding stuff until after the New Year." I shot a hopeful glance at my dad. It appeared that his crossword had just gotten very absorbing.

"Well, you have an idea of how many people you're going to have. And you want to do it outside. And you want to do it in the summer. Didn't you say something about Labor Day weekend? I'd say you've done some thinking about it." I realized my mother had extracted all that information from me, which wasn't even really thought-out enough to be called information yet, in the preceding weeks over the phone. Somehow I instantly felt Andrew was responsible for this. He had set the tone with all his . . . activities! Flying to San Antonio to dine with my parents and announce his intentions, then doing a big romantic proposal, then giving me a ring that screamed big wedding and then wanting to have a big wedding, a desire I apparently shared but wasn't sure truly came from me.

"Mom, I'm asking you. Seriously. Please. I really, *really* don't want to do this now. I really, really don't. Okay?" I felt desperate, which seemed excessive.

"Well that's up to you of course," my mother replied. "I just think you should know that if you wait much longer you probably won't be able to get married in San Antonio."

"Mother! Are you serious?"

"I'm perfectly serious, Kamy. I work with these places all the time. And I know for a *fact*, having talked for many years with the staff at places like the Don Strange Ranch, that they book up years in advance." My mother had worked part-time as a tour guide for ten years. She only missed one out of a hundred questions on the certification test. It was later established the test was wrong. Her authority was considerable.

"So what are you saying?" I asked. "You want me to tell Andrew that if we don't look at these places now we can't get married here at all?"

"Doesn't Andrew want to get married in Colorado anyway?" my dad interjected.

"Not necessarily!" my mother let out, turning to face him with an irritated scowl. "I'm saying that I don't know when you and Andrew are going to be out here again so it seems silly not to at least look. At least you can pencil your name in."

I put my head in my hands. Her logic was impeccable. She was trying to help! And I wanted her help, I really did. So I said, "What do we have to do?"

And she was off. She'd already made some preliminary phone calls. She already had a short list. I tried to discuss things with her like a calm, normal person. How many people, really? What time of day? What sort of place? A DJ or a band? Buffet style or sit-down? Somehow, on that topic, we came around again to the weather.

"You don't want to have a buffet-line outside on Labor Day weekend in San Antonio, Texas," my dad said. "People will be sweaty and hot and uncomfortable in their formal clothes, and nobody's gonna wanna eat in those conditions." My dad had been participating throughout this planning session, whenever he'd had something to say.

"Those *conditions*?" my mother repeated. "I've been to plenty of perfectly nice buffet dinners during that time of year. . . ."

"Outside? With the mosquitoes and heat and the humidity? And the flies buzzing all over the place and landing in the food?"

"Flies!" my mother cried, as though my father had called her mother a whore. I almost laughed. Almost. "*Flies?* You act like rats will be crawling around spreading the plague! For goodness sakes. Flies. At any outdoor event, winter or summer, there are flies! Flies are a fact of life!"

"Calm down, Mom," I said. She bristled. My mother was not going to calm down. The M.O.B. was defending her turf. The F.O.B. never really wanted a piece of it anyway. The next thing I knew my dad was putting the crossword down and getting up from his chair. He was laughing with that no-win-situation, beleaguered-husband laugh.

"Dad," I said, near pleading. "You can help! We should all be a part of it, right? You should come look at wedding sites with us!"

My dad looked at me as though I'd just made a startling joke. "This is obviously an emotional issue for your mother," he said in his low, steady psychiatrist voice. "And I've learned over time that with issues like this, it's better for me to just stay out of it."

"Well," my mom said as he left to go watch the local sportscast, "I suppose that is true if your input is going to be about nonexistent *flies*."

And that was the last I ever heard from my father about anything having to do with planning my wedding.

I<small>N</small> a sense, this was no surprise. I never really expected my dad to be involved in planning my wedding. It wasn't his job. His job was his job, and my mother's job was to take care of just about everything else. This is not to say that my dad doesn't do lots of things in addition to working very hard to provide for his family. He does dad things, like taking out the garbage, replacing doorknobs, grilling outdoors, grocery shopping (this may be particular to his dad list, because he loves strolling aisles of food), and carrying luggage. This is also not to say that my mother didn't work outside the home: she has worked part-time for many years, and has rarely been uninvolved in volunteer work, too. It is my mother, however, who packs the luggage, keeps up with the bills, arranges repairs, does the laundry, does the ironing, runs errands, sends birthday cards, stays in touch with family, cares for her aging parents, and, when she had three children at home, did all the innumerable other things you do when you are a full-time mom. As with many women of her generation, this was how her life worked out, and it was not always okay with her. As with many women of *my* generation, I grew up knowing it.

The story of my mother's life has always loomed large for me, but until I came home that winter, it seemed like a story completely removed from my reality—because my mother (and father) had committed themselves to removing it. My father would never have said to me, as my mother's father said to her, "No man will ever want to marry a woman like you." (Brilliant, competitive, "fresh.") Instead he told me I was beautiful, and praised me copiously for my smarts. My mother never recruited me to be "mother's little helper," as her mother had enlisted her, to wash Monday, iron Tuesday, shop Wednesday, bake Thursday, and clean Friday. Instead she told me, again and again, that I could do anything, go anywhere—that as long as I worked hard, she and my dad would do the rest. My mother's father, on the other hand, an engineer and plant manager in the small East Texas town of Orange, took out a map when my mother told him she'd gotten a full scholarship to her dream college in the northeast, stuck one end of a metal compass into the dot that was Orange, swung the other end out to create a radius of two hundred miles, and drew a fence. "This is where you can go to college," he told his eldest daughter, who was soon to be named her high school's valedictorian. "And you can't go to Austin or New Orleans." Half of the circle was in the Gulf of Mexico.

She was bitterly disappointed, but growing up, my mother had already learned that the world had little to offer a girl. The only traditional female occupation that appealed to her was teaching, and while she hoped it would be something she would only "have to do" until she married and had children, she also realized it would be a good backup in the event that her father was right about her marriage prospects. "I didn't see myself as my own agent of change," she said, "and so I fantasized about marrying a man who would be successful enough to rescue me from a life of drudgery."

She did. My father, who lost his father when he was four and grew up with considerable hardship as his widowed mother worked to support three children, was determined to be a professional and a success. Perhaps because he grew up with a very strong woman, he thought my mom was spectacular and sexy. He also thought she would be a great mom. At ages twenty and twenty-one, the two of them began a life together. My mother taught biology until, at twenty-four, she had me. "I transferred all my ambition to motherhood, even though I wasn't optimistic about it," my mother told me. "I didn't think it was going to be fully satisfying, but I had no other ideas. Then I had you! And I thought, 'Wow!' this is a whole lot better than I thought."

Eighteen months later she had my sister, and, two years after that, my brother Reid. By then it was 1976 and my mom was a twenty-eight-year-old mother of three. My father had earned his medical degree and begun a successful private practice; she was a doctor's wife and a mother—all (and more) that she ever had imagined as a girl. But the world was on its head, and even in San Antonio, Texas, feminism had begun to make her world, and her accomplishments, seem small. She read voraciously about the pros and cons of daycare as she contemplated beginning a career, and began taking coursework at the local university. We had a sitter in the afternoons. In 1983, she was accepted to a Ph.D. program in psychology at the University of Texas in Austin. My dad couldn't move his practice, so my mother bought a Honda Accord and determined to commute. She did it for a year. I was in sixth grade; I became an insomniac. She quit.

Of course it is not as simple as: my mother would have gotten her Ph.D. but she was born at the wrong time, and by the time the world changed she had three children she was determined not to leave or hurt. Lots of other things contributed to what happened, or didn't happen, for lots of other reasons. But in a way the message she sent me *was* that simple. *It's too late for me, but there is no reason for you to sacrifice your ambitions because you are a girl.* And this led me to a vague but dearly held sense of entitlement to a totally different life, as a girl, as a woman, and as a wife. I would never be faced with what Betty Friedan, in *The Feminine Mystique,* called "the mistaken choice," between being a mother and having a career. I would (simply!) have both.

Here was the fantasy: my husband and I would both work outside the home and inside the home, neither of us bearing either load in a grossly disproportionate way. We would be a dual-career couple and a dual-parent couple, too; neither of us would play the stereotypical roles defined by "husband" and "wife." It did not take my engagement, however, to show me that this might be trickier than I'd hoped. Even in LA, when Andrew and I were both working full-time and traveling, I did a little more laundering, cleaning, and social planning than he did, and he did a little more mowing, hauling, and earning. (I was working just as hard as he was, but he was earning a lot more money—something that was particular to our jobs then, but a state of affairs that becomes nearly universal as men and women continue with their careers. Women earn nearly half this country's law degrees, MBAs, and medical degrees, and have for some time now, but they make up only 15.6 percent of the country's law partners, 6.6 percent of its top-earning doctors, and 15.7 percent of the corporate officers in Fortune 500 companies.) On the other hand, Andrew's mother, god bless her, made him start doing his own laundry when he was eight, and he was the one who sewed on my buttons. I had a good one. It wasn't bad.

Around the time of our engagement, however, which coincided with my becoming a graduate student and our moving in together full-time, these minor inequities quickly became more major. I did start doing all the laundry, being home from 8 a.m. to 5 p.m. for the cable guy, and keeping us in toilet paper. And Andrew kept jet-setting. The thing was, this very traditional labor sharing suddenly, terribly, seemed to make incontrovertible *sense*. And we didn't even have children yet! (Leslie, a thirty-seven-year-old mom in LA, said she had a "modern relationship" until they had a baby, at which point they immediately slipped into "the typical wife and husband roles.") But it was hard to argue: why *wouldn't* I pay bills, arrange for repairs, do laundry, and do dishes, when Andrew was earning the money I lived on? (Never mind that I was a full-time graduate student with plenty of work of my own.) And why, when it came to planning our wedding, wouldn't I assume primary responsibility for that, too?

Yes, things between Andrew and me were different than they had been for my parents. But while I may have entertained fantasies of playing the groom ("Just let me get my dress and tell *me* where to show up!" as Felicia, a thirty-three-year-old television executive in New York, pleaded), the prospect of wedding planning triggered some deep, inexplicable, unexpected sense of duty in me. I felt compelled to assume the role of wedding planner, and to prove myself in it. This sense was powerfully reinforced by the structure of wedding magazines and websites, all of which are directed at brides, with things-to-do lists for women, not for men. Little wonder that when I read my first bridal magazine, I felt like I was being given a syllabus. I told myself these lists were for me *and* Andrew to divvy up, but even then, despite Andrew's earnest assurances, I knew it wouldn't work that way. True, it is no longer cool for a man to say "just tell me where to show up." But does that mean weddings are now man's work, too?

No. In all my interviews I found only one case where the roles of bride and groom were truly reversed. A friend of my friend Terry's was not particularly interested in a wedding, but consented to let her fiancé plan one as long as she could have nothing to do with it. He agreed. The deeply entrenched notion that women plan weddings, however, was so powerful that, as Terry told me, "despite the fact that most of the wedding people had never even met [the bride] until the day of the wedding, on the wedding day they all ignored him and constantly asked her questions. At one point the florist said, 'You are the calmest bride I've ever seen,' in response to which this woman pointed to her fiancé and answered, 'I'm not the bride, *he's* the bride!'" The florist was very confused. "Bride" and "wedding planner" are so synonymous, in other words, that if a man does something as bizarre as planning his wedding himself, he becomes one.

Many women go to great lengths—as I did later, pointing proudly to Andrew's "contributions," like visiting wedding sites, florists, and caterers, arranging for alcohol and his own tux, among various other things—to reiterate that *their* man was different, *their* man shared the load! (One woman, in a typical sandwiched woman contradiction, managed to tell me both that "my fiancé is involved almost as much as I am" and "it's frustrating when I feel like he doesn't want to have anything to do with it.") But while bridal magazines flourish, *For the Groom* magazine folded after just two months. With regard to wedding planning, in fact, many women described a division of labor to me that sounded a lot like the running of a modern household: men were "involved," participated in "decision-making," and were responsible for things that were "their area" like liquor, music, and anything technical. But, as one friend put it, "much more of the nitty-gritty fell to me." Her tone of resignation reminded me of Naomi Wolf's description, in her book *Misconceptions*, of women "calling it fair" when they assumed disproportionate domestic duties at home, choosing to ignore the imbalance because they could not see how calling it like it was would change anything.

I also "called it fair," but when it came to planning our wedding, much more of the nitty-gritty fell to me. True, I was between semesters at graduate school but, just as with child-rearing, most women who assume primary responsibility for wedding-planning are also working full-time. "Sometimes I felt like I had so much to do in so little time, on top of a full-time job, that my head would explode," one recently wed bride told me. Wedding work is the first shift of the second shift, and the way couples handle it sets a tone. One wedding guide recognized this, but could only muster the most pathetic kind of faux-empowerment:

> Gone are the days when the groom-to-be's role was simply to show up at the church on time. . . . Ten to one, you'll be doing the lion's share of the work necessary for the wedding and reception, but to let him get off scot-free sets a bad precedent! After all, do you want to be doing all the cooking *and* all the dish washing after you're married?

Hell, no! Yet women who would never tolerate men who won't do the dishes *will* tolerate men who do little more than "approve" choices for their own weddings, failing to see that this establishes precisely this kind of pattern for the future. *Modern Bride*'s fall 2005 issue, with its things-to-do lists aimed exclusively at women, also featured an article discussing the difficulties of the first years of marriage, and again and again brides complained of being tasked with "traditional" wifely duties, like house-keeping. One man explained his refusal to wash a dish by saying, "My dad didn't do that." This made his new wife very angry, but I'd be willing to bet that—just like his dad—he also had very little to do with wedding planning and expected the low expectations to hold.

Most men are not such retro dolts, of course. In fact, as *Time* magazine reported in October 2005, eighty percent of grooms are now "active co-partners" in wedding planning. But what does it take, one wonders, for a man to earn the title of "active co-partner" in wedding planning? Doing *something*, anything? Making phone calls? Showing up for a wedding-related meeting or two? Consenting to be consulted on menus and ceremony details? (It is worth noting, by the way, that according to the study cited in *Time*, 20 percent of grooms still do "just show up," old-school style.) The term "co-partner" calls to mind the term "co-parent," and as many women know, when a man is described as co-parenting, it often means that he actually changes diapers, knows how to prepare a meal for a baby, is willing to go to the park alone with his child on weekends, and otherwise does not treat his offspring as the sole responsibility of his wife.

True, this is a hell of a lot more than the average man used to do at home, and it is progress women should be glad of—god knows it is progress of which many men are proud. I've heard it said that men of my generation, rather than feeling plagued by doubts about whether or not they are "good fathers," find it easier to feel good about their domestic efforts because when compared with their fathers', they are considerable. This can be applied to grooms of my generation, too, who are endlessly praised for deigning to care about any wedding-related thing. As Felicia, the thirty-three-year-old television executive, observed, her fiancé was so enthusiastically praised at the only wedding-related meeting he attended he left "with his chest stuck out!" When Andrew and I went to look at wedding invitations and he spent three hours poring over fonts while I went out of my mind with boredom, the woman helping us kept clucking her tongue and smiling at him sympathetically, saying, "Poor thing! He's so sweet to put up with all this!"

Our culture has changed to embrace the possibility that men "care" about raising children, and a similar shift has permitted grooms to "care" about weddings, too. Despite this, however, it is constantly said that while modern grooms might care about their weddings, they don't care *nearly* as much as brides. With this, I would have to agree. Andrew "cared" about our wedding; I, on the other hand, felt my wedding *reflected my success or failure as a woman* in the eyes of my family and friends—not to mention myself.

No wonder I "cared" more! Certainly there are plenty of women who love doing the things that women are "supposed" to do, and as a result feel far less burdened or pressured into doing them. These women are able to dive into wedding planning with genuine verve. But it is also difficult, if not impossible, to separate a "natural" love of selecting flatware from the approbation women get for possessing it (as opposed to the censure men get for showing a similar interest), and even a woman who loves choosing flatware probably doesn't love being stuck with a gargantuan planning effort all on her own. Women are likely to accept the burden, however, whether they find it extremely onerous or just annoying, because they are judged by their weddings in a way that men are not. Just as nobody blames the father of a baby who isn't wearing any shoes (something I now know from experience), nobody blames the groom if a wedding doesn't have any gift bags. But if I (not we) forgot the gift bags, people were going to look at me. If a wedding stinks, a woman gets the blame—though sometimes another woman, if the mother of the bride clearly did the planning. I do not like choosing flatware, but I wanted to show I could. I wanted to show, in other words, that I would be a good wife.

And as I discovered, to do this I had to show that I could do all those things my mother had done, even if I had a full-time career, too, even if I was a modern, "liberated" woman, even if everything was—as it was supposed to be!—different for me than it had been for her. Despite everything, I couldn't shake the feeling that even though Andrew would never have dreamed of leaving all the wedding work to me, there was a particular kind of labor I owed him as his soon-to-be wife.

I owed. I *owed*? This was the feeling that haunted me when my dad walked out on wedding planning, leaving it to my mom as "her department." Were such things destined to be my department, too? Was Andrew's and my partnership destined to be very like my parents'—even though my parents had told me (not in so many words) that it shouldn't be? The odds were not in my favor. According to a survey the U.S. Department of Labor published in 2004, the average working woman spends about twice as much time as the average working man on household chores and the care of children. Men do more than they used to, yes, but women do *a lot* more than they used to. Seventy-seven percent of American women with school-age children work, and most are still the primary caretakers of their children and the home. Do these women, working just as their husbands do, still feel they *owe?* Do their husbands think so, too?

Not only that, but if couples have a stay-at-home parent, it is almost always the woman who gives up her money-earning job—24 percent of American households have stay-at-home moms, but only 2 percent of American households have stay-at-home dads. Couples often deny the sexism of this by saying their decision was based solely on which partner earned more, ignoring the fact that men almost *always* earn more—because of sexism. As Evelyn Murphy and E. J. Graff report in their book *Getting Even: Why Women Don't Get Paid Like Men—And What to Do About It*, "blatant sex discrimination, sexual harassment, workplace sex segregation, everyday discrimination and discrimination against mothers" cause women to lose anywhere between $700,000 and $1,000,000 over their lifetimes, doing the same work that men do. (This system is most grueling for single mothers, who earned an average of $29,826 in 2004, as opposed to single dads—a much rarer breed—who earned an average of $44,923.) Couples also deny the sexism of prioritizing a man's career by saying that, if a couple has the resources to give a woman a choice, mothers "naturally" prefer mothering to work. For some women this is undoubtedly true. On the other hand, if you are given a choice between working two jobs (mothering and working outside the home) and one job (mothering), most sane people would probably "prefer" the opportunity to only work one.

In other words, progress had given me the "opportunity" to work two jobs, and (as a warm-up) to wedding plan and work full-time. Was this double burden the emancipation my mother and father had imagined for their daughters as wives? Of course not. My parents had always cherished the hope that I would work, and instilled a strong desire in me—a sense of *duty*—to use my abilities not just to parent my children, but to excel in the public sphere. But they'd also hoped I'd have a choice about whether to work, and how much. In other words, they'd always hoped I'd have a husband.

So had I. Case in point: as early as high school, I envisioned two separate lives for myself: one in which I pursued my type-A career with the unadulterated focus that a man could; one in which I devoted all my time and energy to raising my kids. Feeling sandwiched between wanting to mother the way my mother did—full-time—and the career dreams that same mother pressed upon me, I would ask myself: "What will I do when I have children? Will I keep working full-time? Part-time? Stay home while they're young?" Wrenching questions, yes, even when they were only theoretical—but questions that prove I'd always assumed I would have a husband, too. Who else did I think was going to put food on the table if I chose to take time off to be a mom?

Women like my friend Felicia, a black woman whose mother had her at sixteen, did not count on a hypothetical husband when she was imagining her future because her mother (who is now a successful executive) told her she could never count on anyone but herself to take care of her. Women I know whose mothers were left unskilled and impoverished by divorce (an event that drastically reduces the average woman's standard of living, while actually improving the average man's) didn't dare ask themselves either. But I asked, and, consciously or not, I assumed.

Now I was going to have a husband—that I knew. My job description as a wife, however, remained unknown. Or did it? Deep down, I'd begun to grasp one reason I had accepted Andrew's *right* to propose marriage to me. Somewhere along the line I had accepted the idea that as a woman, I needed him—to be financially secure, to have children, to be flexible in my career in order to mother them—more than he needed me.

SHORTLY after the battle of the flies, my mother retreated to her study to send emails and map out an itinerary. We'd agreed to tour places after Christmas. Andrew, as of yet, knew nothing about this. I was not looking forward to telling him. I sat down on the couch across from my dad, who was in an easy chair. The sports were over and he was reading. As soon as I sat down, however, he closed his book with a swift, punctuating crack, looked up at me over his gold-rimmed K-mart reading glasses and scrunched his eyes together quickly, like a double wink with a smile. *We got through that one!* he seemed to say. Yeah, *you* got through it, I thought. But I smiled too.

"Is there any particular kind of scotch Andrew likes?" he asked. "I'd like to have some for him when he gets in. I imagine the man is going to be tired out."

"You don't have to do that, Dad," I said.

"I know. But I *want* to do it." He stood up and clapped his hands together. "After all he's my future son-in-law," he said. "So lezzz go!" We headed for the garage.

I was smiling, but as soon as my father said he wanted to buy Andrew some scotch, I'd tensed. Andrew liked scotch. But he liked kind of expensive scotch. What was I going to tell my dad at the liquor store? Would I make Andrew seem like a guy who spent too much on scotch, making me engaged to a guy who spent too much on scotch, that is, making me a lady who had already lost her grip on the value of a dollar?

I'd always wanted my dad to know that I wasn't spoiled. He'd had a tough time growing up and had had to take lots of crappy jobs to get by. At Stanford (a very cushy place) I deliberately took similar jobs: washing dishes and mopping floors, scrubbing chalkboards, and emptying garbage cans in the engineering building while wearing a Walkman like Carl in *The Breakfast Club*. After college I loved calling to tell my dad about job offers and promotions; he loved to calculate precisely how much money I made per hour, to hear stories of how early I had to get up in the morning and how late I stayed at work at night. I felt like we talked in a special, man-to-man way.

But now? Now I was afraid of disappearing in his eyes into a category of person who was not like him. Now I was accompanying him to the liquor store to buy my future husband a bottle of expensive scotch, wearing a diamond ring that signified the end of being a scrappy survivor in the world forever more, and the beginning of being . . . what?

Suddenly, in the car, I found myself launching into a stream-of-consciousness unburdening, telling my dad a version of all the mixed feelings I'd been having about moving into our big apartment, about my ring, and about suddenly finding myself totally taken out of the equation: amount of money you make = life you're able to live.

"Your mother struggled with this you know," my dad said. I felt a pang when my dad said this. *My mother!* How could I have been so thoughtless? "I think she felt very conflicted about staying home with you kids while I went out and earned the money we lived on. But I'll tell you something. I could not have earned a living, or become the doctor I've become—and in my way, I do feel I've made a significant contribution—without her." As a child psychiatrist, my father has helped a lot of families, and he was absolutely right, my mother has been an integral part of his work. "We've made our contribution together," he said, "and our house is *our* house, not mine."

We pulled up to the liquor store. "You're right," I said. I believed it, but my stomach was in knots. My father was right to share credit for his accomplishments with my mother. But I couldn't help thinking—my mother could have been a doctor, and an excellent one! Certainly child-rearing is a crucial, full-time job when children are young, or still living at home. But women now spend only a third of their lives in the active mothering phase. My father still had his career when his youngest child left home; my mother, with the exception of her part-time work as a tour guide, faced an empty nest.

We bought a bottle of good scotch. "I'm doing just fine, you know," my dad said teasingly when I balked at the price, and of course he was—he had already agreed to contribute a very generous, fixed amount to the wedding, and he was pleased with his no-questions-asked, flat-rate scheme, which did end up working beautifully. With this all-important gesture, he had already discharged his F.O.B. duties admirably. As many women have told me, fund-providing was their F.O.B.'s sole duty, too. "[My father] played the traditional role quite nicely," Mary, a thirty-eight-year-old writer from Chicago, told me. "He wrote several big checks."

Many couples now contribute to the cost of their weddings, or even pay for them alone, but 27 percent of weddings are still underwritten solely by the bride's family. The groom's family foots the bill alone only 4 percent of the time. Very few enlightened types would come out and say that a woman's family owes a man's for assuming the financial burden of caring for her, but the tradition exerts a powerful hold: my very enlightened parents saved money for their daughters' weddings, but not for their son's. (When my brother married they did decide to contribute an equal amount.) It was no mistake that my "maiden name" (which I planned to keep) was later plastered atop every proposal, schedule, and receipt. My maiden name also happens to be my father's name, and the unsubtle implication is that a wedding is a dowry. My *dad* owed! One bride I talked to said as much. "Since the bride is, in some ways, still the responsibility of her parents until she is transferred to the groom, her parents pay for it."

Ultimately my parents, Andrew's parents, and Andrew and I contributed equal amounts to the wedding. But I could see that being able to comfortably foot the bill if necessary made my dad feel very good. And as we drove home, my dad humming to himself while Amber, our late great golden retriever, stuck her head out of the back-seat window as we cruised through the hilly live oak–lined streets, my father's contentment was catching. Yes, Andrew was clearly going to be the breadwinner in our relationship. But so what if our marital/familial duties ended up splitting, to an extent, along traditional gender lines? I was still going to write. Couples have to specialize—it makes no sense at all for two people to *equally* do *everything*. We were a team. We'd be a good one.

We pulled into the garage. My dad turned to me with a look of warmth. "You know sweetheart," he said, "I was talking to Carl [his best friend], and I was telling him how happy it made me that you found a man like Andrew. And he knew exactly what I was talking about, even though his girls are too young to get married yet. I know it's not P.C., but I guess that's something a father feels about his daughters." He squeezed my hand. "You just want to know that they're going to be taken care of."

W H E N my father told me he was glad I was going to be taken care of, I felt a pang of loss. I knew it then: on my wedding day, my dad would feel he was passing the baton not to me, but to the next man in line. And I would stand there looking beautiful while this symbolic transference of responsibility took place—responsibility for *me*, and later, for my children. (As Virginia, a thirty-three-year-old lawyer in Texas, pointed out, the ring also "proves to the father of the soon-to-be-bride that the potential husband can take care of her the way he did . . . or so daddy tells me.") This stung on an emotional level—I wanted my father to take pride in me, to think of me as his equal and his inheritor. It also pissed me off.

Later, however, when I was able to stop obsessing about my womanly role for a minute, it occurred to me to ask myself: did Andrew, as a man, really have the better deal? What my dad said that night stuck with me. *"A father wants to know his daughters are going to be taken care of."* So did the look on his face—the look of a man who grew up without a father, burdened by the responsibilities of manhood at a very young age. Have the responsibilities of manhood changed much over the last thirty years? Or had the role Andrew would be expected to play as my husband evolved even *less* than the role I would be expected to play as his wife?

I believe the answer is yes. Consider the issue of wedding planning, for example—again, an important indicator for the roles played in marriage. What if my father had said, when I asked him to be involved, "Oh, I can't *wait* to look at wedding sites! And I have a great idea for your color scheme! Oh, and when do we get to go look at cummerbunds for Andrew?" To begin with, it would have seemed very unmanly of him to have so much "extra time" when his job was his job; and this means it would have seemed very unmanly of him, period. The *Time* article that described the upward trend in grooms' involvement in wedding planning labeled grooms who paid "assiduous attention to nuptial details" "groomzillas" and "metrosexuals." The word "metrosexual" is a thinly veiled aspersion cast on a man's *hetero*sexuality, and if brides "care" more about wedding planning because they are judged on the success or failure of their weddings, grooms "care" less because if they cared more, they'd risk being labeled brides (that is, women with nothing "better" to do)—as the one man I heard of who took charge of wedding planning was labeled by none other than his own wife.

Again, wedding magazines, websites, and wedding guidebooks enforce this by leaving grooms out and constantly making sarcastic or knowing comments about how little grooms care about anything wedding related. And men enforce this code harshly on *each other*, stigmatizing any man who overdoes his involvement in wedding planning as breaking ranks with masculinity. (Little wonder *For the Groom* folded, when any man reading it would have had to hide it under his bed to keep his friends from seeing it—though it would be perfectly okay to break out the porn.) This attitude is further reinforced by men's magazines and the few books that exist for grooms, books with titles like: *The Groom's Secret Handbook: How Not to Screw Up the Biggest Day of Her Life*; *The Clueless Groom's Guide: More Than Any Man Should Ever Know About Getting Married*; *What the Hell Is a Groom and What's He Supposed to Do?*; and *The Pocket Idiot's Guide to Being a Groom*. (The last is from a series, interestingly, that also has a guide to being the mother or father of the bride, but no *Pocket Idiot's Guide to Being a Bride*, because of course no bride would need such a thing, and if she did, she'd have to hide it under the bed, along with her porn, which also has to stay there.)

It's easy to see how this affects the marriages that follow. The fact that only 2 percent of American households have stay-at-home dads underscores this: feminism has freed women, to an extent, to work and be mothers without risking (as much as they did before) being labeled "masculine" or shamed for their efforts, but it has a long way to go in freeing men to prioritize child care over work, as men who "let" their wives act as the primary breadwinners in their families are still questioned and humiliated. Feminism was permitted to change things, it seems, right up to the point that it would threaten the principal staple of our economy and our culture: man as worker, first and foremost. And women, for all their complaints about men who don't help enough at home or who don't support them sufficiently in their careers, are as complicit in this as anybody.

Again, this can begin with wedding planning, when many women shove their husbands out the door of the florists' or the caterers' the minute they attempt to put in their two cents. An article in *Elegant Bride* noted that "brides often complain that grooms aren't interested in the wedding planning . . . but be careful what you wish for . . . the more he's involved, the less control you will have." As *Esquire's* article "One Hundred Things a Man Should Know About Marriage" warned, "Like it or not, you will defer to your fiancée's wishes in all such matters [wedding planning] and be a better man for it. Think of it as premarriage practice for the rest of your life." Is this a good precedent to set?

I spoke with plenty of brides who saw wedding planning as fun, glamorous, and exciting, and many of them were affectingly grateful to their fiancés for giving them free rein. Not all of them wanted free rein because they were control freaks. But some of them were! As everyone knows, many women *demand* total control of the process, embracing the sexist notion that "men are incompetent when it comes to these things" because it suits this purpose. These same women, however, often turn to feminist rhetoric when their husband's put-on "I'm a man, I don't know how to do that" incompetence inconveniences them at best, and abandons them at worst—times when the issue is not wedding planning but doing the family shopping or caring for a sick child.

Many women, of course, do not assume primary responsibility for wedding planning because they are bossy bridezillas, but because they grew up sandwiched between the idea that they can and should have careers, and the deeply ingrained notion that a man's job is more important than a woman's is. I didn't realize it until much later, but I had internalized this idea, and I'm certain it was a large part of why I felt that while Andrew should be "involved" with planning our wedding, it was my responsibility to support him and his career by managing things in a way that would not unduly interfere with it. And if I'm honest, I know this is because I was counting on his career to provide the primary support for our family when we chose to have children. From adolescence, with the story of my mother's life as my touchstone, I had always wondered how I would redefine the role of wife in my modern marriage. But if I really wanted things to change, shouldn't I have been wondering how to help my husband redefine his role, too?

Women may complain that they are still the primary caregivers in their families in addition to contributing financially, but men complain that they are still the primary earners in their families in addition to contributing to caregiving—feeling they *owe* as earners, and that their wives agree. "I do tend to get pissy in the years when I'm earning more than my husband," Hannah, a writer from LA, told me. "I sort of adopt an 'I shouldn't have to be the one who earns most of the money' attitude, but that's mostly because I'm also the primary caretaker for the kids, and I wind up feeling so overloaded." It would seem obvious that a man working comparable hours to his wife—and perhaps earning less than she—would step up and co-parent. But some men might argue that society is much tougher on men who think outside the role than it is on women. (In an essay from *The Bastard on the Couch*, a single father recounts a judge's refusal to grant him alimony, even though his higher-earning wife had abandoned their children and him.) Andrew did not grow up wondering what he would do when children came along—whether he would work full-time or part-time, or stay home for a few years. In some ways this burdened me because he assumed his wife would wrestle with these questions. But in some ways it burdened him because he could not count on a husband to support him if he wanted to dedicate himself to being a dad.

Women are culpable in enforcing this male-provider code when they refuse to see less ambitious, more "maternal" men as viable marriage partners, even if such a union might make sense. When Sylvia Ann Hewlett surveyed "high-achieving women" (women earning over $55,000 or $65,000, depending on their age), she found that 90 percent were married to men who worked full-time, a quarter of whom earned over $100,000 a year, and only 14 percent of whom earned less than $35,000. "In sharp contrast," she reported, "only 39 percent of high-achieving men are married to women who are employed full-time, and forty percent of these wives earn less than $35,000 a year."

Is this because men don't want to marry their equals? (Or as Maureen Dowd put it, because "men want mommy?") Of course. "High-achieving" women often end up with men who earn a lot because men tend to be threatened by women who do too, and are infamous for choosing nurses over doctors, kindergarten teachers over Ph.D.'s. But it is a two-way street, and women need to ask themselves if they are truly ready and willing to marry men who will play caregiver to their breadwinner. To suggest that such men don't exist is as stupid as suggesting there are no women who would rather work full-time than parent full-time. Do high-achieving women feel that marrying a kindergarten teacher would only call attention to a perceived "masculinity" that already makes them uncomfortable? Or are men even less likely to stay at home, or become a kindergarten teacher, because it would mark them "feminine" in the eyes of men and women both?

If men and women were free to divide the labor in their marriages without facing harsh stigma for deviating from the norm, and, perhaps more importantly, if the workplace supported more flexible, humane, gender-neutral arrangements, it's still possible—perhaps even likely—that a greater percentage of women would emphasize child-rearing, and a greater percentage of men would emphasize earning. Certainly biological instincts and realities would still play a part in the decisions couples make. But they also vary from individual to individual, and, as Francine Prose once wrote:

> The question of whether gender difference is innate or conditioned has been thoroughly raked over, and will be of continuing interest only to someone who has never met a male or female year-old baby. Of course there are gender differences, but probably not as many as there would be if this were a society in which men and women could casually de-

cide which gender wants to be president this term, and which one wants to take care of the kids and Great-Grandma.

I knew that Andrew and I were both nurturing, and both ambitious; that we were both competitive, and both loving. So I wondered: how were we going to decide who took primary responsibility for our children, and who was going to run for president?

Until we had children, it would be hard to know. But one thing was certain: I could not expect my role to change without working to change my husband's, too. "The trick is to make men shift *with* women," my mother told me later. "To let go of the biological imperative of women as nesters, and men as aggressive competitive providers, so that we can all be more totally human."

How wise.

BELIEVE it or not, the wedding coordinator at the hill country ranch we found ourselves touring a few days after Christmas was not concerned about helping Andrew and me be more totally human. She was trying to sell us on the Buckhorn Saloon. More specifically, she was trying to sell my mother and me on the Buckhorn Saloon and largely ignored Andrew, giving me my first taste of the "groom-prejudice" that was to dominate every interaction I had with the expectant, friendly, consummately feminine faces I met at each stage of planning my wedding. Showing up at a club, restaurant, or other venue and admitting to having little interest in china, cake cutters, or lighting design would have made me feel like a man standing with a group of men around a car and, rather than leaning in and taking an interest, walking away and saying, "I'd rather be scrapbooking." (The equivalent of my dad saying, "I have a great idea for your color scheme!")

And so I played the part as best I could. I also noticed that my mother, who, when she's honest, will tell you she has just about as much interest in those things as I do—though of course we were both interested in the essential things regarding my wedding, like where to have it—was playing her part as well, and something about the two of us forcing ourselves to do this (as I saw it) set my teeth on edge. Perhaps it was because my mother didn't seem to see what I saw—I wanted to shout, "Don't you think this is crazy, too? Why am I being treated like 'I won!'? Is this really the most important thing that's ever going to happen to me? And why is Andrew being congratulated for being here while I'm being treated like it's my *job*?" My mother had always been the person I could talk to about issues like these; she introduced me to feminism at a young age, and later she helped me temper the militant, I'm-a-Womyn-now! feminism I brought home from college with me when I was nineteen. But as we toured wedding sites I could not detect a chink in her happy M.O.B. veneer, and it unnerved me.

I began to feel, in fact, that she was one of *them*: the cheery, thrilled bevy of wedding-related women who didn't want to listen to my frustrations or acknowledge my ambivalence. I did not articulate this to myself at the time, of course, but instead acted out exactly as I had as a teenager when my mother had expectations of me I didn't want to fulfill: I sulked and snapped and slouched down in the back seat of my mother's two-door car, feeling every bit the thirteen-year-old forced to grow up. As our days of wedding touring went by, I grew increasingly pissed off at my mom, pissed off at Andrew, pissed off at wedding coordinators, and pissed off at myself for being so pissed off. Many times I managed to hiss the word "*Mom!*" with the exact intonation I'd used in the eighth grade. My mother refused to get angry with me, or even to accept my apologies, saying, "Oh sweetie, *all brides are like that!*"

Really? That scared me even more. And so when Andrew eventually took me aside and told me he still really wanted to get married in Colorado, not Texas, I let it rip.

"Why are you such a jerk about Texas!?" I yelled, out of my mother's earshot but decidedly within his. I yelled for no reason; I yelled despite the fact that I wanted to get married in Colorado, too. "Don't you realize this is my home state!? Are you such a stupid Colorado snob? You can't even pretend to seriously consider this, not even for two days? Do you know how that makes me feel? You're so selfish! God!" It was the verbal equivalent of stamping my foot. Andrew looked at me with irritation and dismay. He had swallowed the breach of our no-wedding-planning-until-the-year-2000 pact with very little anger or resentment. Now he was steaming with both.

"I can't talk to you when you're like this," he said, walking away. I was instantly embarrassed. I was confused. *What's wrong with me?* I wondered. I didn't know. Now I think I was afraid. I wanted to be a good wife, but I was afraid of being a good wife, too.

Later that night, after Andrew and I had made up (we agreed to break it to my mom about Colorado at a later date), I wandered out onto the balcony, which overlooks the family room. It was still and dark. It was late. A fire and Christmas tree lights—tiny flecks of blue, green, pink, and gold—provided most of the light.

I looked down. Directly below me, seated on the big, soft, dark blue leather couch, was my mother. She had a blanket over her lap and was sipping a glass of Grand Marnier. I realized there was music playing softly, Henry Mancini's Christmas album from 1966, our family's favorite. My dad had gone to bed. I walked over to the top of the stairs, smiling. She looked up when she heard the creak of my step.

"Kamy," she said, her eyes shining. "I was hoping it was you."

I came down and sat next to her. I poured myself a ladylike slug. "Oh, Kamy," my mother sighed. "This is so special. Our first Christmas with Andrew officially part of our family. Our first Christmas with you engaged." I nodded. Our *only* Christmas with me engaged, I thought, if I have any control over this at all.

That night, after days of being together without having time to really sit down and talk, my mom and I got down to business. We recapped the engagement. I held my hand up to the twinkling white banister lights to make my ring sparkle. At that moment, I loved it unabashedly. It felt wonderful to let go of the tension that had been building inside me for days. I was ready to O.D. on her approval, and she was happy to oblige.

At the same time my mother's happiness was bittersweet. My engagement made formal what had been true for some time: I did not need her the same way anymore. (As my friend Franny put it, finding a life partner means your mother no longer gets to be your emergency contact person.) So, as the Grand Marnier warmed our stomachs, my mother started the oh-Kamy-when-you-were-a-baby talk. Apparently my wedding had come with another invitation for her, one she had perhaps been anticipating:

In honor of **ANDREW** and **KAMY'S** engagement, you're invited to tell her how much you love her as much and as often as you want, because it's her **WEDDING** and you're allowed! And you're invited to stop pretending that her ceasing to be your little girl is the best thing that ever happened to you and to mourn the passing of your own life, just a little, as it is brought home to you by the passing of your child's.

People need weddings because they are a sanctioned, ritualized forum for much-needed emotional release. Some people don't have traditional weddings because they don't want to give their families the license, and inevitably some family members embarrassingly, sometimes cruelly, exploit it. People often forgive erratic behavior at weddings by saying, "Oh, it's just the *wedding*," as though they were saying, "Oh, she's just *drunk*." But as everybody knows, there are some really bad drunks.

I knew my mother's happiness at my engagement was complicated. And suddenly I was seized by the desire to tell her *my* happiness about it was complicated, too. I decided to communicate through another love we've always shared: literature.

"There's a poem I've become obsessed with lately," I said, hopping up to go to my mother's massive bookshelf. "It's Emily Dickinson. Do you want to hear it?"

"Oh, Kamy. I love it that you love Emily Dickinson," my mother sighed. "I must have done something right."

"Everyone loves Emily Dickinson," I said. "Now listen to this." And I read:

Title Divine – is mine!
The Wife – without the Sign!
Acute Degree – conferred on me –

Empress of Calvary!
Royal – all but the Crown!
Betrothed – without the swoon
God sends us Women –
When you – hold – Garnet to Garnet –
Gold – to Gold –
Born – Bridalled – Shrouded –
In a Day –
Tri Victory
"My Husband" – women say –
Stroking the Melody –
Is this – the way?

For me, the poem sounded a note of triumphant resistance (Dickinson never married) and subversive questioning. Somewhat disturbingly, Dickinson's questions about life as a wife, posed a hundred years before, were not far off from some of those I wanted to ask. "Born, bridalled, shrouded, in a day." On my wedding day, would I be born as an adult woman, bridalled as a wife, the person I was before shrouded forever more? And what about these women so pathetically enamored of the words "husband" and "fiancé"?

Was *this* the way? To this question and others, however, my mother shook her head and begged off. She offered a few insights, but our conversation never resembled the ones we'd had when I was a teenager and we stayed up late discussing feminism and life as a woman in the world. On this subject, at this moment, my mother did not want to analyze or critique, to botch up her buzz. She was retreating from the battleground. She didn't want to fight anymore. She wanted to lay down her arms and pin a corsage on herself, and on her mother too. The break she'd made with her parents' traditional values long ago had been a painful one—something I couldn't really understand. She was tired out, and now she wanted her happy ending, no questions asked.

Not only that, but I think my mother felt that I'd *found* my happy ending. And hadn't I? My mother had never envisioned the burden of the double shift when she'd envisioned her daughters' brave-new-world future, but my ring signaled that I'd had the good luck to avoid this thorny post-feminist fate by doing a very pre-feminist thing: landing a successful man. She had a point. Andrew's income would mean I could write checks to freedom, granting me the privilege of outsourcing tasks like cleaning and, someday, child care. Hopefully I would eventually earn enough to "cover" child care myself (interesting that couples often weigh the *woman's* income against this cost, as though a man doesn't need child care to go to work), but in the meantime, I could still work. I would have the benefits of a traditional marriage—much like hers—without the pain of forgoing my intellectual life. I could work for self-fulfillment, not because I "had" to. Wasn't that the best of both worlds?

I didn't know yet. But even then I knew one thing: while this setup might work for me (never mind my desire to have a partner who truly co-parented, or the limitations I'd face in my career while trying to balance motherhood and writing even with the luxury of help, or the burden of feeling that I "owed" my freedom to my husband), it was hardly realistic for most women I knew. My friend Alexandra, for instance, who worked full-time as a news anchor right through the birth of her second child, eventually quit so she could stay at home. "I do 95 percent of child care in our household," she told me. "He does 100 percent of earning. Feminist that I am, I ended up dab smack in the middle of a 1950's marriage. I am Mrs. Cleaver if she ever went off her pills." Alexandra, pursuing a career that demanded outrageous hours and intense commitment, that couldn't be done from home and was still structured on the assumption that workers have *wives*—felt she couldn't have it all. "I used to be angry at anyone who told me you can't have it all," she said. "I thought they were dream-crushers. Now I think they are brutally honest realists."

This is a wall many women my age hit when they find themselves crossing over from the theoretical to the actual as mothers, workers, and wives. And it's a concern that many baby-boomer mothers seize upon and worry over, I think, often long before their daughters marry, and particularly if their daughters marry "late." Samantha, a thirty-five-year-old editor from New York, felt her mother retreated from the feminist messages she had espoused to Samantha in her youth once Samantha reached her early thirties. "I was surprised considering that through my twenties, my mother was the opposite: pretty dismissive about my relationships, even the ones I took rather seriously, in favor of encouraging me to be my own person, independent, discover who I was without needing a man, etc. Then practically the moment I hit thirty it was, boom, 'When are you getting married?'" Mary, a thirty-eight-year-old from Chicago who recently married, said, "As my mother and her six daughters got older, her messages about marriage did shift. I think she got a bit worried because we all married 'late,' and she may have felt responsible for that somehow." Perhaps Mary's mother, an ardent feminist who had transferred her dreams onto her daughters, had begun to fear, as I believe my mom did, that her generation had taken things too far after all, and, worse, steered their daughters wrong.

This about-face drives a lot of women I know crazy, and hurts them, too. It feels like a betrayal—no, I'm not married yet, but don't you believe I *will* be, and even if I never am, didn't you always tell me that marriage wasn't everything?!

On the other hand, many women of my generation also seem to be asking—*did* the last generation go too far? Clearly some daughters of baby boomers think so. For every mother who dismays her daughter by lurching back into 1950s mode, there lately seems to be a twenty-five-year-old woman as marriage-obsessed as a 1950s coed, eager to trade her suit for an apron and her briefcase for a baby. (In light of this trend a 2005 *Marie Claire* article asked, "Is Marriage the New Dating?") For *The New Wife*, Susan Barash conducted hundreds of interviews with wives from every decade beginning with the 1950s, and concluded that "in the mind of a young twenty-first-century wife there is the belief that finding and holding on to the right partner is of utmost importance. The recent past has shown that career advancement was a hindrance to marriage and vice versa." In a much-discussed article in the *New York Times*, Louise Story reported that a substantial percentage of the women of Yale appeared to have accepted this "fact" as well, and already planned to work part-time or be stay-at-home moms rather than pursue big careers.

In her book, Barash goes on to quote several women who say they are turning to their grandmothers (that's right, their *grandmothers*—like mine, who got an allowance and didn't learn to drive till she was thirty-five) as role models. Barash attempts to argue that these women are empowered, adding a "feminist" perspective to an old approach: "the Cinderella complex, that someone will take care of us, exists with a new component—that of the twenty-first-century wife who views it as required." In other words, "twenty-first-century wives" *demand* to be taken care of by men. (Or, in the immortal words of Destiny's Child, they croon: "Do you pay my telephone bills?/Do you pay my automo-bills?/I don't think you do/so you and me are through.") Sandwiched between the promises of their girlhood and the reality of their adulthood, these women are looking for a way out, and justify taking the old one by saying it's a "choice."

"I think of my mother and her friends as women with dreams," one New Wife told Barash, "mostly failed." The implication is that these were feminist dreams—and that feminism mostly failed. But feminism hasn't failed! It just isn't finished yet! My mother grew up at a time when women were barred from Harvard, when women were forced to quit their jobs when they got pregnant, when husbands were still legally allowed to rape their wives! (The Supreme Court only knocked that one down in 1984.) So much has changed, but there was a hell of a lot to do. So while I am sympathetic to the disillusionment and frustration expressed by these women, really, is *this* the way?

The truth is that work is sometimes boring, petty, stressful, and poorly paid, and in America, it's likely to be brutally time-consuming: Americans work more hours than the workers of any other nation, five hundred hours a year more than the Germans, and two hundred and fifty hours more than the British. In light of this, it has been suggested that women are (simply) saner and smarter than men: seeing that the workplace is hopelessly unfriendly to a balanced life, they leave, often when they have children. "Maternity provides an escape hatch that paternity does not," said one woman interviewed in the *New York Times* piece "The Opt-Out Revolution." Yes, but only if your husband can bankroll it, and only if your husband is content to toil away in a work environment you find unbearable, and *only if your husband is content to stay with you.*

Yes, it has proven difficult, thus far, to make child-rearing compatible with the pursuit of a high-octane career. Certainly one thing fueling the 1950s renaissance is the fear of ending up an unmarried, childless career woman. As Barash also points out, women my age have been the first to enter adulthood under the specter of infertility, and "the fear of being 'an old maid,' a widespread fear of past centuries, appears to be on the rise again." Women in the 1980s were hit with the famous *Newsweek* cover saying a forty-year-old woman was more likely to be killed by a terrorist than to get married (Susan Faludi and others later proved the research wrong)—in 2002, *Time* treated women to this cover story: "Babies vs. Career: The Harsh Facts About Fertility." This scare tactic has obscured the far more widespread problem of ending up a divorced woman with children who, while she probably has a job (most women don't have the luxury of making the "mistaken" choice between work and mothering these days), probably doesn't have an extremely high-paying one, and gets little in the way of child support from a man. Less than two-thirds of the nation's children are now living with married biological fathers, and men now enjoy, as Andrew Hacker put it in his book *Mismatch: The Growing Gulf Between Men and Women*, "freedom that enables husbands to leave their wives and children with little or no social censure and seldom at drastic financial cost." A whopping 41.5 percent of single mothers get *zero* child support, in fact, and of those who do, checks average $3,844 a year. Another reason why men "own" marriage? Because many mothers are now practically begging for their help, and with sex, money, and freedom readily available to men outside of marriage, many men think they should.

In other words the alarmists, while sounding alarms both specious and sexist, have a point. The system is not working! Men should share the wealth! Women need more support to balance work and family! (As Barbara Ehrenreich noted in a *Glamour* article that reported that women aged eighteen to thirty-four did not even rank work among their top three priorities in life, "When we were talking about working and having a family, we meant working an eight-hour day. That's becoming impossible.") They need better ways of exiting and reentering the workforce when they have children, and better child care. They need social policy that recognizes that the 1950s family structure is no more. And *men* need all these things, too. They too deserve better balance in their lives.

"Feminism is about changing the ground-rules," Katha Politt once wrote, "not just entering the game." Going backward is not the answer, and every woman knows it. P. J. O'Rourke has one word for those who wax nostalgic for bygone eras: dentistry. If you are a woman, you can come up with a lot more than that. (Birth control, the right to earn, the right to vote, *pants*.) I love my grandmother, but I wouldn't trade places with her for the world. And I know my mother wouldn't want me to.

AT 2 a.m. I crawled back into bed with Andrew. A little sloshed, it seemed like the right thing to wake him up.

"Andrew!" I said, shaking his shoulder. "What are we going to do when we have a baby?" He didn't wake up. He was exhausted. I studied his face for a long time. I trusted him. I trusted myself. For all my fears about how we would handle the future, I trusted in us, and that was what I had.

Three-and-a-half years later, I got pregnant. As it turned out, Andrew and I had a lot to talk about. It's damn hard, just like I knew it would be.

But that is another story.

five

cℵ

The Dress

My Inner Bride Is Hiding from Me!

O n my last night in Texas, I asked my mother—even though it felt a bit premature given the fact we had no idea where or when we were going to do this thing—if she would fly to New York to visit soon so we could look for wedding dresses together. My eagerness to begin was helped along by my mother's well-argued case, made via newspaper articles, magazine clippings, and other sources, that I had to find a dress *at least* nine months before my wedding, as wedding dresses, apparently, take as long as new human beings to be assembled. And this meant, if we were thinking of having our wedding as soon as August, that I was already a month behind. (When it came to wedding-planning timetables, this was to become a constant state of affairs.) "Why don't you come out in early February?" I asked her. "Really?" she said.

"I would never consider looking without you," I told her. I meant it. Or at least I meant I would never buy something without having gone to look with her *at some point*. (Wearing my mother's dress was not a possibility—it had been her second choice and she'd never really liked it herself.) And as we planned the trip I realized I was genuinely excited. Of all the wedding-related activities that lay ahead, shopping for a dress

seemed like it would be *fun*. All those Texan event planners, one or another of whom had asked me to imagine making my grand entrance on
a boat, or in a horse-drawn cart, or through a flower-covered entrance-
way, had whet my appetite to see myself in white.

Other than that, I'd given little thought to what it would be like to see
myself dressed as a bride. I was excited about wearing an unforgettable,
once-in-a-lifetime dress. I wanted to look hot and thin. That was about it.
Most wedding dress buying guides go no deeper than this, either: in all
my research I found very little about the wedding dress's meaning, and a
lot about the right kind of dress to buy if you're "plus size," "thick waist,"
"wide hips," "big bust," "tall and thin," or "petite," as *InStyle Weddings*
dubbed these "anxiety-producing" shapes in its spring 2000 issue.

When I asked women what they thought the wedding dress symbolized, I got a lot of one-line answers like: "A wedding," "Tradition,"
"The bride," and "Something fancy you can't spill anything on that you
wear once in your life." As Felicia, the thirty-three-year-old television
executive, put it, "I plan to wear a white dress not because of any tradition, but because I like the clean, simple look of a white dress. You'll
most likely see women in every other color of dress at your wedding,
but chances are you will be the only one in white."

Is this really all there is to it?

No. Like diamond rings, white wedding dresses have universal meaning, meaning that extends beyond women as individuals. Like the ring, the
wedding dress tells us something about what a bride *is*, or is supposed to
be, and about what a wife is supposed to be, too. And while many women
eventually adjusted to the sight of themselves in white, almost all of the
women I talked to vividly remember the shock of their first encounter with
themselves as brides. (An ecstatic experience for some; not unlike Sarah
Jessica Parker's outbreak of hives on *Sex and the City* for others.)

I will certainly never forget mine.

My mother and I agreed on February. But soon after leaving Texas, I
thought: February? February to look with my *mom*. But did *I* really
have to wait until then?

So in late January, there I was. Standing in the middle of a small, sunny bridal boutique in Los Angeles, temporarily immobilized. I was surrounded. Dresses lined either side of the room, hung from metal poles affixed to the ceiling. There was a breeze, but the dresses weren't moving, either. ("I was amazed [at] how heavy most of the dresses were," Amanda, a twenty-nine-year-old writer in New York, remembered. "I could barely carry two at a time, and I'm a strong person.") While their bodices appeared slack and easy to differentiate, and thus semi-approachable, their skirts presented an intractable white and ivory mass, and it seemed that if I wanted to view one, thrusting my entire arm length into a crevice would be unavoidable. I could not quite bring myself to thrust. My friend Clara, who had made the appointment for me to get into this place, was parking the car.

How had I gotten there? Just after New Year's, on a cold, dark winter afternoon in New York, Andrew had showed up to meet me in a café and, with a mischievous grin, presented me with a gift: a stack of bridal magazines about three feet tall. Well maybe one foot tall. At any rate they were formidable. It was officially the year 2000: time to start planning. So he'd picked them up at a subway magazine stand sort of as a joke, and sort of as a way for us to dive in. I'd whimpered and complained and then we'd opened them and I'd found that the only thing I could deal with were wedding dresses. Votive candles, flowers, caterers, invitations, things-to-do lists twelve months long—what was I supposed to do with those? We didn't even know where we were going to get married yet! So I looked at dresses, and Andrew did too, and we decided that it wouldn't hurt if we went and looked at them in New York together, before my mom arrived.

Except you can't just waltz into Saks, for example, and look at wedding dresses. For one thing, on Sunday the bridal salon is closed—roped off like a night club. Every other day, you have to have an appointment. Trying to "walk-in" to the Saks bridal salon in New York City is like trying to walk into Per Se on a Saturday night in Reeboks and jeans. You are obviously a tourist. It had then occurred to me, however, that we were going to be in LA the following weekend, and that my friend Clara had just gotten married there in October, and that she might be able to help. So I called her.

"Do you think we could go to a few places in LA while I'm there?" I asked her. "I just want to get a feel for it before my mom comes to New York." I told her about attempting to go with Andrew in New York. "You took *Andrew?*" she said. "What were you thinking?" This seemed very silly to me. Andrew loves to shop. I love to shop with him. How fun would it be to try on different wedding dresses and let him see? But Clara made me promise that in LA I would leave Andrew at home. "You obviously have no idea what this is like," she told me. On that point, she was absolutely right.

As indicated by my inability to make a move toward the dresses. I looked to the doorway for Clara. No sign of her. But just at the point when I was beginning to attract inquiring, less-than-friendly stares from the sole saleslady in the shop, Clara bounded in, went right up to the desk, and announced our presence. "This is my friend Kamy," she said, "and we have an appointment for her to try on wedding dresses." The woman told us she'd be with us momentarily. Clara turned to me and grinned. "Let's go, bridey!!"

Clara was an eccentric, smart writer/photographer/surfer-chick, a thirty-two-year-old who inherited some money and with it an innate boldness in that sort of boutique that I didn't have. She had also dated women for ten years before she fell in love with a man and married him, and as a result may have come at the whole thing from such a clearly unconventional perspective she could enjoy it wholesale. She did not hesitate to begin bushwhacking through the dresses with bravura. Pressing each gown back with the palm of her hand, causing the hanger to make a swift, scraping sound, she looked it up and down, and, if interested, grabbed its side to partially free it from the line for better viewing. Then she either called to me or moved on.

I was nervous, and approached more gingerly. I felt insecure and tomboyish, like an impostor who'd slipped into a fancy party wearing the wrong outfit. But what was wrong with my outfit? I was wearing black pants, a knit top, and the black Nine West half-boots that were issued to every working woman at that time when she moved to the East Coast. I strode in with my thumb under my purse strap and my thick, wide heels slomping (my mother's word for it) along the floor, feeling every bit the slouching androgyne I was when I was ten and Aunt Patsy asked me, with concern and a twinge of reproach, why I never wore dresses. But now I was going to wear a dress. Big time.

Keeping one hand in my pocket, I peeked at a price tag: $1,500. I tried not to blanch visibly. The saleswoman, who was finishing up some paperwork, glanced at me priggishly. Then she saw my ring and smiled. Emboldened, I began imitating Clara's method. Only I was giggling and glancing at Clara every ten seconds to say things like "I can't believe I'm doing this! I'm getting married! I'm going to wear one of these things! This is so bizarre!"

"What are you looking for?" the saleswoman asked nicely, approaching.

"I don't know," I said, avoiding eye contact. "This is the first place I've tried." She smiled. *And?* "Um, I guess I was thinking of something very simple and straight, you know, a Carolyn Bessette kind of thing," I added. At that time, every woman in the country who preferred pants to crotchless clothes thought she wanted a dress like the one Carolyn wore to marry JFK Jr. Slinky, silky, and without petticoats, it had one foot in the sexy-tough, tradition-busting door and one foot in the I'm-no-girly-girl-but-if-I'm-going-to-do-this-thing-I-might-as-well-do-it-right door. The second door has a much longer name, however, and in the year 2000 it appeared to be exerting a more powerful influence. Clara's dress—a 1999 Vera Wang actually featured in a fashion magazine (with Clara in it) because a hot LA designer in attendance had dubbed their wedding her favorite—had been anything but slinky. It had been downright poofy, in fact.

"How did you envision yourself, when you were a little girl?" asked the saleswoman, who was about sixty-five and looked exactly like my sixth-grade English teacher, Mrs. Larabee. "What kind of dress did you imagine yourself in?"

I racked my brain, and, to my consternation, found nothing there. I smiled blankly. I'd flipped through magazines, yes. I'd been to weddings, yes. But I realized I had never tried (or hadn't been able?) to plug myself into one of those outfits.

"Every woman has pictured herself in some kind of wedding dress, at least once," the saleslady informed me confidently. "Just think back on that."

At that point I felt that my wedding-dress blank was not a cool, independent woman thing, as I'd hoped, but instead a freakish deficiency. (Too bad my friend Felicia wasn't with me. She later exclaimed, "Are you kidding?! That's something invented by the bridal industry to make girls like me feel like shit!") As it turns out, every magazine or website that gives any advice about wedding-dress shopping suggests calling to mind the dress "you've always imagined." Then, without attempting to alienate the women who may not (gasp!) have had anything in mind, *The Knot Book of Wedding Gowns*, for instance, gently continues, "Dream a little. Get in touch with your inner bride. Close your eyes and envision yourself walking down the aisle. What do you see?" But I had not read this book, nor any other book or article, before entering my first bridal boutique. And now that I was there, on the spot, my inner bride was hiding from me.

Clara appeared at my side. "Let's put her in several different styles so she can see what she likes," she suggested. The saleswoman nodded. I breathed a sigh of relief. We picked out two sleek Carolyn gowns and three full or "poofy" gowns, ranging in size from big, to bigger, to Super Size. The last had to be hung (it did not *have* to be hung—it could have stood alone without any assistance) outside the fitting room because, when released from its confined position on the dress-squashing display rack, it snapped open like an umbrella, and brandished spokes of tulle that could have put somebody's eye out.

The saleswoman asked me for my bra and shoe sizes, and soon reappeared with an exhausted looking brassiere, a pair of pointy white satin pumps, and an armload of headpieces and veils. (Important tip listed in all wedding-dress shopping guides: bring your own brassiere.) I stripped, sheepishly, down to my underwear. I was wearing a dark green cotton pair from Victoria's Secret that sagged in the back. I was mortified. I stepped into the pointy pumps. The saleslady helped me hook up the brassiere. My pooch hung out between the bottom of it and the top of my underwear. The saleslady held a hand up in front of my pooch and mimed flattening the roll of flesh down. "Control top," she said. *Where does the fat go?* I asked my friend Franny later. "Control top hose compresses your organs together on the inside," she replied. Wow.

I took a deep breath. We decided to try a sleek, silky dress first. I slipped it from the hanger. It was satiny and limp, and I pulled it on over my head without much help—if I'd needed to, I could have done it alone. Elegant, with a scoop neck and a low-cut back, it hung in shimmery pools around my ankles on the floor. I stepped out. "Ooh, pretty," Clara breathed. I walked slowly around the store, staring at myself, smiling at myself, twisting around to wave at myself over my shoulder. In it, my movement was effortless. The dress felt comfortable, even familiar— not unlike a black crepe floor-length dress I'd worn to black-tie events with Andrew. It would have been sort of normal to wear it with him in his tux. The saleswoman approached me with a veil. I balked.

"Oh no," I said. "That's okay." I had never imagined myself wearing a veil—perhaps because I associated veils so closely with the mental, sexual, and physical confinement of women who are forced to wear them; perhaps because it seemed like the ultimate expression of demurral and virginal modesty. "I'm always shocked when I see a bride wear a veil over her face," Amanda, the writer, said to me. "It's so old-fashioned and rooted in nothing pro-bride/woman." Clara, however, who is very pro-woman, had worn a veil. (I'd forgotten that.) She shook her head at my svelte slip-dress.

"You need something more bridey, baby," she pronounced, grinning. She hoisted the Super Size from its perch, and whipped it around for a 360 view. "Try a full one. I *never* thought I would want a full one, but that's what I got." The saleslady concurred, and ushered me back behind the fitting-room door.

"If it's right," Clara added, "you'll know."

If it's right, I'll *know*? This sounded like a bit much. But Clara was simply sharing Rule Number One of wedding-dress shopping, as dictated by the experts: You are not just shopping for a wedding dress, you are shopping for the physical incarnation of *yourself*. Know thyself, and you will know thy wedding gown. (Weddingchannel.com has a series titled "Who Are You?" intended to help women find a dress.) The right dress would express my "bridal personality." As Maria McBride-Mellinger advises in her book *The Wedding Dress*, "What is fashion but an opportunity to express your identity? What is a wedding but an occasion to affirm your identity? And what is a bridal gown but a chance to revel in the fantasy of all you ever wanted to be?" (Yes, a woman named "McBride" has written a whole stack of these tomes.) One popular criticism levied at brides who don't look quite right is that they pushed fantasy too far, failing to look like "themselves." *Have the good sense to choose a dress true to your identity!*, the experts warn, *but don't forget to find a dress that embodies "all you ever wanted to be!"*

"I melted in front of the mirror," one woman told me, as she described trying on her dress in tones reminiscent of a romantic encounter. "It was meant to be."

Tall order. No wonder women become so hysterical about wedding dresses. No wonder they are whipped into such a frenzy at Filene's infamous wedding-dress sample sale that every single dress, according to Jacqueline Geller in *Here Comes the Bride*, is gone in thirty-two to forty-six seconds. What if you can't find yourself? What if you can't afford yourself? What if you don't look good in yourself? What if some other bridezilla buys yourself—the last one in your size!—first?

I looked at Super Size. If this was my fantasy self, it was news to me. I could not suppress a burst of laughter. "Just try it!" Clara called encouragingly from outside. I slipped out of the satiny dress, and, back in my green underwear, borrowed pumps, and brassiere, confronted the gown. I could not begin to imagine how to put it on.

With help. Like all clothing that is utterly feminine, big, poofy bridal gowns make a woman awkward and dependent because in bride-and-groom-stereotype-land, men take action, while women wait to be rescued; men are doers, while women get done. Princess Diana's dress, which in 1981 ushered in an era of renewed "romanticism" (that is, big,

poofy bridal gowns), loaded her down with forty yards of taffeta, crino-
line, and lace. In 1994, Celine Dion wore a seven-pound crystal head-
piece and had a twenty-foot train that required all eight of her sisters to
carry it. (Amazingly, she carried her own head.) According to the catalogue for a wedding dress exhibit at the Victoria and Albert Museum in
London, in 1933 Margaret Wigham, later the Duchess of Argyll, wore
an eighteen-foot train. She found it, in a classic English understate-
ment, "considerably difficult to manage." My dad has always said that
the luxuries the middle and upper-middle class seek are based on the
desire to live like royalty. Certainly the notion of wearing a dress that requires numerous attendants to assist in its donning fits with that.

Super Size had nothing on the Victorian hoopskirts of the nineteenth
century, some of which required ceiling-mounted pulleys to lower them
onto their waiting wearers. But an attendant was needed. In order to get
into this dress, I had to stick my hands straight up over my head like a
little girl and point them in the direction of an unwieldy, circular mass
of material being handled by my experienced attendant. Wobbly and
blinded, I then had to search out, with fingers flailing and a mouthful
of tulle, the tiny constricted circle of the waistline—the light at the end
of the tunnel. I became so disoriented as I attempted to locate and
squirm through Super Size's coaster-sized waistline I nearly toppled
over. Once emerged, however, I did not attempt to yank the dress down
farther. Instead I stood stock still, staring at myself in the mirror, as the
panting saleslady completed the task. Another word women used again
and again when describing the experience of seeing themselves in a wedding dress for the first time? *Surreal.*

"Well," the saleslady said. "I can see you like this one." Like was not
the right word. I was transfixed. I couldn't speak. And right then I knew
that my mother should have been there with me. Seeing myself for the
first time in a wedding dress, a bona fide, ball-gown wedding dress, was
indeed a once-in-a-lifetime experience, and my mother had known this
even if I hadn't. This dress in particular, a four-thousand-dollar *gown*, an
avatar of the form, with its boned strapless bodice and its spectacularly
full skirts ("extreme fullness of skirt," stated the V&A catalogue, "reflects

the significance attached to the wedding ceremony"), altered my appearance in a way that no piece of clothing I'd ever put on had before. And I knew I wouldn't feel quite this way—surprised, overwhelmed, emotional—even when I tried on other dresses again.

Clara called to me. I turned, smiling hard at the strange feeling that pulled at my throat, and as I did my skirts swooshed around me. I lifted them up as gently as I could, as I'd seen princesses do (in Disney movies?), with both hands. I prepared to step out to face the wall of mirrors outside.

"Just a minute," the saleslady said, grandmotherly for the first time. "*Now* would you like a veil?"

I nodded. Without thinking I knew that without a veil, Super Size would not "be all that it could be." Would anyone dress up as a bride for Halloween—or a bachelorette party, for that matter—without one? In *How to Be a Bride (And a Flower Girl, Too!)*, a popular present for flower girls, young brides-in-training are told, "Brides can wear whatever they like, but the most important thing is a *veil*." It was clear to me that I, too, was playing dress-up—though the most adult, expensive game of dress-up I'd ever played—and in this light my philosophical objections to the veil suddenly seemed beside the point. The saleslady plucked various veils from a chair in the corner until she found the perfect one, sheer with a tiny strip of creamy satin around its edges. She placed it on my head. At that point my back was to the fitting room mirror, so I couldn't see myself. Then she reached in front of me and pulled the veil's blusher over my face. "Now," she said.

I walked out, and, in the wall of mirrors before me, saw . . . my inner bride. Or at least: an outer bride. Her face was shrouded, but beneath the veil she was smiling from ear to ear, because that's what she does when she freaks out. I stepped up onto the wooden box, which acted as a pedestal. *A bride!*

"See?!" Clara said, clapping her hands delightedly.

It was me standing there, but in a very real sense, in a sense no piece of clothing had ever brought about before, it wasn't me at all. I wasn't supposed to be *myself* in that dress! All that talk about a woman finding a dress (or a ring, for that matter) that is distinctly "her" obscures the fact that things like the dress are meant to obscure, to subsume the self into a larger entity, a shared cultural thing. The veil and the majestic dress had distilled my entire person—my entire being—into a feminine ideal. And this ideal also drew, as the proposal and the ring had, on the idea that femininity is best expressed by passivity, appearances, and silence. Any part of me that might have contradicted it—my often masculine body language, my slomping booted feet, my tendency to spill sauces, my ability to *move* freely, and even my sarcastic, foul mouth— all were erased or restricted by the gown, by ritual's purposeful erasure of particulars.

I had not been prepared for the power of the traditional, historical clothing to overwhelm me, to set me into a continuum that connected all brides, past and present. "More than anything," said Mary, a thirty-eight-year-old writer from Chicago, "[the dress] symbolizes a rite of passage . . . a communion with other women who have 'put on the dress.'" I sensed this too, and felt at once transcendent and utterly confined. After all, communing with other women who've put on the dress means communing with women who for much of history were kept in an effective state of slavery. When I read Sheryl Nissinen's comment in *The Conscious Bride* that "brides may be especially comforted to learn that their modern anxiety is echoed by women who lived over two thousand years ago," I thought—my anxiety stems precisely from the fact that it is *not* modern, but echoes the anxiety of women who lived over *two thousand years ago*!

While the ring talked to other people about me like a gossipy sidekick, the dress silenced me with an incontrovertible authority, and in some ways this was more frightening. It made me into a thing—an offering, to be exact—a publicly understood expression of consent. And assuming such a posture made me undeniably beautiful, because female beauty has always been about surrender. To achieve such a state of feminine beauty, however, a state I had always resisted and fought against but which, deep down, I had always longed to effortlessly inhabit, was intoxicating.

The saleslady took my hand and had me walk to the far end of the store, so I could see myself from far away—as, she said, "your fiancé will see you on your wedding day." Suddenly it seemed comical to me that I'd thought of dress shopping with Andrew. I've always been attracted to romantic drama, and I loved the idea of *appearing* before him this way, like the awkward girl in the movie who gets a makeover, then walks down the stairs with a nervous smile to greet her open-mouthed admirer, soundtrack booming. "I definitely wanted that moment," my friend Jessica told me, explaining why it was so important to surprise her husband with her dress on their wedding day, "that 'I am so lucky to be marrying this woman' moment. A beautiful dress is part of that."

"This is the kind of dress young boys dream about," the saleslady said sotto voce, pressing her advantage. "He has always imagined you walking toward him, looking like this." An ad! And a good one. Tears sprang to my eyes. "This is the dress," the saleslady said confidently. Apparently crying, in her mind, was the clincher. Numerous women cited tears—theirs, their mother's, or even the saleslady's—as evidence they'd found *the one*. Oscar Wilde, on the other hand, once said that all bad poetry springs from genuine feeling.

The saleswoman turned to Clara. "See how she glows?" I walked around some more. I pulled the veil back over my head. Some people on the sidewalk outside the store stopped and stared. Clara walked around me in a circle, studying my face.

"It's not you," she pronounced.

"Oh come on," I said. "Should it be?"

"Of course!" she cried. I gave her a look. "Well, within reason," she said. "You can't get married in those Levi's you wear every day."

"Sure I could," I said, smiling.

"You *could*. But do you want to?"

No, I thought. I guess I don't.

FOR a few days afterward, despite the fact that it had felt like "a costume, not clothing" (as one friend described many of the dresses she didn't like), and despite the fact that it had made me feel like an actress playing a part, as another woman complained, visions of Super Size danced in my head. Andrew was primarily responsible for bringing me to my senses—the look he gave me when I described the dress to him, even in the most general terms, snapped me right out of it. It wasn't right. It was one thing to look like a bride, it was another thing to look "like a Barbie on top of a huge round cake," as Alexandra, a mother of three in New York, quipped. I wanted to look real, to feel authentic, to feel like myself, but I also wanted to be recognizably, definitively a bride. And I believed that I could find a wedding dress that would let me be both.

Many of the women I spoke with expressed similar goals. Mary, who wore a long ivory satin gown to her wedding, said, "One thing that struck me favorably about the dress was that I still felt like me in it—a very dressed up me, a me wearing an unmistakably bridal-looking white dress, but still recognizably me. Whereas, many other dresses I tried on that day and on subsequent days of shopping felt more like costumes for a performance rather than dressing for a real occasion in my life." Amanda, who wore a light dress of raw silk with a few inches of train, told me that "with the other dresses, I felt like I was a piece of cardboard, and the dress was in charge—the star of the show. When I tried on my dress, I felt like it was me that came through. . . . I didn't feel controlled by my outfit." Jessica confessed, "If it were really me it would have been a miniskirt, but my dress was a version of me—the romantic, ladylike me." (For good measure, Jessica "funked it up" by wearing platform shoes that no one else could see under her full-length gown.)

Years later, I asked my mother if she thought a lot about finding a dress that was "her" when she got married. The question itself amused her. When she was shopping for a wedding dress in 1968 she was twenty years old. She did not agonize about finding a wedding dress that would not overwhelm, betray, or undercut her individual identity. She felt triumphant about *assuming* an adult identity, period, and about announcing this assumption by wearing a white wedding dress. In her bridal portrait my mother's expression is animated and awake, in stark contrast to the dull docility my grandmother—married in 1945 to the kind of man who liked her that way—exhibited in hers. But my mother's lace chapel-length train and encumbrance of skirts still meant largely the same thing they'd meant when my grandmother had worn a similar ensemble: she had achieved, as she put it, "a woman's number-one priority in life: to get married."

"Marriage was a rite of passage into adulthood for me," she told me. "It was an emancipation! I had no rights when I got married. I was in college, living in a dorm that served in my parents' stead, monitoring everything I did. I had no money. And being your father's wife was infinitely preferable to being my father's daughter."

In 1968, obviously, things were just beginning to change, and the idea that women can and should have an adult identity outside of marriage (as well as the right to marry without ceding their civil rights, as used to be the case) was taking hold. In the 1970s a bride could hardly avoid making a statement about a woman's "place" with her choice of dress; during that anomalous time, personal style was inevitably political. When Bianca Jagger wore a white pantsuit with a neckline that plunged to her waist to marry Mick in 1971 (she was also four months pregnant), *that* was political; when Tricia Nixon got married the same year wearing silk organza in the Rose Garden and danced with her dad to "Thank Heaven for Little Girls," that was political, too. (Across the country in San Francisco, an LSD-dropping band of cross-dressers named the Cockettes made a film called *Tricia's Wedding*, with Goldie Glitters as Tricia.) In 1971 everything was political, whether people liked it or not. The whole country was engaged in a conversation not just about women but about race, war, and a whole host of other issues, and while you could choose not to participate, you could hardly ignore it was happening.

By the year 2000, however, I could easily have asked, *what conversation?* My wedding dress would not be seen against the backdrop of a raging debate about women's rights. The political upheaval and social changes of the 1970s, we are told, cut veils, tiaras, pearls, and petticoats loose from their historical fetters, freeing them from the weight of the crushing restrictions on female growth that gave rise to them in the first place. By the year 2000, *The Knot Book* could easily begin by saying, as it does: "The wedding gown. It's loaded with symbolism. It's laced with history. It has gone in and out of fashion. But what ultimately makes it the dress of all dresses is that it is a serious statement of *personal style*." Weddingchannel.com's "Who Are You" series lists a range of bridal personalities like horoscopes: Are you The Diva? ("No one has to tell you how to make an entrance . . . you love gowns that rustle . . . and drama in unexpected places.") The Classic Bride? ("We can see you falling in love with a strapless A-line gown of candlelight duchess satin.") The Natural Bride? ("Your look is angelic, ethereal, radiant, natural.") No— you're The Fashion Plate Bride! ("You've always known that the designer you spent your girlhood worshipping would take you down the aisle.") Worried about the pesky meaning attached to veils? Don't! All you have to decide is whether you are a "veil bride" or a "hair bride," as *The Knot Book* says, and get on with it.

Dot, a forty-two-year-old graduate student living in California, felt this. "I didn't have to cope with any gaps between who I am and what the white dress meant. Everyone else coped with them before me. I think women have been liberated from that, since the pill was invented in the sixties." And wasn't this a gift? I could have my wedding cake and eat it too! In 2000, Madonna got married (for the second time) in a castle wearing a ball gown that was straight out of Cinderella. Gloria Steinem got married that year, too. (She did not wear a white dress, but when the founder of *Ms.* becomes a Mrs., it says a lot.) The question, we have been led to believe, is no longer *why* wear a traditional wedding dress, but why *not*?

If this is the case, however, why the concern, voiced again and again by women I spoke with, and reiterated by wedding-dress designers' relentless emphasis on "personal choice" (and by the endless choices they put up for sale, the sheer quantity of which flabbergasted my mother), about finding a dress that doesn't conflict with your sense of self, that doesn't *undermine who you are*? This urgency makes it obvious that wedding dresses, far from being benign statements of personal style, still have meaning that individual women do not control, but with which they feel they have to contend.

The first, most obvious thing symbolized by the white wedding dress? Virginity. This is also the first meaning women my age scoff at, and it is easy to see why they consider it irrelevant and outdated. As Felicia, a television executive in New York, put it, "Honestly, if we all sat around thinking about what a white dress meant and the true tradition of why brides were supposed to wear them . . . no one would be able to wear white! Are there still women who don't test drive the car before they sign up for a life-long lease agreement?" Hannah, a writer in LA, was four months pregnant when she wed in white, and as she noted, "'Virginal' was pretty far from my mind." Samantha, an editor who recently married, put it this way: "It didn't bother me that it was white and yet my fiancé and I had been living together for almost three years already—that's more common these days than the alternative. Most brides aren't virgins anymore, but most still wear white, so perhaps the tradition, [and] what white symbolizes, is changing."

To the extent I even stopped to consider the issue of wearing white, I simply told myself that whether I liked it or not, just about everyone at my wedding would assume I wasn't a virgin, and therefore wearing white (well, ivory) wouldn't be hypocritical or against my principles, it would just be nice.

Except. While I believe it's true that white no longer symbolizes literal virginity—as Queen Victoria surely intended when she wore white for her 1840 wedding to Prince Albert, inaugurating the white wedding dress tradition—it is also true that a woman wearing a white wedding dress makes a statement about her sexuality, a statement men are not asked to make when they marry. Emmy, a twenty-four-year-old historian living in Pennsylvania, captured this in an unexpected way when she told me: "I felt a little uncomfortable wearing white because I am not a virgin. But I absolutely rebelled against the idea of proclaiming that in public at my wedding." In other words, Emmy wore white because *not* wearing white would be the equivalent of making a public proclamation about her sex life (a powerful incentive for women to conform to this tradition, by the way), which means that wearing white does, in fact, make a statement about her sexual past, understandable to all. Or, perhaps more importantly, the white dress makes her sexual past disappear, much to the crowd's relief and delight.

Women are not just redeemed from being "unchosen" when they marry. They are also redeemed from the shame of being sexually active, unmarried women. The "double-standard," as every woman on earth knows, still exists, as amply evidenced by numerous obnoxious, successful-marriage manuals for women, written by both women and men, which say things like (to give only the tiniest sampling):

"Many men want their woman to be virginal, but with natural porn-star talent."
—from *Closing the Deal: Two Married Guys Take You from Single Miss to Wedded Bliss*, by Richard Kirshenbaum and Daniel Rosenberg

"A man will break up with an otherwise perfect woman who has 'wife potential' simply because she slept with too many guys. Why is this so important to a man? Well, men don't want to be associated with a woman who is considered a tramp."
—from *Marry Me: Three Professional Men Reveal How to Get Mr. Right to Pop the Question*, by Bradley Gerstman, Esq., Christopher Pizzo, C.P.A., and Rich Seldes, M.D.

"No matter what a man will tell you, they all secretly measure how quickly you sleep with them against that secret perception of acceptable wifely behavior they've got locked away in their brains."
—from *Stop Getting Dumped!* by Lisa Daily

Even *The Conscious Bride*, written in gentle, new-agey tones and clearly sympathetic to women, describes the search for a wedding dress as the search for "the pure virgin, the silk-petaled lily, the delicate drop of dew. The gown is the primary symbol of maidenhood. . . . A woman wants to be a princess on her wedding day . . . the consummate symbol of innocence, virginity, purity, and maidenhood." Nissinen knows perfectly well that her readers are unlikely to be *literal* virgins. But given our society's deep ambivalence about female sexual freedom, she is absolutely right in saying that sexually active women want their sexual past sanitized, purified, and erased when they marry, because it still isn't really okay for a woman to have one. In the South, as Elizabeth Hyatt reported for the *New York Times* in 2002, growing numbers of brides are choosing to become born-again virgins before their weddings, abstaining for weeks or months before they marry even if they have been living and sleeping with their fiancés for years.

This phenomenon is largely confined to religious conservatives, but *Marry Me* was a nationwide bestseller, and while it never suggests that a woman abstain from sex once she's found "the one," it actually provides a fucking *chart*, which is literally a Fucking Chart, illustrating the maximum number of sexual partners a woman can have by a certain age and still expect to be considered "marriageable." Dubbed "The Prostitute Formula," the authors suggest that mothers share it with their daughters early so they can "plan ahead." On the one hand I found this to be insulting, outrageous, and infuriating (I may have actually thrown the book across the room at that point), and on the other hand it struck a chord, upsetting me so greatly precisely because, as a woman sandwiched between the sexual revolution and the enduring power of the double-standard, I'd always felt guilty, confused, defensive, and ashamed about being a sexually active single woman, even as I'd felt entitled to being one. I was always more comfortable in a monogamous relationship because it made my sex life "okay," and if I'm honest I'll admit that one reason I was eager to wear white was that it would make my sex life unassailably respectable, sanctioned, and safe for the first time since I was eighteen.

I wanted to show everyone, in other words, that in the end I'd become (or always had been?) a good girl. I wanted the uniformly approving looks reserved for women in white. But is it really progress that women are now free to *act* the part of the "pure virgin," as Nissinen puts it, "the consummate symbol of innocence," even when this role directly contradicts and undermines the choices they've made in their single lives? Why should they have to pretend? Once again, the slave always acts more than the master.

This dynamic is so powerful that it overwhelms, as with so many things relating to weddings, the understanding between individual men and women. Andrew did not want, need, or require me to "perform" my virginity at our wedding, or to wear clothing that announced that my sexuality was now being put safely under his proprietorship. Like many grooms, he respected my sexual freedom without judgment or disapproval. One woman told me she did not mind that her husband forwent the traditional Jewish "kittel"—a white tunic worn over the groom's wedding suit to signify his spiritual purity—because "he was pure in all the ways I cared about." Andrew felt the same way about me. But the pressure to produce the image of controlled, chaste female sexuality for the crowd was more powerful than our privately held views on the subject.

Meanwhile, Andrew was not even remotely expected to make a big public display of offering his "husband-material" sexual purity to me when he walked down the aisle. Men are so totally entitled to a sexual past that guys like the authors of *Closing the Deal* feel free to tell women that men, when it comes down to it, just like to "*stick it in.*" (*Sorry, girls!*) As with other things regarding marriage, grooms are seen to be giving something up when they marry (sexual freedom) while brides are seen to be gaining something when they walk down the aisle—a man's public proclamation that they are good girls after all, or good enough, at least, that they did not suffer the fate of girls only "good-for-now."

There is a twist, however, as there usually is for sandwiched women. Modern brides are burdened not just with the traditional task of conveying purity (the veil, the white or ivory dress, etc.), but also with the very modern task of looking sexy and hot (dresses backless to the butt, red-carpet cleavage, and so on). Where women used to be tasked solely with showing the world what a chaste, pure wife their husband was acquiring, donning high-necked gowns and covering their bodies in lace, women are now tasked with showing the world what a gorgeous, sexual wife their husband is acquiring, too, sporting low-necked gowns and showing skin in places that make grandmothers blush. (As *Modern Bride* reported in its fall 2005 issue, low-plunging dresses are at the forefront of design, and undergarments like Victoria's Secret's Very Sexy Push-up Plunge Strapless Bra are required to cope.) Modern brides are supposed to advertise the purification of their sexual pasts *and* the va-va-voom auspiciousness of their grooms' sexual futures, too.

Wedding dresses, in other words, are not just statements of a bride's personal style—they are wrapping paper for the gift publicly presented to a man on his wedding day: a woman's body and her sexual favors, which from that day forward will be his alone. The element of surprise, to which women rapturously refer when they talk about wedding dresses, symbolizes the presentation of this gift, and men do not surprise women with their wedding attire because men are not offering their bodies as presents, their sexual services as marital booty, or their appearance as a commodity for their wives to show off. (They have already made their gift of financial patronage with the ring—*their* surprise.) Surprise is only possible when reciprocity is impossible, and in the case of the wedding dress, it is.

In keeping with this, grooms wear a uniform that varies only infinitesimally from one man to the next, while brides wear gowns designed specifically for the occasion, never to be worn again. According to the Condé Nast Bridal Infobank, 98 percent of grooms rent from a "formalwear specialist," spending an average of $110 on their tux, while the average bride's dress costs more than seven times that. The exponential difference in cost, like the difference between the money spent on a woman's diamond engagement ring and a groom's corresponding—*nothing*—reiterates one of weddings' key lessons: marrying is not of equal importance for women and men. Wedding is *so* much more important for women, in fact, that while a man may rent what is essentially a work-a-day outfit dressed up in black and a bow tie, the bride must buy something that shows that nothing in her life matters as much as becoming a wife.

Do these costumes really reflect the state of affairs between most couples marrying today? Few modern brides, after all, would describe themselves as born-again virgins or gift-wrapped offerings, and few grooms would describe themselves as their brides' saviors or owners. Why present the bride to the groom this way, handing her to her groom? Why not have both partners walk into the back of the church, hall, synagogue, or other space at the *same* moment, perhaps escorted by their parents, to regard each other with mutual surprise as they see each other's clothing for the first time, clothing that dresses neither partner in the trappings of virginity or fantasy or sober uniformity? And why not walk down the aisle together, like two adults who have already made a life together, on equal ground?

Perhaps because deep down, many women have internalized the lessons the wedding dress teaches: that female sexuality outside of wedlock is shameful; that to be feminine and beautiful is to be passive and physically restrained; and finally that a woman gives herself to a man in an elaborate, expensive, once-in-a-lifetime gown because when she weds he makes her a wife, and this is the most important gift she'll ever receive, a gift she must show herself worthy of. Many men, consciously or not, have internalized these lessons, too.

Andrew and I certainly had, though we were light-years away from recognizing it—in no small part because while we may have internalized these lessons, we had always done our best to *reject* them. Whisked into a world of women as I shopped for my wedding dress, however, deliberately isolated from my husband-to-be and plopped into a separate sphere (or alternative universe, it sometimes seemed) in which my doubts and discomfort were alternately squashed and stoked by the massive machine of the wedding industry, I found little room to breathe, let alone think. And so I didn't.

In 1968, when my mother got married, she did not get the dress she wanted. I've known this for as long as I can remember.

"I can still describe it," my mother said wistfully as we headed out for our third day of dress shopping in New York. "It was satiny, without a long train, cut along princess lines." *Princess lines?* Two days of wedding dress shopping and I still had no idea what she was talking about. "It was soft, natural, and white, with very little lace, short sleeves and a broadly rounded neckline—not low-cut, but like a semi-moon. I could draw it." I assured her that wasn't necessary. "But it was $150, and my cheapo dad made me get the one that cost $90." She went on to say what she always said after telling me this story: I should get the dress I really loved, whatever it cost.

It was appropriate for her to reiterate this just then, because that morning we had an appointment at Vera Wang. We had been everywhere else. It was our last appointment, and we were both excited but nervous, too. My mother was nervous because she never goes to places like Vera Wang. I was nervous because I was not sure I was prepared to spend the amount of money that Vera Wang (Very Wealthy) extorts from brides for her wedding dresses. But I had a feeling I was going to find one of them irresistible. I believed the hype. It was convenient for me to believe it, mostly because believing it would absolve me of responsibility, somehow, if I (or my parents, or Andrew's parents, depending on which part of the wedding-money pot you wanted to count the dress against) shelled out for a Very Wealthy dress. Clara had told me with the utmost seriousness that I should not even enter Vera Wang if I was not prepared to buy. Otherwise I would be setting myself up for heartbreak, because her dresses were in "such a different league" that I would surely find The One, and afterward no other dress would compare.

The collection, I knew, *started* at $1,700. "I don't know if we should even be going to this place," I said to my mother, bouncing my knee up and down crazily in the cab. I had a sick feeling in my stomach, like I was sliding down a slippery slope, losing my grip on reality. (I was.) "Don't be silly, sweetheart," she said, gently placing her hand on my knee to still it. "We are looking for the right dress for you. The most perfect dress for you. And when we find it, we will get it!" I smiled, grateful for the rationalization. More and more, I was warming to the idea of buying my way out of the panic I was feeling about being The

Bride. I wanted reassurance, and Vera Wang had serious wedding authority. The words "Vera Wang gown," in fact, resounded with it.

I calmed myself with the thought that I'd already found two other dresses I liked very much. I'd probably buy one of them! One had a strapless bodice with beading across the top, and full skirts. The other one I can no longer remember.

Andrew knew about all of them. He was following my progress closely from Japan, where he was again working on a deal. He had reassured me about my trip to Vera Wang the night before, with his characteristic evenness of temper. "Just go, have fun, and stop worrying about it!" He encouraged me, perhaps because my Aunt Patsy is not the only one who has asked me why I don't wear more skirts. Andrew asks me too, and has always nudged me toward heels and sexy, feminine clothes.

I don't know what I think about this. I don't tell him to wear muscle shirts to show off his bod. One night I made him walk around our apartment in my three-inch mules (we wear close to the same shoe size), and of course he did very well for the grand total of ten minutes that he wore them, and congratulated himself for refuting my assertion that they were akin to foot binding. But I can certainly say now that I was not just looking for the right wedding dress for me. I was looking for the right wedding dress for him, too. He loomed large every time I walked out of a dressing room and looked at myself in white. (That saleslady had really known what she was doing with that whole "this is the dress every boy has dreamed of" bit.) And the ring he'd given me—simple, clean, elegant, and very expensive—had given me a certain notion of what he'd like.

He'd also, not subtly at all, asked me if I was going to take one of my friends to look at whatever dress I picked out. I had to admit it was a good idea. So my very stylish friend Caroline was meeting us at Vera Wang for quality control purposes.

"Honey," she said as we walked up to the door, "get ready for this. There's a lobby." And there was. Vera Wang on Madison Avenue is located, in a stroke of genius worthy of this former designer for the former

Ralph Lipschitz, now Ralph Lauren, in the 1930's era Carlyle Hotel. When you enter, you are downstairs. The dresses are upstairs. Very upstairs. It reminded me of the carpeted, gilded, impeccably appointed lobby of a country club spa in Texas. I was seized by the feeling of being an all-wrong impostor again, and it's possible that I would have actually taken my ring off and handed it to the well-coifed receptionist like a credential if she'd asked me to.

Upstairs, however, as the attendant began to bring out the dresses, I found myself beginning to relax. The dresses were indeed simple, clean, and elegant. Full of "effortless grace," "sophistication," and "style," just as the website promises. "Modern" and "urbane," just as the reviewers rave. The term most consistently associated with Vera Wang is modern; she makes a point of using it herself.

"I adore the challenge of creating truly modern clothes," Wang said in one online article, "where a woman's personality and sense of self are revealed." One could argue that Vera Wang has made a fortune off the exact sort of anxiety I felt about whether or not I could wear a traditional wedding dress and still retain my sense of self as an adult, modern woman. Vera Wang has succeeded in catering to women like me by preserving bridal traditions with her gowns while at the same time designing dresses that make it clear that the bride dressed herself. She is also expert at stoking the fires of bridal-romance fantasy until they reach money-burning temperatures. "For most women a wedding gown represents far more than just a dress," she writes in her sixty-five dollar book *Vera Wang on Weddings*. "It is also the embodiment of a dream, perhaps one she has nurtured since childhood. In this fantasy of idealized happiness, the groom represents perfection and the face of all human possibility. The instant a woman becomes engaged, however, all that energy and passion gets transferred to her dress. What follows can be something akin to madness." It's madness all right. And it got to me too.

I didn't think it would. My appointment lasted an hour, and eight or ten dresses in I still hadn't found *The One*, or at least not one I had to have. I'd just had fun, I thought, playing high-end Kamy-Barbie (I'd been provided with a very nice bustier) while my mother sat next to Caroline on a taupe-colored sofa, her back perfectly straight as always, a look of contentment on her face as she smiled and nodded with pleasure at various styles. Then the saleswoman decided to bring me something different, unlike the sort of dresses I'd asked for when I'd come in. The gown had a French name. (They all have names, like second homes.) It was stunning. "Oh yeah," Caroline said, winking. Even seeing this thing on the hanger, we all knew I was in trouble.

This dress wasn't strapless. It had tiny, straight, silk spaghetti straps instead. It also had a slightly curved neckline that gave me a little décolletage, and a low back that was slightly curved too. It wasn't poofy either. It fit snugly over my hips, and then flared outward to form a fluted skirt, bolstered by petticoats. (My friend Franny still insists it was poofy. "Deal with yourself!" she says. "Totally poofy white dress!") But it wasn't even white! It was ivory, with a subtle, broad crisscross pattern of lace overlaying it. And it came with a veil. "I didn't think I would want a veil," Clara had told me, "but it gave me a sense of privacy and inward meditation that was so nice." This comment had made a lasting impression on me. The idea of privacy, when the time came that I would be stared at by a few hundred people in such a state, sounded incredibly good, and I had been pairing veils with almost every dress I tried.

This dress, however, was different from any other dress I'd worn. I put it on, and for the first time since Super Size, I looked at myself in the mirror, and I started to cry.

I'm going to get married, I thought. And when I do, I'm going to look like this.

DAYS later, I wasn't so sure. Not surprisingly, the gown I loved was more than $1,700. To buy one of the $1,700 dresses at Vera Wang, which were so "simple" they were like cars without air conditioning or power steering, was to buy a dress just to say it was Vera Wang and miss out on lots of other beautiful dresses that had more going for them at the same price. To buy this dress, which fell into the middle of the Vera Wang price range, was to buy something unlike anything else I'd seen.

But it was also to spend a lot of money on a dress I would wear only once in my life. Considered that way it was unjustifiable. (The owners of Kleinfeld's, in *How to Buy Your Perfect Wedding Dress*, attempt to counter this with a chapter titled "A Wedding Dress Is Forever." Nice try.) The majority of women I spoke with could not, and did not, pay nearly as much. The winner of the wedding-dress bargain sweepstakes paid fifty dollars for her wedding suit; another bride got a Vera Wang for $99 on eBay—though it was platinum blue and she suspects it was a bridesmaid's dress in a former life. I paid a lot more, but in that dress I just *knew*, and that seemed, well, worth it. My mother, Andrew, Caroline, and everyone else I talked to assuaged my guilt, but I always hoped my dad would never find out what I'd spent, which should have told me something about how over-the-top it was.

But . . . *it was The One*! What did that mean? Did it mean I was comfortable in it, that it was *me*? No. Early on, I had concluded that I was never going to feel like "me" in a wedding dress; more important, I'd decided that this was appropriate. I'd asked myself, reflecting on how strange I felt in almost every wedding dress I tried: *should* I feel like I'm dressing up in white for a black-tie dinner? Shouldn't the whole thing be far more extra-ordinary than that? Yes, the event itself was what mattered. But why deny that clothing can play a crucial part in signifying the meaning of the event? And how would I do that if I didn't wear a traditional wedding dress? I wanted my dress to serve as a constant reminder that what I was doing was singular and sacred, and my desire to participate fully in one of the few culturally shared rituals our society has left was very powerful indeed.

This argument had its merits. One of the things that discouraged me most as I looked for a wedding dress was how bereft of real meaning it all seemed to be. Joseph Campbell, who wrote about ritual and myth across world cultures, lamented in his interviews with Bill Moyers that, as with many rituals in American life, the wedding ritual that once conveyed "inner-reality" had now become "merely form." Life had changed so much over the last fifty years, Campbell contended, that it had been impossible for ritual to keep pace, and the ritual clothing brides wore reflected this gap. Wedding dress has not changed as radically as women have, and the wedding industry knows it—one reason they instruct brides to concentrate solely on form and dismiss more difficult questions of meaning. But, like many other women I talked to, I wanted to believe there were meaningful connections between me, my dress, my community, and historical custom. So I employed yet another bit of sandwiched-woman, contradictory logic. *I am wearing a traditional wedding dress because I want my clothing to have cultural and historical meaning*, I told myself. *But to the extent it undermines and insults me, I reject the cultural and historical meaning of the wedding dress.* Ta-da!

This is the method of choice for the majority of modern brides: they "pick and choose," not wearing a veil over the face, for instance, or wearing ivory instead of white, or going strapless or trainless or otherwise -less, and thereby removing what they find offensive or problematic while preserving the recognizable, traditional garb. I am sympathetic to this approach, and I still think it's a reasonable strategy—in the absence of a new kind of wedding dress, the only alternative, as I saw it, was to invent a totally new outfit, and at the time I felt this would have been a public proclamation of the void. I did not want to be a walking reminder of the void at my wedding! This was partly due to a sense of longing common among women my age, I think, for an era we never knew, when there were rules, stability, and well-defined sex roles (but roles that infantilized women, *don't forget!*), a time when tradition and individual reality were largely in-sync. It was mostly, however, because I didn't want to be different.

When it came right down to it, concern over other people's opinions (those other people again!) was the most powerful force of all in my choice of wedding dress. I may have told myself it was for spiritual reasons, but more than anything I was willing to be uncomfortable in order to make everyone else *comfortable*, because if everyone else had been uncomfortable, I would have been even *more* uncomfortable, and more than I wanted to participate in ritual or dress myself up like the perfect virgin/porn-star (my dress was somewhat sexy), I wanted to conform. I wanted to say "I am just like you." I also wanted to say, of course, "I am just like you . . . except wearing a more beautiful dress, with more toned arms, and more special hair." Competitive conformity also drives women to traditional wedding dresses, and if I'm honest I know I wanted to excel at it.

As always, my mother was one of the most important "other people" I wanted to please. And just as she surprised me with the intensity of her desire that I marry, she surprised me with the intensity of her desire to conform to various wedding traditions, beginning with the dress. (Wedding-dress sellers have found a way to profit from the conflict between mothers and daughters about the traditional and the modern, of course: the designer Monique Lhuillier told the *New York Times* that many of her brides are buying two gowns, one mother-pleaser for the ceremony and one modern model for the reception.) My mother tried to smile when I tried on a satiny-slip of a "modern" wedding dress the first day we shopped together, but it was clear it left her cold. She wanted to see me in the full getup, and, I realized, had been anticipating this for some time. Andrew has said that when it came to our wedding, I clung to the tradition-map a little too tightly, fighting him when he wanted to veer from it. My mother, however, often seemed to be holding this map up between my face and hers, shouting out directions.

"It is traditional to do a bridal portrait to display at the reception!" (?!) "Everyone knows the bride marries in her hometown, and if you don't I will have to explain to everyone that you don't like where you're from!" "I'd like to appear on the invitations as Dr. and Mrs. James S. Wicoff, not as James and Kathleen!" "I won't walk you down the aisle with your father. I can't do it, Kamy. I just can't." The last one was the worst. I could choose to overrule her about other things. We got married in Andrew's hometown. I put my mother's name on my wedding invitations. (Who is "Mrs. James S. Wicoff?" I asked her. "It's the formal way of doing it," she said, "and if you aren't going to consider my opinion, I don't know why you bother to ask.") But I couldn't make my mom walk me down the aisle. "I didn't know a lot about the traditions surrounding weddings," said Jen, a twenty-seven-year-old graduate student living in Denver; "however, my mom made damn sure that I knew and followed as many as possible. . . . I was a little surprised at how much it meant to her." I was surprised, too. What was that all about?

One easy answer was that, like me, she was looking for help during a stressful time. In a post-feminist era where the old map has flown out the window, and the new one hasn't been constructed yet, reaching for the old map in the form of etiquette books and the like can be a very useful tool for planning a wedding. Etiquette manages tricky relationships and situations by codifying them, and minimizes decision-making by supplying rules. In communicating wedding etiquette to me, my mother was trying to play the traditional role of the Mother of the Bride; but our battles about it called attention to how ambiguous that role has become. (One advice book I read said the only definite job a modern M.O.B. has left is to tell her daughter she looks beautiful.) My mother never had a chance to plan a wedding—her mother planned hers, and I'd made it very clear that I was going to plan mine. Sometimes this made her feel left out, looking for ways to be in.

Another fairly easy answer is that my mother had been envisioning my wedding for some time, and had cherished ideas about what it would be like. She'd always imagined, for instance, watching me walk down the aisle with my dad. She couldn't part with this image, and I didn't have the heart—or the spine—to make her. After I got married and my mom and I could talk about it more easily, she sent me a little book by Ilene Beckerman called *Mother of the Bride*. I always wished she'd given it to me during my engagement; Beckerman is funny and honest, and the book helped me see things from my mother's perspective—something I had difficulty doing at the time.

"I wanted my daughter to be happy," Beckerman writes. "'Well, just as long as you're happy,' I'd say. I was lying. What I really wanted was for the things that made me happy to make her happy." I never thought marriage, and a traditional wedding, would make my mother so happy. But I'd also never stopped to think about how much my mother, and many other women of her generation, might have longed to put that raging political "conversation" they lived through in the 1960s and 1970s behind them, and call it quits. Is it possible that big, poofy wedding dresses were also all the rage in the year 2000 because a bunch of baby-boomer moms, with big late-nineties-boom budgets, were thrilled to think that despite the battering it has taken (a battering for which they may feel responsible), marriage had survived, and it was time to sing *Celebration* in a big white dress, without regrets and please, *please* without politics?

It's possible indeed. It's called backlash, and my mother wasn't alone in getting caught up in it. Clearly I got caught up in it too. Weddings bring out the conventional in everyone, and the ambivalence about convention in everyone, but too often we cope with our ambivalence about the conventions by clinging to them all the more tightly. Looking back on it now, I wish I'd been braver. I wish I'd looked at my wedding not as a time to forget about the past or my politics, but as a time to think about those things and make choices that—rather than contributing to the continuity of custom—contributed to the continuity of human growth, and capacity for change. I suppose I didn't know exactly how to express our inner reality in a wedding. I did know I wanted to say, "I am just like you."

What did wearing that wedding dress with a veil over my face mean in the year 2000? Maybe it meant I was free to wear it. Maybe it meant I still felt like I had to.

So what *would* I wear, a friend asked me, if I had it to do over again? I don't know exactly. I'd have to go shopping, but I wouldn't shop in bridal boutiques; at this point I can't think of one good reason to spend what they charge, much less to walk down the aisle in white or in ivory, either. Believe it or not, I might take a cue from an earlier era, when women—particularly non-royal ones—simply made or ordered the "best dress" they'd ever had to wear on their wedding day, in blue, brown, or any other color (but almost never in white, since most women planned to wear the dresses again and white was very impractical). I suppose I too would go looking for my "best dress," something beautiful but functional, below the knee but not to the ground, flattering and light and grown-up and, yes, *me*. I'd seek out a dress that was special, perhaps more costly than the dresses I normally buy, and definitely more feminine than my everyday wear—to the extent that feminine means flattering to the female body, and that femininity means freedom to experiment with one's appearance in a way that masculinity forbids.

But I would not dress for a part that was only partly me, and I would not dress in a way that undermined my adulthood or erased my past. I would dress for myself, for Andrew, and for that larger thing that was our wedding. And I would trust that my participation in the ceremony of marriage—not the act of hooking, fastening, and battening myself into a wedding dress and, as a result, into its messages—messages I could not control—would have been sufficient reminder that I was doing something singular and sacred that day, and probably would have helped me see just *what* a lot more clearly.

LATE the night I tried on the dress, I called Andrew. My mother would have given me privacy if she could have, but there was nowhere else for her to go in our loft except into the bathroom. So I talked to him with her nearby, trying not to listen, but having difficulty restraining herself from backseat-phone-talking, something I do too.

"I found a dress," I told him.

"*The* dress," she whispered, as though to herself.

"It's pretty incredible," I said.

"Pretty incredible?!" my mother cried, looking at me and smiling adoringly.

"Did Caroline like it?" Andrew said.

"You're a jerk!" I said, reproaching him for his lack of confidence in my taste.

We laughed. Convinced with regard to the romantic impact of wedding-day surprise, I didn't describe it to him in detail. Andrew told me that he trusted my (and Caroline's, apparently) judgment. He told me that if I'd always be thinking of that dress even if I chose another, less expensive one, I would just have to get it. Going into Vera Wang in order to provide myself with just such an excuse had worked. Talking to him, part of me felt sure I would make him incredibly happy when he saw me walking towards him in that gorgeous, exquisite gown. At the same time I felt guiltily hesitant. Could it possibly be right to kick off our wedding planning by buying a dress like this?

Then Andrew said something that made me feel like I'd done the right thing.

"As long as the dress is formal," he said, "you know, elegant. Because I want our wedding to be like that. Formal and elegant but a really fun party; a really good show."

Well then. I had to get it, or so I thought. The next day I went back with my mom, along with another close friend, to see the dress again. It was still breathtaking. The salesperson took Polaroids. I signed the paperwork, which was not inconsiderable, and oughtn't have been considering the size of the transaction being made. It was done. I had a wedding dress. Now all I needed was a wedding to wear it to.

six

~∞~

The W.C., Part One
The Wedding Consumer

When I chose my wedding dress, I officially became a bride. This was because seeing myself in a wedding dress thrust me into a confrontation with myself as bride, wife, ersatz virgin, gift-wrapped girl, and, finally, high-end Kamy-Barbie. It was also because as a woman in white, I found myself struggling with issues of history, tradition, and where I fit in. But mostly it was because after I chose my wedding dress, I bought it, and when I did I spent an amount of money that would normally be acceptable only if one were buying a flat-screen TV. "I think that was the moment I really felt myself go into 'bride' mode," said Mary, a thirty-eight-year-old writer from Chicago, "when I slapped down my AmEx for a $2,000 dress."

The phrase "it's your day," when trumpeted by wedding magazines and websites, really means "it's your day . . . to spend more money than you ever dreamed possible." Many brides resist this, or set out to, but every year millions of dollars are spent to coerce the reluctant into spending more than they budgeted (Condé Nast's Bridal Infobank relishes this, reporting that 43 percent of couples spend more on their weddings than they planned!), and the already eager to spend more than they have. (Record numbers of newly married couples now begin their marriage saddled with wedding-related debt.) If bridal boot camp trains women to be wives, there may be no single skill more aggressively drilled into them during their engagement than that supreme function of the American woman: spending money.

"Why is it never said," Betty Friedan asked in *The Feminine Mystique*, "that the really crucial function, the really important role that women serve as housewives is *to buy more things for the house?*" Speaking of brides over the last ten years, as the wedding industry has mushroomed at a rate surpassing even Martha Stewart's wildest dreams (or perhaps not), why is it never said that the really crucial function, the really important role that women serve as brides is *to buy more things for the wedding (and for the house!)?*

According to Martha Barletta's book *Marketing to Women*, a whopping 85 percent of all consumer buying decisions in this country are made by women. In light of this, it is unsurprising that from the perspective of the Wedding Industrial Complex, "bride" and "customer" are synonymous. When Friedan wrote *The Feminine Mystique* in the 1950s, she cited a marketing company report that described engagement as a woman's "rehearsal of the material duties and responsibilities of marriage," and brides as dreamy romantics with "a product-centered outlook." This language is downright quaint when compared with the cynical avariciousness exhibited by the modern wedding industry. Consumer advocates Denise and Alan Fields quote the publisher of *Brides* as saying, "Never before in a woman's life, and never again, is she going to be worth this much money to a marketer." The internal tag line of *Brides*, this man went on to say, was "Where love meets money." Given the fact that bridal magazines have an ad-to-article ratio resembling a catalogue's, the motto is apt.

It's easy to see why wedding profiteers are so filled with glee. The women of Generations X and Y have fueled explosive growth in the wedding trade. Since 1990, the average cost of a wedding has gone through the roof, from $15,208 to $26,327 in 2005. Since the year 2000 twelve new bridal magazines have made their debut, and the total number doubled between 1996 and 2005. *Modern Bride* magazine, in conjunction with Roper Starch Worldwide, published a report in 2001 titled "Your New $100 Billion Customer . . . The Engaged Woman," announcing that engaged women have different "spending priorities" from single women, and will spend fifty billion on wedding-related items and a further fifty billion on "cars, homes, furniture and more."

My wedding dress was the first purchase I made as an engaged woman, but there were to be so many more. Over the next eight months, as I assumed primary responsibility for planning what would become a two-hundred person, formal, sit-down wedding on top of a mountain in Colorado, I slid quickly down the rabbit hole into that surreal universe where it is so important to have frosted flower vases you will spend hours in the New York summer heat trolling stores to find them (and then pay to have them shipped), where you say the word "wedding" to a caterer and the price of petit-fours is suddenly four times higher than it would have been if you'd said "birthday," where a hotel wedding coordinator can tell a bride (as one told my friend Jessica) that she "has to have" a special utensil for cutting her cake, and like a Stepford bride–bot she does not protest, despite being "flabbergasted," but instead goes to Hallmark and slaps down her credit card yet again. I got a kick out of insouciantly referring to the wedding consultant we eventually hired as our "W.C.," but the "C" was not so much for consultant as it was for consumer and customer, and the truth was that the W.C. was me.

At some point in late January, Andrew and I made it official: we wanted to have an outdoor wedding, in August, somewhere in the vicinity of Boulder. (I broke it to my mother as gently as possible, and agreed to an engagement party in San Antonio so we could celebrate with my parents' friends.) Years before, dreaming of his wedding day— yes, Andrew did this—Andrew had also decided this event should be a sit-down, formal dinner, perhaps black tie, for three hundred people. "Do you *really* think we're going to have *three hundred people*?" I kept asking him, as though I were saying, "Are you *really* trying to *kill* me?"

As it turned out we ended up with less than two hundred—exactly as predicted by the mystifyingly accurate formula that says you will have as many guests as invitations you send—but Andrew was thrilled at the idea of getting so many friends and family together, and for the most part I thought it sounded good too. The question was, where were we going to do it? And how, with so little time to plan?

It did not seem to me at first that we had "so little time to plan." At first it seemed to me that seven months was ample time, an assertion I stubbornly maintained even when faced with the exhaustive things-to-do (a.k.a. things-to-buy) lists detailed in the fat, glossy stack of wedding magazines I had recently acquired. They all began with "one year ahead," which put me "five months behind," but, as I told Andrew defiantly (and hopefully), this *had* to be scare-tactic hype. Not only that, but upon deciding to plan a wedding in Boulder while living far away in New York, we had also decided it would behoove us to enlist some professional help. We were going to hire a wedding consultant, and I was confident that as soon as we did, all my fears would be assuaged. Instead, however, our telephone interviews with potential wedding consultants in Boulder succeeded in scaring me at last.

Prior to making the calls, I dutifully printed out a list of thirteen questions suggested by theknot.com, which read like an advertisement for wedding consultants, probably because it was written by them (The American Association of Bridal Consultants was listed as a source). "Will the consultant devise a master plan mapping out all the little details, from announcement to zebra-striped decor? (This will clue you in to organizational prowess and a willingness to keep you in the loop on every matter imaginable.)" and "Can the consultant score you some discounts with any vendors? (Consultants bring volume to favored vendors; often they'll reciprocate by slashing prices or throwing in extras.)" My first problem was that after clicking the link and calling to request a directory of Colorado consultants, I was told I could expect it to arrive in four to six weeks. Four to six *weeks!*? I panicked, but only briefly, as my ever-resourceful mother-in-law-to-be got us several names from friends in four to six days. The only problem was that after five or six phone calls, we still hadn't been able to get as far as question one. Instead we got stuck in the initial general-information phase.

"Three hundred people, mountain views, 'rustic meets black tie,' a site that's no more than half an hour's drive from Boulder . . . sure, it's possible," the wedding consultant would say, clearly not thinking out-side the box, as Andrew very much wanted our consultant to do, but at least treating us like rational people. Then she would say, "And this is for the summer of 2001?" August *2000*, we'd answer, at which point we'd earn a condescending sigh or, in one case, an outright laugh. August 2000! Three hundred people! Seated black-tie dinner! Spectacular mountain views! Ha ha ha! Good luck! One candidate Andrew spoke to (we took turns making the calls) said, "I'd be happy to see what I can do, but at this late date you will have to be flexible."

Andrew hung up. "Flexible? You haven't even made one phone call and you're already telling me I have to be flexible? Loser!"

If we'd been okay with getting married at a country club, or in a hotel ballroom, it would have been different. But Andrew had a fantasy in mind, a fantasy I'd come to share: the place needed to be something natural, not corporate or weddingy, the place needed to be, in his words, "untouched." (That was where he lost me. "Untouched! What do you mean *untouched*? Like, no indoor bathrooms, untouched!? Where is my grandmother going to go to the bathroom?") There were, as it turned out, a few places in Boulder that fit our bill while also being official, real wedding sites: restaurants, parks, barns, and ranches converted for the purpose of hosting events. These sites had staff and seating and indoor bathrooms and even buildings people could enter after the outdoor cer-emony. But they had all been booked months beforehand, as most of the wedding consultants could tell us without having to make any phone calls at all.

Engagements now last longer than ever—up from an average of eleven months in 1990 to an average of seventeen months in 2005—

and this means that wedding sites are booked further ahead of time than ever. It isn't hard to guess who benefits from couples spending such lengthy periods of time in the "engagement period" (or, as Condé Nast's Bridal Infobank calls it, the "year-round shopping spree"), months when brides have "no price resistance," also according to the publisher of *Brides*, months during which they can save up money for the "perfect wedding"—just as De Beers convinced them to save up and defer engagement rather than forgo the perfect ring. The industry has succeeded so completely in grimly, firmly convincing couples that they *must* plan this far ahead, however, that one bride who planned her wedding in "just" five months told me she was frequently asked by the incredulous if she was pregnant.

It doesn't take sixteen months to plan a wedding. I spoke with women who did it in ten weeks or less, and even heard a beautiful story about a woman who, because her mother was dying of cancer, put together a formal wedding complete with caterer, florist, photographer, and men in custom-fit tails in five days. The catch, however, was that she had to get married on a Monday. Because while it may not actually take sixteen months to plan a wedding, as long as there are brides willing to wait in order to get their hands on the most popular spots, it can indeed require twelve months notice to book one.

I, for one, felt humbled. Bitch-slapped by unseen brides who'd just beaten me at a game I didn't want to play. "We're not going to be able to get married this summer, are we?" I sighed. I looked up at Andrew and smiled ruefully, feeling very sorry for myself. "That's okay. I don't mind. We'll do it in a year and a half. So what?"

"Sweetie! There are a million places all around Boulder that are just big, beautiful open spaces, and for anyone to tell us we're too late to put a bunch of chairs in a field and stand out there and get married is total bullshit."

We started laughing, a tad hysterically. We were just going to put a bunch of chairs in a field and stand out there and get married! What was the big deal?

"One more," he said. "Want to call?" I shook my head. He dialed.

He began speaking with one Marci Barton, of Perfect Planning International. He kept speaking, which was a good sign. He outlined our vision. He began tossing out various possibilities, and then he began saying, "So you think you might be available for a weekend in February?" A huge grin spread across my face. Marci Barton. The last name on the list. Marci with an "i". I bet she used paint pens to put a heart over the "i" in junior high. I bet she knew how to French braid her own hair. A real *girl*.

Andrew and I had come to share a wedding fantasy, but our fantasy wedding consultants were different types. Andrew wanted someone who could execute, "run an audible" and do "due diligence" (all phrases he uses at work), a crack negotiator who knew how to use Excel, a wedding CEO. I wanted to hire a woman who excelled at all the things about being a woman I'd never been any good at—namely, shopping, makeup, and crafts. To me, a wedding consultant was a lifesaving flotation device to wear around my waist as I bobbed up and down in the vast, unfriendly foreign ocean of corsages, dinner plates, space heaters, seating assignments, and "save-the-date" letters that, according to the magazines, I was about to be tossed into. A wedding consultant also seemed like a nanny; a way for those with means to outsource women's work, thereby diffusing tension over the double shift.

Naturally I wanted to hire a woman who would make me look good. I did not know if Marci Barton knew how to tie a perfect pashmina, but I hoped so. I did know that she was saying yes and at the moment, that was enough.

At last Andrew hung up the phone. He was scribbling things on a piece of paper. "So?" I said. "Did you hire her? Was she great? Was she creative and totally kick ass?"

He shrugged. "She was nice." He was teasing me a little. *"Nice?"* I repeated.

"Yeah. Nice. She was very nice, I would say. And she was open-minded, didn't seem to think that putting it together for August was a problem at all."

"No problem at all?"

"Totally doable," he said. "Absolutely." Walking up behind me, Andrew rested his chin on my shoulder and kissed my cheek. "I say we go to Boulder and see what she comes up with. We've either found somebody really resourceful, or we've hired the only wedding consultant in Colorado stupid enough to think we can do it."

A FEW weeks later, as Andrew and I walked into the ballroom on the top floor of a hotel conveniently located near the Denver Airport (upon further reflection, and after further panic attacks, I'd decided we should at least *look* at a few wedding sites that would actually come prêt-à-porter), I nervously squeezed Andrew's hand, scanning the room for Marci Barton, my wedding savior. I was looking for high heels, I was looking for a smart black pencil skirt, I was looking for a clipboard and blush. Instead I found Marci Barton, undoubtedly as nice as she could be (Andrew had that right), but who looked not like a cheerleader, but like a gym teacher instead.

Not a gym teacher in Andrew's fantasy W.C. way (like a general), not like my junior high gym teacher, who hurled red rubber balls at us with such ferocity during dodgeball that she frequently made us cry. Instead Marci Barton looked like an easy-going, chaperone-the-dance, sweatpants-and-New-Balance-tennis-shoes kind of gym teacher. She was a few inches shorter than I was and tended to stand with her feet planted shoulder-width apart, rolling forward on her toes when she wanted to make a point. She had light brown hair, layered and curling-ironed, which framed her face and fell just above her collar. Her face was round, as were her eyes, and her nose was small and flat. She did not appear to be wearing lipstick. I felt sure that she drove a minivan, lived in a recently built subdivision, and didn't swear. My W.C. fantasy didn't swear either, but she was a ruthlessly correct, interior decorator Prom Queen.

"You must be Andrew and Kamy," she said, pronouncing Kamy like Tammy, as almost everyone does, and holding out her hand with a smile.

"It's like Amy with a K," I said, closing my hand around hers. (One person actually took this to mean my name was Amyk.) Marci apologized with a nervous laugh. She was nervous! Not only was she nervous, I realized, she was more nervous than I was. Upon this realization, a funny thing happened to me. My disappointment gave way to something new, something pleasurable and empowering. Seeing that Marci was not feminine perfection incarnate but instead just like me—or better yet, not even as cool or fashionable as me—I felt something I had not yet felt as a bride: self-confidence. Or, perhaps more honestly, superiority. Pathetic but true: Marci's homegrown niceness had made me feel feminine, fashionable, and fancy by comparison. I live in *New York City*, I suddenly found myself thinking, the capital of urbanity! As far as this Marci Barton person knows, all that urbanity has rubbed off on me! And then I thought, maybe it *has* rubbed off on me! Looking around the ballroom with a critical eye, knowing instantly it was not the right place for us, I said to myself: *I can do this, dammit. I am going to show good ole Marci Barton a wedding the likes of which she's never seen!*

In other words I felt superior, self-confident, and *competitive*. My big beautiful ring really had filled me with guilt, anxiety, and a feminist desire to prove myself as an equal to Andrew. But it had also filled me with a desire to show off. To prove my worthiness as a new member of a class that could afford to host a formal black-tie wedding for three hundred people, many of whom had been to a lot of formal black-tie weddings before. The truth was that from the time I got engaged, two voices had been competing for attention inside my head: one angelic, sincerely focused on the meaning of it all, intent on being genuine, generous, and unpretentious, and one demonic, perched on my other shoulder whispering things like, "Vera Wang! Caviar! Twelve-piece band!"

My little demon, however, had an advantage. It was backed up by an entire, well-funded chorus. Bridal magazines, wedding websites, and, naturally, on-site wedding coordinators all stood ready to throw gasoline on any spark of desire I had to competitively, conspicuously get wed, and at the conclusion of our tour the Denver hotel's coordinator did her part by producing a gigantic notebook filled with (what else?) other people's wedding photos. "This is just to give you an idea of what we can do," she said to me. What she really meant, of course, was: "This is just to give you an idea of the competition." Undoubtedly the name-dropping, status-spending, keeping-up-with-the-Star-Joneses tack often yields good results for wedding vendors. As Kathy, a twenty-seven-year-old analyst from Atlanta, put it, "There's an increasing sense that you have to at least 'match' how wonderful/extravagant/elegant, etc., the past weddings you've been to are . . . it's got to be bigger and better than the last one." Mary, a thirty-five-year-old writer in New York, put it this way: "Weddings are now a competitive sport."

And page after page of this giant, three-ring photo album spelled out the terms of the game. Illustrating an endless list of wedding "requirements," things one absolutely had to buy, rent, or mortgage one's house for in order to have the perfect wedding—since of course it is necessary for a wedding to be perfect—the display was designed to intimidate and to prod. The wedding industry, well aware that it can't grow by upping the number of weddings each year, a number that has remained steady for decades now (though gay marriage could expand the market for the first time, an expansion *Forbes* recently estimated could yield a "windfall" of 16.8 billion dollars), has hit upon the obvious: it can *only* grow by upping each wedding's cost.

"We initially planned on getting married in our hometown in Vermont," Sidney, a twenty-nine-year-old scientist, told me, "but as I talked to the club's wedding planner, she started to manipulate our plans. I understood it was her job to make as much money on our wedding as possible, but she insisted on all kinds of extras, more food, more decoration, more, more, more!" Sidney finally had a meltdown, but, more important, she had the guts to pull out, and ended up planning a wedding in a Florida church followed by a beach picnic cookout. Many brides, however, tackle the gap between their resources and their wedding dreams by assuming the role of bridal bargain hunter. This, too, is appropriate training for a wife-to-be: wives have long been charged with managing family finances, with making a little bit go a long way. And as women plan weddings many defend "bride-mode" by saying it is decidedly *not* slapping down an AmEx for a $2,000 dress but rather finding the exact same dress (ha!) marked down by half on eBay. This is an admirable way to do battle with the business (see the excellent *Bridal Bargains* by consumer advocates Denise and Alan Fields)—but just because you buy at a bargain doesn't mean you aren't buying into a system that asks way too much in the first place.

Bargain hunting can also be tough when brides are made to feel ashamed for even considering cost cutting with regard to their big day. "Everyone struggles with what it's 'worth' to them," said Diana, a thirty-one-year-old software developer from California. The wedding industry stokes this, naturally, as it stands to profit. Its message, as one bride put it? "If it's important, you'll pay a price that shows how important it is to you." This is one reason so many wedding vendors get away with "the wedding tax."

"The most insane thing I discovered," said Amanda, a twenty-nine-year-old writer from New York, "was that you say 'wedding' and prices quadruple. Who are these people who have made it their livelihood to unabashedly exploit people who want to join their lives together? I'm imagining a special circle in hell for them." Felicia asked angrily, "Who the hell has forty thousand dollars laying around that they can throw away on a wedding?" Not many people. As a *New York Times* article with the headline "For Richer or Poorer, to Our Visa Card Limit" observed, the cost of an average wedding now represents more than five months' wages for a middle-income family. As more couples marry later in life and foot the bill for their own weddings (as of 2005, 27 percent of weddings were paid for by the couple alone), more couples begin their marriages in debt.

It is not just young couples who get into debt, of course—with wedding costs skyrocketing and the pressure to host ever-more-extravagant three-day events increasing, parents can find themselves in debt, too.

(The *Times* article featured one set of parents who, not wanting to appear "cheap," accrued so much debt to pay for their daughter's wedding they found themselves struggling to buy groceries.) There is something sinister about the wedding industry's faux-feminist "articles" saying that in this day and age, it is antiquated for *only* the bride's family to pay. After all, these people are all for ramming tradition down one's throat when it means buying the bride a thousand-dollar dress. Clearly jettisoning sexist traditions is not their concern. In this case the real message is "the more, the merrier." As Condé Nast's Bridal Infobank happily reports to its advertisers, more than one party now contributes to 45 percent of weddings, and as the average cost of a wedding increases, one headline announced with celebratory triumph, "so does the number of people paying for it!"

In some cases, however, debt, bargain hunting, and pooled resources still aren't enough. But that doesn't stop some couples from having lavish weddings anyway. It is a tribute to the power of the industry (and, of course, to people's vanity) that when the bride, groom, and both families still come up short, the "latest trend," according to a May 2005 article in the *Wall Street Journal* titled "To Have and Hit Up," is to register for wedding contributions. (Many couples, apparently, ask guests to pitch in for wedding costs while still expecting to receive traditional gifts.) Wells Fargo has set up "wedding accounts" where guests can deposit cash to go towards photography, caterers, and everything else now "required" at a wedding, and savvy vendors have begun to add a registry feature to their websites. Jennifer Watson, a San Diego wedding photographer who has done just that, told *WSJ*: "I'm constantly looking for ways to fine-tune so the client's money goes further." What she really means, of course, is that she is constantly looking for ways to get *more money*, and if her clients' runs out, she "fine-tunes" by creating a registry that helps them get more money from someplace else.

We were lucky. We were not going to have to beg, borrow, or steal in order to have the wedding we wanted, and this meant I was going to be spared a lot of stress. (My friend Jessica, whose first check for the reception bounced—the second one cleared!—said that worrying over money was the worst part about her wedding, something I heard a lot.) Our pooled resources had created an enviable budget. But if this made me happy, it made the hotel's wedding coordinator even happier.

"Now *this* was a spectacular event," she said, warming to her subject and to the prospect of getting our business as she turned to the last wedding displayed in her book. "As you can see the ballroom can truly be transformed by the right florist." She was right. The room, dreary and banal, suddenly appeared opulent, almost luscious, draped with lilies and roses from end to end. It was an impressive feat. Marci nodded her head vigorously in agreement, checking Andrew's and my faces for a reaction. "Wow," Andrew said, poker face intact. "How much did that cost?" The coordinator initially pretended to demur, peppering us with a few more details regarding this high-society fête, namely with regard to the wealth and status of the family that had bankrolled it.

"How much were the flowers?" Andrew persisted.

"About fifty thousand dollars," the coordinator said, with studied matter-of-factness. *Big deal!* she implied. *If you want to do it right, that's what flowers cost!*

Fifty thousand dollars. At that, we said goodbye.

As we walked out, Marci, still getting to know us, said, "It seemed like you guys liked the way the room looked for that last wedding." Andrew laughed. "That room could *only* look good if you spent fifty thousand dollars on flowers!" Marci laughed too. She really was down-to-earth, and seemed relieved that we were not the fifty-thousand-dollars-on-flowers types. I felt relieved too. And again I experienced a pleasurable feeling of superiority. Ha! *We* were not going to spend fifty thousand dollars on flowers! *We* were not suckers! *We* would never spend that much money to get married . . . in a hotel ballroom where everybody else gets married, too!

What were we willing to pay for? A wedding that was unique, different, memorable, and, perhaps most importantly and yet again, "us."

This concept is a relatively new one: just as my mother laughed when I asked whether she'd sought a wedding dress that was "her," she marveled at the lengths Andrew and I were willing to go to in order to create a wedding that reflected "us," too.

More than any single thing you hear about planning a wedding these days, you hear this: plan something that reflects *you* and your identity as a couple. Don't do it like everybody else does, magazines and wedding coordinators urge, do it *your* way! What is this all about? In part, it's about the anxiety baby-boomer children feel as they confront marriage, an institution they have all seen wrecked by divorce. Just beneath the loud protestations of "Our wedding is *different!*" can be heard the frightened plea, "Oh please, *please* let it be different." At the same time the strenuous emphasis on individual identity shows just how deeply my generation absorbed the lesson that any compromise of the self within marriage leads to miserable, bad, failed marriages, and in this case individuality is emphasized to say, "But we are still the same!" or, more desperately (if less succinctly), "We are not going to become embittered, marital clichés! We are going to remain deliriously in-love individuals . . . who just happen to be married!"

Yet for all this, 99 percent of Condé Nast Bridal Group readers have formal weddings, meaning that for all their emphasis on expressing individuality, when it comes right down to it very few weddings are *truly* different. Perhaps this is because piled on top of the urge to differentiate from marriage's dismal record over the last thirty years is the resurgent, misplaced urge to identify with marriages past (like those of the 1950s, hence Susan Barash's "New Wives" who cite their grandmothers as role models) . . . while still, of course, rejecting the drawbacks of a less enlightened time (Valium-popping, embittered women, martini-swilling, embittered men) . . . while still longing for its perceived stability . . . in other words, once again, a thicket of sandwiched, contradictory desires about weddings that, faced directly, could cause couples to opt for the beach barbecue. Fortunately the wedding industry has relieved us of the difficulty of discussing these underlying issues by expertly exploiting them. Want/need to have a wedding that displays your individuality *and* reassuringly displays your conformity? You can do it! Just *personalize!*

Increasingly couples anxious to make their conventional events "different" do so by personalizing, also known as paying extra to put their unique stamp on every scrap of paper or glassware their wedding guests might touch. In 2000, the year I got married, one of *InStyle Weddings*'s cover stories was "Your Day, Your Way: 101 Ideas For Making It Personal," and *Brides* advertised "50 Ways to Personalize Your Wedding." Since then, the emphasis on the personalization panacea has only increased: *Brides'* winter 2005 issue featured monogrammed M&Ms on its "hot list," and its wedding-spy column reported that western weddings had spiked a demand for monogrammed wedding boots. "It makes sense," reported theknot.com in 2005, "with more and more attention paid to personalizing every wedding detail (and with more and more couples worrying about their friends co-opting their fabulous ideas), designing an invite that'll stand out is challenging." Don't despair! the website enjoins, just click here to order Asian-influenced, floral-designed papers *sewn* onto the backs of yours! And maybe if you do, *your* marriage will work out, maybe *you* will perfectly embody traditionalism and modernity, maybe *you* will retain your individuality while still being a Good Wife!

The trend toward personalizing is not as deep as all that, of course. There is another, less complicated reason to personalize everything from confetti to hot sauce (to name a few of my favorites from theknot.com's "Personalize It!" boutique): it is a handy way to display wealth. In this sense, personalization is simply a new twist on a very old game. Weddings have always been an opportunity to display power and status, but now, as Marcy Blum, a New York wedding planner quoted in the *New York Times* piece "Perfect Wedding: $5,000 Cake, Hold the Simplicity" observed, "it's not enough to show you're rich, you've got to show you're creative." A well-to-do New York couple cannot get married at the Plaza anymore and expect everyone to get the message: they now have to transform the Plaza into fifth-century Ireland and send everybody home with monogrammed hunks of peat. Personalization also dovetails neatly with weddings' narcissism, again something that isn't new. And when a couple takes personalization to the point of designing a wedding logo that, among other things, they beam onto the dance floor, they are not resisting self-abnegation. They are staring at themselves in the mirror and making everyone they know stand around and clap.

Andrew and I had been to enough weddings to see most of this before: we'd received wedding invitations that were twelve-page photo albums featuring portraits of the bride and groom shot in soft-focus alongside their favorite poems; we'd attended weddings that seemed more about advertising an astronomical price tag than they were about two people beginning a marriage. I may have had a little "Vera Wang!" demon on one shoulder, but I had enough sense to avoid turning my wedding into a branded, marketed, tacky me-fest. Andrew and I wanted our wedding to be unique, yes. But we also wanted it to be natural, unassuming, and relaxed. The ballroom wasn't right for this, or for us—that we knew. That weekend, however, the right place eluded us completely.

Not only did the right place elude us, but the wrong places acted on me like a steady drip of acid rain, eroding my confidence in our ability to carry off our fantasy and increasing my irritation exponentially as I walked around university halls, amphitheaters, dinner theaters, country clubs, and even the top floor of a parking garage (with a view!) in Boulder (Andrew's mother suggested that one—as a fundraiser for the arts she is expert at the resourceful and the cheap), all the while enduring Andrew's extremely annoying practice of pointing at any open space we drove by and saying, "What about right there? Why can't we just do it there?" The rush of confidence I experienced during that first appointment had completely evaporated by the last.

Finally, at the very end of the weekend, we found ourselves at the Paintbrush Ranch. By that point the Paintbrush Ranch had assumed enormous importance. The word "ranch" had caused Andrew's eyes to light up, and all weekend I had been clinging to the idea that this place was The One. Marci had suggested the same thing, registering our tepid reactions to other sites and saying, "Just wait till we get to the Paintbrush Ranch!" But when we got there, Andrew, his mother Caryl, and I simply couldn't agree about it.

The ranch was high up, at seven thousand feet. It had multiple meadows (Andrew had a vision of me walking toward him across a meadow, ivory skirts in hand as I high-stepped over mountain grass, an image I'd admittedly been totally charmed by) but due to its being in a valley surrounded by trees, somehow there were no mountain views from any of them. The meadows were also swampy and covered in horseshit, and the only place it seemed reasonable to set up a reception tent was on a flat, red-dirt parking area the owners of the property had leveled in a field. We were offered the use of the lodge at the top of the steeply inclined driveway, a portion of which the owners lived in but the rest of which they rented out for events, but the space was too small. Andrew insisted we could make it work, while I snapped at him for being so doggedly naïve (at the same time wanting desperately to believe him), and Caryl thought the whole thing was plain crazy.

In answer to all our questions about whether it really could work, Marci either said, "Absolutely, totally doable," or "Weellll." As it turned out, these were her two favorite phrases. I was beginning to think she would say, "Absolutely, totally doable" if we requested that the Aspen leaves change color, just for our wedding, in August.

At one point, while we were touring around the place, Andrew took me aside, out of Marci and Caryl's view. He took my hands in his, and looked straight into my eyes. "What's going on?" he said. "Every time I make a suggestion you're jumping all over me. We're all just trying to figure this out."

"I just think that you're not being very practical about this, that's all. Maybe we can't just put up a tent somewhere you know? You can't just drive around pointing at fields and saying, 'Why can't we do it there?' You can't do that!"

"Hey, hey," he said, hugging me. "You're really upset."

I was really upset. I was shaking.

"You haven't been yourself lately," he said. "It's like you haven't been yourself since we started talking about planning this wedding." All this searching around for "myself," and he was absolutely right. I didn't feel like myself at all.

We were silent. "Do you still want to marry me?" he asked, smiling.

"Andrew!" I threw my arms around him. We stood like that for awhile. "Of course I do. Of course I know that. I never doubt that. Not for a minute." I didn't.

"I just don't think it's as impossible as you think it is! You have to have vision! And you don't want to get married at a country club do you? Or any of those other places we saw?"

I shook my head. No. "I don't know what's wrong with me," I whispered, my eyes filling with tears. "I can't seem to, I don't know. I just want to do this, that's all. I don't know what's wrong with me. Why it makes me so upset. I had just hoped that after this weekend, we'd have a place, and we'd be able to start hiring all these caterers and florists and vendors and start taking care of all this crap, and after all of this we haven't found anything." More than anything, I wanted to say, I can't find myself in all this. I can't *see* myself in it, anywhere. But I didn't know how to say that.

Inexplicably, or so I thought, I was feeling an increasing sense of isolation. I felt like I was being negative and pessimistic about something I should have been positive and optimistic about; like I was acting like a spoiled brat instead of a can-do bride; like I was overreacting to everything, from the very idea of planning to Marci Barton's ho-hum. But in my isolation, I was not alone. Wedding websites like theknot.com, weddingchannel.com, and indiebride.com get thousands more posts to their "non-wedding-related" message boards than to any wedding-related subject. Every year, thousands of brides feel a sense of nagging isolation and anxiety they can't name either.

Men, however, don't seem to share it. It angered me that Andrew was so stupendously free of wedding-related angst. There is no book called *The Conscious Groom*. There are no online chat rooms for the "someday groom" or the groom who is on the verge of a nervous breakdown. Is this because men are emotionally repressed? Is it because men don't feel that weddings are their job, and as a result feel almost no pressure when it comes to planning them? Or is it because women, deep down, and contrary to the infinite talk of male commitment-phobia, actually fear married life more than men do, despite seeming so much more desperate to enter into it?

I believed that asking myself a question like that, at that moment, would have sent me off the rails, and so I kept such thoughts at bay. Now I wish I hadn't. I think facing my feelings would have helped a lot. Standing there at the Paintbrush Ranch, however, all I knew was that I needed a place to get married, and fast. I felt an agitation I could not shake, and assumed it would be soothed when we finally walked into, or onto, just the right spot. And a few weeks later—as even the indomitable Andrew was beginning to give up hope, and Marci Barton continued to come up empty (aside from the not-quite-right Paintbrush Ranch)—Andrew's even more unstoppable mother came through. Friends of hers knew an elderly couple living on what they described as one of the most beautiful pieces of land in the Boulder area, with a meadow, a pond and a view of the Continental Divide that took the breath away. For once, it was exactly as advertised. We flew to Colorado, drove up to the ranch, took one look, and said yes.

A FEW minor technicalities regarding the Cushman Ranch. Its sole structure was a mobile home that housed Lewis Cushman, his wife, their three perpetually shedding cats, and two huge shaggy dogs. This ranch was also covered in horseshit, and was guarded by an insane attack horse that reared up and nearly charged my mother and me during one of our visits. (The horse, we were promised, would be carted off for the wedding day. Julia Roberts riding a horse in a wedding dress is one thing, my being chased by a horse while wearing my wedding dress was another.) It had no power source sufficient to power the kind of wedding we were going to have. It was *very* high up at eighty-five-hundred feet, an altitude that had the potential to cramp the party's dance fever and inspired us to rent some just-in-case oxygen tanks for sea-level denizens and the elderly. As with wedding consultants, we had to inter-view multiple caterers before we found one who did not laugh us out of the room, but eventually a formal, large wedding in a rustic, natural place began to materialize—with considerable input from Andrew and considerable output from me.

In the end, we bused two hundred people to the top of a mountain and had an unbelievable party. We had a clear-topped tent strung with tiny white lights, we had candles floating in frosted vases on the tables, we had grilled steak, a dance floor and a band, and sky-blue programs tied with white ribbon. We had a string trio on the grass. We asked our family and friends to send us poems, movie lines, song lyrics, book ex-cerpts, or advice about love and marriage, and compiled them into a photocopied book that everyone could take home. I have my regrets: I regret being price-gouged just because I was getting married, I regret taking as much money as we did from our parents, I regret making such a big deal about the vases and a few other things. We certainly could have spent less. But for the most part we avoided personalizing with products rather than with our personalities, or getting so caught up in the hype we forgot we were planning a wedding, not an inaugural ball, and the little world we made that day is one of the things about my wedding that, even after all my analyzing, I *don't* regret one bit. It really was a once-in-a-lifetime chance to have everyone we loved in one place, and to have a really great party (at one point I did karaoke on stage in my V.W. gown, if that gives you any idea), and I'm glad we did.

At the same time, there is no denying that the once-in-a-lifetime ra-tionale has gotten way out of control. Too often it becomes code for "obscene-waste-of-money-and-time," and the insatiable mass-media appetite for celebrity weddings doesn't help. These celebrity weddings are often underwritten, indirectly, by non-celebrities, as the rich-and-famous get freebies from jewelers and dressmakers in exchange for publicity, and regular people pay the same jewelers and dressmakers ex-orbitant amounts to have what the Zeta-Jones-Douglas's had. Some regular people (with regular budgets) have resorted to offering ad spots to their vendors, printing ads in their programs or displaying business cards next to cakes in exchange for goods. The madness, in other words, flows freely between the business and the brides: bilking couples for every dime when they have "no price resistance" is wrong; confusing a perfect wedding with a perfect marriage is wrong, too. One would hope that there is a point (and there *is* a point) when enough is enough. I'd like to think Andrew and I knew what it was, but sometimes we surely didn't.

In the end, however, I believe weddings should be a gift a couple and their families give to others, and in that spirit it's nice to be as generous as you can. (Giving people pictures of yourself as a "favor" isn't generous; paying for food, wine, and music for your friends is.) To what extent, however, have weddings become about getting rather than giving? Yes, being a W.C. means buying things for your wedding and for your house. But it also means asking other people to buy things for you and your house, too. Half of an engaged woman's output as a "100-billion-dollar customer" comes from the money spent on the wedding itself, but the other half comes from the 50 billion dollars in sales a couple's engagement generates for the makers of everything from DustBusters to linens to flatware. And these goods are usually acquired by way of that other "time-honored" wedding tradition: spending hours in the aisles of Bloomingdale's, the store's full-time wedding-spending consultant in tow and scan gun in hand, registering for them.

⌘

seven

The W.C., Part Two

Showers, Scan Guns, and Girly Clothes

One wedding guidebook referred to the search for the wedding dress as "the shopping trip of a lifetime," and several women I spoke with were candid about enjoying their wedding-dress search precisely for that reason. But the modern-day ritual of registering—which has come to resemble that old gimmick where a store grants a lucky winner the chance to race through its aisles scooping up as much loot as she can while a timer ticks away—is the *real* shopping trip of a lifetime. When else can you pick out everything you ever wanted for your house, or for yourself (increasingly couples register for much more than household items), and then expect other people to buy it for you?

"I thought the best part about the wedding was that people get to 'buy things for the bride,'" quipped one woman I interviewed, and she was only half-joking. Marketers love marriage because it joins a man's income with the womanly habit—drilled into them from birth—of shopping with it. Marketers love weddings even more, however, because registries send women shopping with money not just from their husbands, or from their own incomes, but from everybody they know.

It must be said, of course, that the tradition of registering for wedding gifts has many sensible, sweet reasons for being. For young couples and couples who have never had the money to invest in kitchen appliances, crystal, or matching plates, it is a wonderful and right-minded thing for family and friends to pool resources and help them set up house. "Neither one of us had 'grown up' things," Diana, a thirty-one-year-old from California, told me. "We had just moved in together after moving out of living with roommates." Lori, a thirty-five-year-old university dean from Boston, said, "I believed we should get certain things to have in our home forever. It is a little silly, but in our case we never could have afforded matching dishes and sheets and silverware otherwise!" In the finest spirit of a house-warming party, wedding gifts can be wonderful things. In the worst spirit of a present-grabbing, booty-licious, materialistic free-for-all, wedding gifts can simply be more things, things, things—things that nobody really needs, and more things than anybody really ought to expect other people to buy for them.

ANDREW and I initially planned to skip the registry altogether, not being in need of dishes or sheets, and ask people to donate to selected charities instead. (A charitable organization called the "I Do Foundation" offers a nice compromise: if you register using their site, a small percentage of people's purchases at participating stores will be donated to a charity of your choice.) But after some pressure from our parents and others we agreed to register for crystal, silver, and china in addition to listing the charities, and also to set up a fund at an art gallery where people could contribute towards the purchase of a piece of art. Another reason we gave in and registered? We'd been convinced that people would insist on giving us "real" gifts rather than donating to charity, and if we didn't pick some out ourselves we'd get a lot of stuff we didn't want.

This turned out to be absolutely true. Many of our guests donated to the charities, but we also got all kinds of things we didn't want. This is another sensible reason to register—as Anna, a twenty-eight-year-old writer from New York, said, "We weren't planning [on registering], but we learned a lesson from my brother and his wife, who didn't register and ended up getting a bunch of things they can't use. We always joke they now own ten crystal chickens." Anna and her fiancé, in addition to registering, set up a house fund to which people could contribute. Several couples I spoke with did this, and it seems like a nice idea in the spirit of the event. Registering for wedding gifts, to my mind, made sense; it seemed reasonable both to appreciatively welcome gifts and to give their givers some guidance. Having a wedding shower at which I would fish for even more gifts from the very same people, however, was quite another.

I may have had somewhat mixed feelings about registering, but I didn't have mixed feelings about showers. I didn't want one. I'd like to say this was solely because I wanted to avoid putting yet another burden on my friends—most of whom, I knew, were already planning to fly to Boulder for our wedding, stay in a hotel, and buy us a wedding gift, too. But there were other reasons. Again, I felt silly and stereotyped by the assumption that because I was the woman, I, and not Andrew, would want to sit around and ooh and aah over lingerie and cookware (two things Andrew oohs and aahs over quite a bit more than me). I also felt vaguely sick, like a person who has eaten too much chocolate, at the amount of consumption surrounding my wedding already, and was not particularly interested in celebrating the purchase of more stuff, or in handing more cash over to the marketers who'd been circling over my head ever since I'd gotten engaged. Perhaps less high-minded, but no less compelling, however, was my powerful aversion to the idea of sitting around opening presents in front of people. And I really, really didn't want to play games.

"I hate the embarrassment factor," said Leslie, a thirty-seven-year-old stay-at-home mom in LA, "the stupid games about how many kids you're going to have, or getting wrapped up in toilet paper." Amen. I once attended a shower where the women in attendance were blindfolded and forced to play "pin the tail on the groom," in this case a paper plate with the unfortunate groom's photo plastered on it in effigy. He had no interest in actually being there, and who could blame him?

Many showers are childish in this stereotypically female way, reacting to the impending marriage with giggly, "Kamy and Andrew sittin' in a tree" silliness that suggests the woman in question really *is* a virginal girl, or at least ought to play one for the crowd. Traditional showers, to me, reflect the discomfort our society feels regarding female adulthood, and as my adulthood was already under attack in so many ways as a bride, I hoped to avoid this one.

Surprise, surprise, I had a shower anyway. "It's just another thing on the list of things you're 'supposed' to do, isn't it?" said Leslie, who ended up having one, too. "The few ideas I had for doing this entire process 'differently' were quashed by my family, and I didn't have the force of personality in my mid-twenties that I do in my mid-thirties," she added—so, like me, she went along. (I'd like to think if I'd been a bride in my thirties I'd have successfully resisted, but who knows.) My mother really wanted me to have a shower, and my best friend's mother, along with some of my mother's best friends, wanted to give me one, and to refuse the offers of these loving women seemed (incredibly) infinitely more bratty and self-centered than sitting in the middle of a room opening presents I'd asked for in front of people who'd felt obligated to buy them for me.

PEOPLE don't just feel *obligated* to buy shower gifts, of course—some people genuinely enjoy giving them, and look forward to wedding showers in general. While most women I interviewed agreed that the trend toward having multiple showers is excessive (increasingly, brides-to-be have two and sometimes three showers before their weddings, frequently piling on by making one "coed"), most also thought showers were "fair and fun," as Dot, a forty-two-year-old graduate student from Oakland, California, put it. What goes around comes around, she went on to say, and while you may buy a lot of gifts over time as a shower guest, eventually you're the one to get them, too.

The problem, of course, is that not everyone finds themselves in the position to get them. I mostly talked to straight, married women when I asked about showers and wedding registries, women who had both given and received. But until very recently, it was not acceptable for same-sex couples to be on the receiving end of this ritual, even as they were expected to give just like everybody else. (A gay friend of mine has a policy of not giving anything costly, one I completely respect, and for our wedding presented us with Dr. Seuss's *Oh, the Places You'll Go!*) Not only that, but as Jaclyn Geller points out in *Here Comes the Bride*, a heterosexual, monogamous woman who lands a husband is treated as if she has "earned" these gifts (one ad for the Macy's registry reads: "True love should be rewarded"), when everyone knows that finding a life partner is to a large extent about luck. "Because the source of these accolades is a romance," Geller writes, "a hit or miss relationship based on a series of random intangibles—the inequity of the marriage custom is truly grotesque." Unmarried men and women who may not have been so lucky in love are expected to chip in when their friends tie the knot, and may never be shored up this way themselves. By withholding this gift bonanza from anyone who doesn't marry, of course, the society also makes marriage extremely attractive to anyone considering skipping it—a powerful form of coercion. Wouldn't it be more fair, as Geller suggests, to give all women "showers" on their twenty-fifth birthdays (interestingly, she leaves men out) to honor their passage into adulthood and help them set up house—a burden all adults shoulder whether they are married or not?

This elides one of the principal reasons that the tradition of showering married couples with gifts endures: implicit in the custom is the notion that heterosexual couples who choose to marry are also likely to have children—perhaps society's main concern, when it comes down to it—and their unstated commitment to reproduce is their true claim to the financial support of their families and communities when they marry. Laurie Essig, arguing in *Salon* that the state should not favor heterosexual, monogamous relationships over others, said that to the extent the state *should* offer extra support to any committed pair, it should only offer it to couples who become parents. "Why should anyone get societal privileges," she asks, "let alone gifts, when he or she marries for the fourth time at age sixty-eight with no intention of ever becoming a parent?" The gifts, in other words, are intended for new families, not just for marrying couples.

Very few people, when buying yet another Cuisinart blender for yet another bride and groom, consciously think to themselves: "I'm not giving you this just so you can stay footloose and child-free, and make margaritas with it for the rest of your life! I'm giving it to you so you can purée baby food at 5 a.m. like the rest of us!" But the entitlement many people feel—particularly people who have already married and had children—to openly harass an engaged people about having babies partly stems from the notion that weddings merit major appliances because weddings signify an assumption of responsibility by two heretofore "irresponsible" (a.k.a. immature) single people. Never mind that it is not necessary to procreate to be of use to society, or necessarily of use to society to procreate. Couples have long accepted wedding gifts with the tacit assumption that they are accepting them not just on behalf of themselves, but on behalf of their families-to-be.

Unmarried women, however, are invited to *many* more gift-giving events than their male counterparts, and bear a disproportionate burden in the gift-giving department. As women marry later in life, this has only become more pronounced. Are single women supposed to financially support all these new families, while unmarried men don't?

"I do think it becomes a bit unfair, and much more expensive, when women have to go to bridal showers, baby showers, etc., while men (who only have bachelor parties) just have one night out of fun," observed Nazneen, a thirty-two-year-old unmarried doctor from Philadelphia. The *Sex and the City* episode where Carrie realizes how much money she's spent on a friend's wedding, wedding showers, and baby showers and concludes it is her turn to be showered (she announces she's getting married to herself and registers at Manolo Blahnik) is legendary for the catharsis it provided single women.

I knew this, and it was one of the reasons I subtly let my friends know that they would not be expected to attend the shower that had been planned for me in San Antonio. As a result, my shower, held on a June weekend that recorded some of the most dramatic downpours in

San Antonio's history (talk about showers), was mostly attended by my mother's friends (many of them my friends, too, since they were women I'd grown up with) and a few members of the family. Since her mother was cohosting the shower, Devon, my best friend from high school and a bridesmaid, was there, too, and she and my sister helped me feel somewhat less weird as I sat on a chair in Devon's spacious living room—isolated by the several feet of distance between me and my audience of ladies—opening gifts and reading thank-you cards out loud with my legs crossed, wearing a girly outfit.

The girly outfit, of course, was a must. One woman recounted walking into her first shower to discover every woman in the place, from little sisters to the bride's grandmother, wearing ultra-feminine garb. There were "skirts galore, pale colors, a few hats, all just screaming 'women women women here!' It was like something out of the *Stepford Wives*," she said. "Compared to them, I looked like a major dyke." This woman never made the same mistake again, and I already knew better. I wore a lightweight ivory sweater and a matching skirt with flecks of gold, with summery heels to boot. The wedding shower, decorous, proper, and intergenerational, is one of the crucial tests of a bride's qualification to become a bourgeois wife. Does she know how to conduct herself at a coffee, tea, or ladies' lunch? Does she know how to chat, how to sip, what to say, and what to wear? There is a debutante element to the shower, as an aspiring wife mingles with established wives (or other aspirants, all of whom have also been given the opportunity to display their skills in this department), being introduced and, one hopes, welcomed into their ranks. In this sense shower games are a form of hazing, as humiliation and initiation always go hand-in-hand.

At my shower, however, I was very grateful to find that the few ground rules I'd set were faithfully followed: there were no games, no gimmicks, and very little lingerie. The shower was not, however, coed, though Andrew had been invited to "stop by" towards the end and help with the gift opening. I was anticipating this eagerly, as it seemed very odd to me to open the gifts alone, especially since, at Andrew's inspired suggestion, we had registered for . . . camping gear.

There was a theme for the shower: our honeymoon. We planned to take a three-week, high-low road trip through Wyoming, Idaho, and Montana after the wedding, alternating between camping and staying in fancy hotels. Devon's mother had a very cute cake made, with a little bride and groom in sleeping bags. And somehow opening Camelbaks, Leathermans, field guides, and topo maps in front of a group of women sipping Mimosas while holding tiny plates took the edge off for me. It made some of the guests noticeably uncomfortable (my prom date's mother, who I adore, told me in her soft, thick Texas drawl that she couldn't bring herself to buy a Camelbak because "for the life of me I just couldn't figure out how you'd *clean* it"), but considering how uncomfortable I felt opening presents in public—something I had not done since childhood birthday parties at swimming pools and roller rinks—this only seemed fair.

It's possible that a number of the guests were uncomfortable too, or at least bored, not with the camping gear, but with the opening-presents-in-front-of-everyone routine. Sitting around watching another woman open presents irritates a lot of women I know, including Devon, who later told me, "I'm happy to go to a luncheon in honor of someone, but *why do I have to watch them open presents?!!*" Why indeed? While women my age have adopted the male custom of the bachelor party, men have not reciprocated by having male-only showers, and one woman speculated that this was because "guys [don't] have the patience to watch other people open gifts for forty-five minutes . . . I think they lose an appreciation for that after about age twelve." (This reminded me of Dave Barry's line: "There comes a time when you should stop expecting other people to make a big deal about your birthday. That time is age 11.")

I am certain that the reason guys don't have guys-only showers, however, is not because they are more mature than women are. Instead it is because shopping and displaying one's purchases is a socially prescribed way of displaying one's femininity, and, again, one's fitness to be a wife. A woman is judged by the gifts she registers for; wedding-shower guests are judged by the gifts they bring; this makes the public exchange of gifts essential to a shower's function. Brides are also expected to show off their wifely manners by publicly, gracefully, and gratefully *receiving* gifts—another decidedly female duty. Male-only showers have not come into being largely because it would humiliate a man to play the acquisitive, grateful dependent in front of family and friends, and it would also humiliate a man to assume the role of eager shower-guest, showing off his shopping. (At coed showers, the presence of women makes the presence of men "okay.") Women have also long been taught to believe that their acquisitions—their furniture, their china, their "things"—are crucial to their identities, their very sense of who they are in the world. And as with the wedding dress and the ring, wedding marketers stress this by co-opting the language of romance when they speak of that perfect marriage between a bride . . . and her stuff. In an ad for its registry in *Brides'* winter 2005 issue, Target encapsulated this with the tag line: "When you find the right registry *you just know.*"

The shopping showcase that is the wedding shower has been known by another name, too, of course: conspicuous consumption. Despite the fact that the majority of wives now work outside the home, the notion that women achieve status by being *able* to shop, i.e., by having husbands who make shopping possible, while men achieve status by not "having" to shop, i.e., by acquiring wives who will shop for them, has proved difficult to dislodge. "Women are brought up into a culture where they will be evaluated according to how they look, what they wear, and, even still, how rich/successful a husband they can 'land,'" said Mary, a thirty-eight-year-old writer from Chicago. "So most women end up being shoppers and measuring their own success, to some extent, on how much they have to spend and how well they spend it." It's hard to imagine men acknowledging they spent time scouring the mall (or the Internet) shopping for one another—they have better things to do! It's easy to see how proud they feel when their wives have the means and taste to shop successfully in their stead.

Men are beginning to participate more in all levels of the pre-wedding, gift-giving bonanza, of course. All-male showers have not come into being, but coed showers are on the rise, and fully 95 percent of grooms report participating in registering—something brides and their mothers used to do alone. Andrew and I registered together, and though I didn't see a lot of other men at the store that carried our china (which leads me to think that many grooms' "participation" comes in the form of "input" rather than slogging through hours of shopping), very few men entirely opt out of the scan-gun shootout. Once again, to the extent that all things domestic should not be treated, from the outset of a marriage, as a "woman's department," this is a good thing. Even so, coed showers are yet another excellent example of the wedding industry taking contemporary couples' discomfort with an outdated, sexist tradition and saying, "You're right, it *isn't* fair! We too believe in equal opportunity—to buy more stuff! If your man doesn't like cake pans, why not register at Home Depot *and* Bloomingdale's, and have as many showers as you need to be sure you get everything you want?" If men, too, became reliable W.C.'s, the wedding business would love it. The more, the merrier.

Despite increased male "participation," however, showers and the kinds of gifts couples register for *are* still considered a woman's department, and the traditional gifts of lingerie and cookware continue to dominate the ritual. (I received some despite my shower's theme.) The custom of giving lingerie originates from a time when showers served the critical function of preparing virginal brides for the wedding night; the custom of giving cookware from a time when showers outfitted women to be housekeepers and cooks. Showers, then, with their emphasis on the domestic, also enforce this notion of the wifely role, and many women silently accept this even when it has nothing to do with their reality. "I'm a terrible cook!" Emily, a thirty-seven-year-old professor from Pennsylvania, said. "On the other hand, my *husband* loves to cook. He's the one who registered for everything at Williams-Sonoma, whereas I got a little pang of terror every time I saw one of those presents because I had no idea what half of those utensils were used for. These showers are a throwback to a pre-feminist era, and part of me finds them insulting." One reason men don't have showers? They aren't being formally prepared for marriage by older men, because marriage is not to be their main occupation.

I resisted—and resented—this idea: hence the camping gear. But considering the fact that 93 percent of brides are given showers (94 percent of whom register in time for the event), part of me was also happy to have one. I probably would have felt like a loser if no one had at least offered to host a shower for me, and a lot of things about my shower were really nice: seeing my mother's friends and my friends' mothers, gathering together with women of different ages—something I would not do at my bachelorette—drinking champagne and cutting into that cute cake. It was fun to have Andrew, too, who conducted himself beautifully upon arrival, oohing and aahing over sleeping bag liners, never once treating the afternoon with macho, sarcastic disregard—maybe because he picked out all the gifts. But the casual, warm, at-home engagement party my parents threw for us that night was nearly perfect, and suited us much better.

Fundamentally, the idea of giving a wedding gift is a good one. It's *nice* to give gifts. It's nice to get them! Is it necessary to give two or three gifts to a couple getting married? Absolutely not. Is it okay to use your wedding as a way to load up your home with stuff that has nothing to do with establishing a home, and everything to do with an opportunistic shakedown (hello, digital cameras)? What do you think?

To the extent that a particular couple really needs all the help they can get in setting up house, a coed shower is clearly preferable to holding a women-only one. At least that way there is some notion that the task of setting up house will be equally shared. If I had it to do over again, I'd opt for a casual engagement party like the one my parents gave us, or even a gift-free, all-woman lunch, because I do agree with Geller's contention that the "coed" panacea, presented as an example of increased equality between the sexes, often reinforces the tyrannical togetherness of coupledom instead. Undoubtedly, however, it must be acknowledged that more than anything, expensive shower gifts—particularly in light of the fact that the average cost of attending a wedding has climbed to $500 a person, not including airfare, and members of the typical bridal party shell out thousands for the "privilege" of participating in them—are simply too much to demand.

In 1968, my mother had a traditional southern wedding. She and my dad got married in the afternoon in her hometown church, and afterward they had cake and punch. There was a rehearsal dinner but it was only for those who actually needed to rehearse, and nobody in attendance would have expected to find a gift bag in their hotel with a schedule, snacks, and bottled water in it, much less to attend three days of wedding-related events. As one woman pointed out, some of this has changed because our lives are increasingly peripatetic, and many more guests travel to weddings nowadays. (Forty percent, according to an article in *Mother Jones*.) It's nice to acknowledge their efforts with a bottle of water or two, she said, and by spending as much time as possible with them.

The demise of the cookie-cutter, cake-and-punch wedding has had other positive results, too. As Kathy, a twenty-seven-year-old analyst in Virginia, observed, "The pressure [to have] the increasingly extravagant expensive wedding is not a change for the better, but the greater variety of what's acceptable for a wedding is definitely good. For instance, a wedding in a park officiated by a justice of the peace may have been sacrilege in our great-grandmother's era, but it is considered a beautiful acceptable wonderful wedding today." This is certainly true—though a couple marrying in the park is likely to find that even such a modest event costs plenty. (Amanda, a writer in New York, had a friend's "rustic" nuptials in mind as she set out to plan her own, only to discover the couple had spent $18,000. "How did they spend that much?" she and her fiancé wondered. "We found out how very, very quickly.") And lately the couple who marries in the park distributes personalized parasols to the guests. And then there is the couple who does a "simple" wedding on the beach—in Tahiti.

Weddings, truth be told, have always been a competitive sport among those who could afford to compete. But the pressure to compete even when you can't afford it has become enormous (as the modern media has catapulted people from feeling pressured to keep up with the Joneses down the street to keeping up with the ultra-rich on their television screens), and the pressure to have a "perfect" wedding to show how much you care about your relationship, your marriage, your family, and your friends has become enormous too. What *is* a perfect wedding?

As uncertainty about marriage and tradition grow, the wedding industry acquires more and more power in providing the answer to that question, and, almost exclusively, it targets women with its message.

Only the most minor effort is made to shame men into being perfect grooms or registering for perfect gifts or planning perfect weddings—though certainly the pressure applied to women is intended for men and their wallets, too. But just at one of the most sensitive times in her life, a time when she is preparing to marry and likely undergoing an identity shift—or crisis—that can be extremely difficult to manage, an engaged woman is subjected to the most vigorous assault America's formidable mass-marketing machine can possibly make upon her. Everybody wants a piece, and women try not to come apart. It is ironic but not accidental that when this happens, women, trained to seek "retail therapy," often seek solace from the very same retailers, marketers, and consumer magazines that are assaulting them. But as Francine Prose observed in an article about websites aimed at women, the counsel women are offered by these providers falls "far short of suggesting that we examine the source of the pressure, or that we begin to push back, or that we face the problems that no amount of shopping can solve."

When I talked to women about America's wedding madness, several of them mentioned that in other countries, things are different. Sometimes this was to say that in other countries it's worse, though for consumerist extremism Americans are hard to beat. But I also heard about places where it sounded better. In Scotland, for instance, as Sidney, the scientist from Vermont, described it, "they first have the ceremony in the late afternoon with only closest family and friends, they then have a sit-down dinner at a restaurant somewhere with those guests, and then they are off to a reception hall and the rest of their extended family and friends come to have drinks, cake, and dancing for the rest of the night. And most of the time those guests BYOB!" Terry, who married in England, simply said, "There was a huge difference in what seemed 'necessary' for our wedding in England versus what seemed necessary for my sister's in DC." Another woman I interviewed was driven crazy by her Israeli husband's casual way of distributing wedding invitations; in Israel weddings are "much larger, up to five hundred people, yet somehow much less formal"—apparently you invite the village to stop by and party. American weddings, for all the effort lately to make them personal, often feel strained, and no amount of money or "personalization" can cover this up. In the end, it feels as though all those unanswered questions, big, important ones about marriage, about gender roles, about monogamy and divorce, hang around no matter how hard you try to ignore them or how much money you spend. Leaving them unanswered seems to leave participants feeling both uneasy and over-eager—unable to treat a wedding as a natural part of life, they clamor for the scripted, over-produced shows couples now feel compelled to put on, as though they were trying to distract themselves and everyone else from something . . . troublingly, *from the thing itself.* But working to close the gaps between our ideals about marriage and our experience of it, our fears about wedding and our hopes for it, would be a lot better than covering them up with monogrammed fabric that costs us thirty dollars a yard.

eight

※

Beauty Day
Walking the White Carpet

I remember the moment it sunk in. I was in an elevator with a friend of mine, riding down from an outdoor rooftop café where we'd just had a delicious lunch—which for me was not a low-carb salad but a high-mayonnaise sandwich. "I'm stuffed," I said. Then, in keeping with years of training and habit, I took a quick look at my faint reflection in the elevator's glass and added, "I can't believe I ate all those french fries!" I laughed. My friend, a gay man with a perfect body who (usually) treats me like gold, gave me a faint half-smile, quickly, critically scanned my body from head to toe and back again, then said: "You're going to get a personal trainer before the wedding, right?"

I think I managed not to crumple right there. But the jolt of unwanted awareness, the sudden stab of panic and self-consciousness I felt as I realized it wasn't just my relationship that had been made public property by my engagement but my *body*, my appearance, my arms, butt, stomach, and legs, unnerved me. As a bride, I wasn't just supposed to create a perfect wedding. I was supposed to make a perfect me.

The oft-repeated phrase "It's your day!" could also be completed this way: "It's your day . . . to look the most beautiful you've ever looked in your life." This is not just an opportunity, it's an order, and every year millions of brides find their bodies, from the hair on their heads to the hair on their vaginas, the object of endless discussion and scrutiny. (Hopefully the hair down there will be the object of only two people's *actual* scrutiny, but the bikini wax has become a crucial component, in the words of one spa, of the beauty "bridal bouquet.") During the course of my engagement I found that almost every time I saw a friend or relative, he or she—but mostly she—commented on my appearance more than ever before. (This is saying a lot, because most women spend the first minutes of any meeting commenting on each other's appearance.) For the most part, the commentary was positive. "You look great!" people said encouragingly. But they said it as though they had entered my house knowing I was currently putting considerable money and time into renovating it, and in a way this was exactly the case. If you count the dress and the engagement ring, the average couple spends nearly 30 percent of their wedding budget on the bride's appearance. That translates into an average of about sixty-five hundred dollars. And Andrew and I spent more than the average.

How important is a woman's appearance on her wedding day? "It's basically the whole point of the wedding," said Mia, a thirty-year-old literary agent in New York. "It is probably the most important thing, as all eyes are on her and it is what *everybody* talks about," said Stephanie, a thirty-three-year-old recruiter from Florida. "Every bride I know diets more, works out more, and puts herself through immense pressure to be 'perfect,'" observed Melissa, a thirty-two-year-old executive from New Jersey. "I can only imagine what it must be like for someone who feels un-beautiful on her wedding day," speculated Alexandra, a forty-two-year-old mother of three: "Devastating."

To say that a groom's appearance is less important than the bride's is somewhat like saying that a broom closet's appearance is less important than a foyer's. "These last few weeks," Amanda, a twenty-nine-year-old writer, reported as her wedding drew near, "I've been at the gym at 6:30 every morning. I'm currently sitting here with White Strips on my teeth. My next seven days? Friday, makeup lesson; Saturday, facial;

Wednesday, humiliating spray tan; Thursday, hair trial; Friday, nails; Saturday, hair. Meanwhile, the groom's big grooming plans include buzzing his hair in the bathroom. His wedding day preparations will be: wash face, brush teeth." Leslie, a thirty-seven-year-old writer in LA, contrasted her and her husband's pre-wedding beauty preparations this way: "I dieted, let my hair grow long to have lots of hairstyle options, and went for experimental makeovers with various makeup artists. It worked, I looked better than I usually do. My husband did nothing except accidentally stab himself in the forehead with a screwdriver the day before the wedding."

"Are you doing everything you can to look your best on your wedding day?" an online quiz posted on theknot.com asks worried brides-to-be. If you aren't, the barely concealed subtext reads, you'd better, and ads for beauty products helpfully pop up all over the site—just in case you're wondering what doing "everything you can" means, exactly, or how much it costs, or where to buy it. True, more men get buffed and waxed for their weddings now than used to, though this is not necessarily something to take heart in. (A groom featured in the October 2005 *Time* article "Metrosexual Matrimony" took his groomsmen to get manicures and eyebrow waxes the day before the wedding, arguing that this was not "superficial" but "artistic.") The general attitude about grooming the groom, however, still comes to something like what James Douglas Barron describes in *She Wants a Ring—But I Don't Want to Change a Thing*: "Make sure your nails, teeth and hair look, human."

I looked forward to being a beautiful bride. I hoped to experience the pleasure one gets from being pleasing to the eye. I hoped to glow, shine, exude joy . . . and have toned arms, professionally plucked eyebrows, the right lipstick, the right shoes, good highlights, styled hair, underlined eyes, and décolletage. It's easy to dismiss any critical discussion of brides' obsession with beauty (and the assembled guests' obsession with it, too) by saying, *it's only natural to want to look your best for such an important event*. Well of course it is! But it is one thing to look your best, and another thing to look like somebody else; it is one thing to be healthy, and another to undergo surgery; it is one thing to go to the gym regularly, and another to have five pounds of weights concealed in your bouquet to show off your triceps as you walk down the aisle, like one bride described in *New York* magazine. Again, the question is, why are men merely supposed to "look human"—or even just plain handsome in a tux, smelling nice with neatly combed hair—why are men viewed as a bridal *accessory*? ("Let's be real," one woman said with regard to groom-grooming, "he's more prop than anything else.") Is it really because men don't care, or because, as another woman suggested to me, women are just "more shallow"?

During my engagement, as I found myself thinking about my appearance more than I had since junior high, and spending more money on it than I ever had in my life, I knew, deep down, that it was not just because I wanted to "look my best." Looking my best meant something entirely different for me than it did for Andrew. Looking my best meant expending valuable time, money, and energy that he could—and did—expend elsewhere. Once again and as always, I was being sent a powerful message about my job as a woman, a bride, and a wife, and once again I heeded it. Andrew had flexed his manly muscles by buying me a big diamond ring. My job was to show that I was worth it.

A FEW weeks prior to the wedding, following the advice of various magazines and websites, I scheduled a beauty day: haircut and highlights, a dress fitting, and a makeup lesson. The morning was hot and humid, overcast and still like most July mornings in the city. It was also a Thursday, which meant that Andrew was getting up to go to work. Since the end of May when classes had ended, wedding planning had been my work. It had nearly become a full-time job, something I still couldn't believe—but to paraphrase Betty Friedan, wedding work expands to fill the time available. So that morning, as I rose early in order to make a 9 a.m. hair appointment uptown, I felt a certain sense of pride at beating Andrew out the front door. Yes he was off to work, but I was too.

Wedding planning was the first kind of labor I owed as a wife, but making myself beautiful was the second. Beauty-work is also part of the second shift: women shop, primp, and make up on top of working full-time while men (with "better things to do") shower and shave. As a single woman I had also owed this labor, but as a single woman it felt like an investment: something I did to up my value as the seller in the marketplace, the pitcher of a product. (The language of product-marketing permeates land-a-man literature: *The Rules* are introduced by a section titled, "First the Product—You!" *Closing the Deal* suggests the "artful use of marketing" to sell yourself to a man, and *Find a Husband After Thirty-Five* coaches women on developing a "personal brand.") Arguably appearance ought to be more important for a single woman than for a bride: certainly Nazneen, a single, thirty-one-year-old doctor, has felt this. She gets enormous pressure from her mother to lose weight—pressure she never got before—because she "still" isn't married.

Brides, however, are under enormous pressure to lose weight, too, and in general to look "the most beautiful they have ever looked in their lives." I knew I was no longer selling a product to potential husbands but displaying a product that had already sold—a fact that supposedly makes beautifying for one's wedding a peaceful, happy joy, unlike the tense insecurity of putting one's "game-face" on for a night out at the bars. But as a newly acquired asset, hundreds of people would soon be traveling from all over to evaluate, comment on, and photograph me, and that thought scared me to death.

After all, I wanted everyone to *like* looking at me! I wanted to be admired, to succeed! But I especially wanted Andrew to be dazzled. I wanted to make him proud. "I want to come down the aisle and have him think I look amazing," Amanda said, partially explaining her White Strips.

I also wanted this, not just because I love Andrew and I love the look on his face when I look good. I wanted it because I knew my beauty was my gift to him, as the ring had been his gift to me. I also wanted it because, believe it or not, I *still* felt I had to sell the idea that being married to me was going to be great for him. After all, men fear marriage (so the story goes) because they fear being stuck with one woman forever, and if that woman doesn't look gorgeous on her wedding day, mightn't he rue his commitment anew? Another reason women work hard to be beautiful brides? Their work represents a pledge to continue working hard on their appearance for the rest of their lives, thereby making their husband's sacrifice of other women's favors "worth it." As Virginia, a lawyer in Texas, put it, "If you don't look your best on the day you are getting married, what more can you or your future husband look forward to?"

Tellingly, Virginia asked not just what more your future *husband* could look forward to, but what more *you* could look forward to—because it is not just the groom who hopes his bride will stay beautiful forever. The bride hopes so, too. Yet another reason a woman's beauty takes on such immense importance on her wedding day is the unstated belief that it's all downhill from there. *It's her day* is also a way of saying, *it's her peak.* Fear of aging underlies the intense anxiety about appearance many brides feel. As Naomi Wolf put it, women die two deaths: one as a beauty and one for good. Some might say that the second death is less terrifying. At least you aren't alive for it.

"People are more afraid of looking old than actually dying," Mia, the literary agent, commented, adding, "wrinkles and sagging skin and fat carry more of a stigma than cancer." She said "people," meaning men, too, and in New York this probably applies more than it does in other parts of the country. Still, wrinkles, sagging skin, and fat are met with far more derision and disgust when they appear on a woman's body than on a man's (a slew of wrinkled, aging, yet still sex-scene-eligible Hollywood leading men come to mind), and the majority of the people more afraid of looking old than dying are women. A woman fears dying as a beauty because individuals internalize their society's assignation of their value, and society values nothing in a woman (or a bride) more than beauty and youth. Men may be more afraid of *being* old than dying, but if they are successful enough in other ways (society values them for making money) at least they can soothe the ache by sleeping with hot twenty-year-olds.

As the average age at marriage rises, of course, women are less and less likely to be in their "prime" when they marry—if by prime one means that brief moment when you are past puberty but pre-metabolic-slowdown. (From a purely physical standpoint, nineteen would have been more like it for me.) The beauty business knows this very well, and has made piles of money with each uptick of the average age a woman walks the aisle. At twenty-seven I was young, but not so young I didn't feel pressure to do "everything I could," meaning things unnatural and expensive, to look beautiful on my wedding day.

My first appointment in this quest took me to the tony, very midtown salon I'd been visiting ever since I'd acquired the means. In the elevator I was joined by two women older than myself (we were all looking at each other while pretending not to look)—one in her mid-to-late thirties, I guessed, blonde, cold, and haughty, and one who was either in her fifties and had had very bad plastic surgery, or was in her seventies and had had pretty darn impressive plastic surgery, as there was nary a wrinkle on her immobile, tight, and emaciated painted face. I felt a frisson of pride at being twenty-seven then, an absurd but satisfying feeling. I remembered the cover of a men's magazine I'd seen proclaiming the ideal woman to be aged twenty-eight, suggesting, I guess, that men should just keep dating twenty-eight-year-olds and break up with them every time they turned twenty-nine. These women needn't have seen the article to know the score: I was younger than they, and therefore at an advantage.

There would always be somebody younger than me, too, of course. My sense of superiority was as fragile and transient as it could possibly be, and, as it was based on something unearned and un-earnable, it was just plain wrong. But rather than questioning the emphasis put on my youth as a bride, my barely repressed fear of aging fueled my determination to milk the moment for all it was worth. This was one way being engaged was not good for my soul: my inner diva, competitive and peacock-like, had been given free rein and lots of encouragement to come on out. A cartoon in *Closing the Deal* captures this with its depiction of an ultra-thin bride saying, "And when I think of all those hyper-competitive women out there who want to kill me, I'm even happier." Normally I too would have referred to "all *those* hyper-competitive women," assuming a world of difference between *those* women and down-to-earth, kindly me. But I secretly relished the idea of having my day, one day to be the belle of the ball, one day to indulge my vanity without reproach, one day to openly bask in other people's envy. It would have shamed me to admit it but I never had to—I was a bride and I was entitled to this, no questions asked. It was my day . . . to be a shallow narcissist. Whoopee!

As I stepped out into the reception area, the little buzz of anticipation I'd experienced in the elevator was pleasantly greeted by crisp, sun-filled space, despite the fact that it was a gray day outside. Every wall in this particular salon was painted a warm golden-yellow, and recessed into the golden-yellow ceilings were bright white fluorescent lights softened by large swathes of white nylon draped beneath them. As I checked in, however, I discovered to my dismay that I and the younger-looking woman were both going to see the same colorist—Reno, whom I had never met.

Reno (pronounced Renault, like the car) was tall and broad-shouldered, had a deep, dark tan and dark hair that he had grown out and colored blonde on the ends, and moved with unhurried economy, as though he was reserving every ounce of his energy, like a large cat. He attended to the other woman first, whom he apparently knew well. It was a good twenty minutes before Reno sat me down in a chair, poked around my head, asked me a few questions that, due to his thick French accent, I could hardly comprehend, and gave me to understand he would be with me shortly. He then returned his attentions to the woman sitting next to me. She resumed talking to him as he moved with languid serious-ness and concentration around her head, carefully lifting strands of hair and painting them with the white, smelly stuff that would make them blonde.

"I'm staying at an apartment over the weekend because I could not get a hotel, everything is completely booked—all my friends from London are coming in on Saturday but I'm flying out this afternoon." Reno did not look up. "What was it that you put into my hair last time that made it so shiny?" At this, a look from Reno, but a completely blank one. "You know you put it on my hair and it was so shiny, what was it?" Reno's expression upgraded from blank to questioning. He then resumed staring at and working on her hair, shrugging. "A conditioner?" she tried again.

"The gloss," he said.

"Gloss! Can you do that again?" Affirmative. "I am so excited to go to St. Tropez alone. You can't imagine what it's like going there with kids. You can only leave them with the nanny so much, and you just can't be hung over. Oh I can't wait! Isn't that awful?" Reno shrugged again.

Suddenly, as I worked on the crossword in the *New York Times* (attempting to buttress my claims to superiority over this woman in still other ways), I noticed something. This woman was not wearing a wedding ring. In all likelihood, I realized, she was divorced. And I thought, *she is probably dating, and, things being as they are, she is probably being forced to compete with women my age for men her age or ten years older. She probably worked very hard to look perfect on her wedding day, but now she has to work even harder to look good enough to marry again.*

Nowadays women don't just face the fear of aging, they face the fear of getting divorced when aged. I still think of plastic surgery as the nuclear option—though I realize it is now placed by an alarming number of people in the category of "pedicure"—but my friend Jessica said one reason she's toyed with the idea of breast augmentation is because "I hate the idea that at some point, god forbid, I may lose my husband, who thankfully is not a boob man, and I'll have to start all over again, dating guys, wondering if they're disappointed in my chest size." It's harder to sell a used car than a new one, but it's harder still if the new ones come with "standard" features you never had installed.

Many women I interviewed expressed disgust at the idea of plastic surgery while seeming comforted by its existence, glad to have it as an option in an uncertain world. In his book *Diamond: History of a Cold-Blooded Love Affair*, Matthew Hart described the cold-blooded logic behind diamond marketing this way: "Men want sex; sexual attraction is a transitory asset for a woman; she had better exchange it for something with better liquidity." This cold-blooded logic also applies to some marriages. Many women who leave their careers or scale them back once they've bartered youth/beauty/fertility for security are left impoverished by divorce, and at a considerable disadvantage as they re-enter the marketplace, both as workers and as daters, older than they were before. If the woman next to me was indeed divorced, however, she had clearly retained some serious liquidity in her exchange, leaving her wealthy enough to buy some of her beauty back.

So many beauty treatments, of course, are as much about signifying wealth as they are about beauty; a facelift may look unnatural or downright weird, but you have to have thousands of dollars of disposable income to afford one, and a woman displays that as much as anything when she gets one. The more money a bride spends on her appearance, and the more obvious it is how much she spent, the more she shows off her groom's wealth, in this case using her *body* as a status symbol, a far more radical demonstration of her status as a possession than donning the diamond ring. Brides are pressured to show that they have the resources to conspicuously consume facials, and to pay for the dizzying number of beauty treatments "necessary" to look good. (In its October/November 2005 issue, *Modern Bride* featured five of the "best big-day beauty treatments," and included laser skin treatment, "an aggressive resurfacing treatment" that involves "zapping thousands of dots of skin over three to five weekly sessions.") You could say that by choosing a woman like me, not much of a shopper or a maker-upper, Andrew had demonstrated his security by eschewing the kind of mate who would display his success that way. You could also say that Andrew was getting it both ways by teaming up with a mostly au naturel woman while slapping a big rock on her left hand. You could also say I was getting it both ways by taking two hundred dollars of his earnings to get my hair highlighted while telling anyone who'd listen that I didn't care about that sort of thing.

But I did care. A few hours and one partially completed crossword later I was blonder, and it looked great. I felt soothed. I smiled the smile reserved for those moments when you look into a mirror and feel truly pleased, regretting only that my awful companion for the morning had left thirty minutes before, when I still looked like a science project with cotton and Saran Wrap all over my head. I was born a blonde but like most people I didn't stay one, and when I was fourteen I justified (with some help from my local hairdresser) highlighting my hair partly by arguing that it suited my "coloring." I hardly know what I would look like with a head full of brown. I'm not sure I'll ever find out.

EMERGING from my morning at the salon, I got into a cab and headed uptown to the Vera Wang Maids boutique (across from the flagship salon) where fittings for bridal gowns are done. I was very nervous. At my last fitting (which had also been my first), I had discovered, much to my dismay, that my rib cage was too big for my dress. Not the always troublesome area around my stomach, but my *rib cage*, as in, my bones, as in, an area no amount of cross-training could shrink. The women waiting on me had eased the dress up over my chest, brought each side around my sides, pulled them toward the zipper in the middle and found zipping almost impossible. I, on the other hand, when zipped at last, could not expand my chest enough to breathe. Considering that I would already be running the risk of hyperventilation at my wedding (due to nerves *and* high elevation), this did not seem like a good arrangement. I could not imagine how such a thing could be fixed, but had been assured that it would be, and as I walked into the reception area of the boutique I unconsciously touched my palms to my ribs, as though to compress them. My bridal body was supposed to be perfect, I knew.

There was a reason I had so much trouble finding any discussion of the historical meaning of the wedding dress in all the wedding "literature" I read. When I asked, "What does the wedding dress symbolize?" one woman answered: "The perfect body on the perfect day." If websites, magazines, and guidebooks are any indication, she was exactly right. Forget the weddingchannel.com's "Who Are You?" bridal personalities of the Natural Bride, the Fashion Plate, and the Diva. Instead focus on the real you, as described in *The Knot Book of Gowns*: "Pear-Shaped" (do choose a basque waist or strapless gown that will cover your bottom half and focus on your better half); "Boxy" (don't choose a sheath or dropped waist that will make you look even more boxy!); "Petite" (do remember the key word here is "elongation"); or, my favorite, "Arm Issues" (don't choose cap-sleeve gowns, which highlight the upper arms).

I didn't get a personal trainer, but for four months I did go to the gym five days a week most weeks, and fretted over my body more than I ever had in my life. And as I waited for my dress to be brought into the quiet, grand dressing area, with its peachy walls and its pedestal surrounded by three floor-to-ceiling mirrors, I hoped like hell I'd made my body good enough for it. In my bag I had my shoes and the bustier I'd bought from Vera Wang, too. This time, I was wearing white underwear.

In a moment, I was going to strip down and expose my body from every possible angle as I donned the gown, and I felt grateful that in this fitting room the lights were warm and forgiving. I was fit and trim, though not as trim as I had been a few weeks before when I'd gotten the flu and puked for three days, after which, disturbingly, I received more compliments on my figure than I'd ever gotten in my life. Like many brides I had lost some weight, though I hadn't officially dieted and I don't know how much weight I lost; also like many brides, I thought I should have lost even more. Most brides do officially diet; in 2004 the Fairchild Bridal Group reported that nearly 60 percent of brides want to lose at least ten pounds. In an interview with the *Pittsburgh Post-Gazette*, Rosie Amodio, an editor at theknot.com, used the term "bridal-rexia," and put the percentage of bridal dieters at seventy-four.

"For a bride to be," write the authors of *The Wedding Dress Diet*, "figure flaws seem to become a matter of life or death . . . even if you're well-proportioned or at your healthy body weight, flabby arms, jiggly thighs, or a pot belly may still be a problem." Healthy, in other words, does not cut it. To its credit, *The Wedding Dress Diet* discourages brides from *literally* making figure flaws into matters of life or death, relating cautionary tales about brides who put on weight between fittings, or ordered, optimistically or masochistically, dresses a size too small in the first place, only to find themselves dangerously desperate to lose weight with little time to lose it. One bride did such an extreme version of Atkins her tongue swelled up, causing a great deal of pain, not to mention difficulty speaking, for days. Another attended a seven-day "fasting" camp where only water was served. At least, however, it made her thin!

According to one of the book's authors, brides (after athletes and pregnant women) are the largest group of people concerned about their weight, and if I felt a nagging sense of isolation as I coped with other aspects of bride-dom, I couldn't have had more company in this one. "Bridal boot camps" have proliferated in gyms, and, as one trainer told *New York Magazine*, "[Brides'] single mindedness can be scary." Some women extend their dieting obsession to their bridesmaids—Laurie, a dance instructor from Denver, found herself in a place called "Suddenly Slender" where she and the other bridesmaids "stripped to our underwear, got wrapped up in bandages soaked in a 'secret solution,' put on plastic bags and a raincoat over the bandages, and worked out on an elliptical machine in this getup while watching *Big Trouble in Little China*. Everyone's measurements were smaller [afterward], but I'm sure it was from dehydration." Another bride threatened her sister with bridesmaid excommunication if she didn't get "serious" about losing more weight, because daily walking didn't cut it. Brides reserve the harshest treatment for themselves, of course: the most outrageous story I heard came from wedding-dress designer Monique Lhuillier, who told the *New York Times* that one client had her jaw wired shut for two months in order to fit into her size eight dress.

It is easy, when hearing stories like these, or when picking up *People* or *US Weekly* and reading about the seriously crazy lengths celebrities go to in order to get the perfect silhouette (or a sickly, diseased looking one), to look at your own attitude about your body and feel pretty damn good. You probably should. But women are also told these stories precisely to distract them from thinking more critically about the behavior they have come to consider "reasonable." Lara Flynn Boyle, Calista Flockhart, the Olsen twins, and other famously thin celebrities allow the average woman to binge, purge, peel, wax, Botox, and pop diet pills (and, as a matter of course, to stare at her own body in the mirror with fear and loathing), all while saying—well at least I'm not like *that*.

The forty-billion-dollar-a-year weight-loss industry depends not only on the emaciated fashion model, of course. It also depends on super-sized chili fries (the slogan "you deserve a break today" has particular power when women are assaulted at every turn with comments about their weight). Both are necessary to guarantee the yo-yoing dieters that are the bread and oleo of the business. *Everything* depends, however, on making healthy, non-airbrushed, un-surgically altered, endlessly varied female bodies hard to see.

"I don't often see 'real' women's bodies nude," said Susan, a twenty-seven-year-old from New Orleans. "I like it when I get a glimpse of real-life women and remember that we really *can* look different and it's okay." (Dove's recent "Real Beauty" campaign heartened me until I realized it was launched in order to promote their new "firming" cream: "Dove defies 'lookism' and celebrates real curves"—which you can get rid of by purchasing its special new firming cream!) Growing up in Texas, I went to a health club that required women to wear bathing suits in the steamroom, and in junior high I perfected the art of changing clothes without exposing any part of my body in public. Not until I was in college and began swimming regularly at the pool did I see, almost every day, naked female bodies, of all ages, all sizes, and all shapes. It was tremendously liberating. I wished I'd grown up seeing them all my life. But being a typical American girl I still felt anxious about being undressed in broad daylight. And when the three employees of Vera Wang entered the room while I stood nearly naked in my underwear, shoes and bustier, I felt insecure, saggy, and inadequate—and eager to get on with things.

My heart rose, however, when I saw the gown again. For a minute my body disappeared, and the dress was all I could see. The handiwork of the crisscrossing lace overlay was meticulous and beautiful, the ivory fabric lustrous and warm, the tiny spaghetti straps satiny and delicate—all just as I had remembered. Still, I knew that even this dress would not make my flawed body disappear for others when I walked down the aisle. It used to work that way. As the *New York Magazine* article "Here Comes the (Buff) Bride" pointed out, "Traditionally, it was always the gown that took center stage at a wedding; whatever shape it was in, the bride's body was at least partially hidden under layers of taffeta and tulle. Today, however, the opposite is true . . . the trend toward dresses that exhibit more flesh and less flash has put the body at the forefront." *Brides* November/December 2005 issue featured dresses that "show off skin, linear shapes, and soft volume," a euphemism for dresses that had big holes cut out of them around the hips, ribs, and even over the belly. There were no holes in my dress, but it was form-fitting, and my exposed back, chest, and arms were going to be as much a part of my bridal presentation as it was. If my body didn't look good, my dress wouldn't either.

This time, as the attendants pulled each side of the dress around my chest to zip, I took a deep breath and held it in. But this time, as promised, the bodice fit me perfectly. The women who were helping me oohed and aahed, complimented my figure, my taste, my arms-without-issues, and as they did I found myself feeling close to them, wanting to talk, to tell them all about the wedding and where it was going to be, and all about the bridesmaids' dresses and the quest for frosted vases and to ask them about themselves, whether they had done this before or yet, and if so what they had worn, and if not how beautiful I knew they would look. In her book *The Beauty Myth*, Naomi Wolf wrote:

> Ironically, the myth that drives women apart also binds them together . . . on one hand, women are trained to be competitors against all others for "beauty"; on the other, when one woman . . . needs to be adorned for a big occasion, women swoop and bustle around her in generous concentration . . . these sweet and satisfying rituals of being all on the same side, these all-too-infrequent celebrations of shared femaleness, are some of the few shared female rituals left; hence their loveliness and power.

The swooping and bustling was lovely indeed, and for the first time I looked forward to more of the same on my wedding day with my bridesmaids. "In my long history of behind-the-scenes bridesmaid-dom," said Carrie, a thirty-eight-year-old marketing executive from

Philadelphia, "I've never seen a bride who didn't enjoy 'beautifying.'" Part of this stems from the comforting feeling of being rallied around rather than scrutinized; when you are a bride, beauty is briefly a team sport. Or perhaps it's more accurate to say that it's an individual sport with a supporting cast. Most women reject the idea that bridesmaids dresses are ugly for a reason (so as not to outshine the bride), but most also believe that while many brides want their maids to look good, they don't want them to look *too* good.

So there I was, in my bridal uniform again, and this time I didn't want to take it off. *I only get to wear it once,* I thought ruefully, while still feeling glad I was going to get to wear it at all. After awhile, I had to step out of it. Alone again, as I got back into my everyday clothes, I felt an uncomplicated happiness. I was going to be a beautiful bride, and this made me feel fit to be one. "I think every woman wants to feel special, admired, and deserving of love on her wedding day," said Laurie, the dance instructor in Denver, "and looking beautiful will help her feel all those things." A beautiful bride, in other words, *deserves* to be a bride. Her beauty is what she brings—and what she owes.

My last appointment for the day was also nearby (I was stuck in a kind of midtown beauty Bermuda triangle) at a "skincare center" co-founded by a prominent dermatologist and a well-known makeup guru. I have no idea how I found my way to that place in particular, but the combination of medical practice and makeup counter powerfully underscored the cosmetic industry's presentation of ugliness as a disease, with beauty products and services as its cure. (Mani-cure? pedi-cure? are my toes sick, or do they just have cuticles?) Technicians in white coats periodically appeared, summoning their waiting patients, and it was impossible to tell whether they were there to help a given woman pick out blush, peel off the top layer of her skin with acid, or both.

Of all bridal beauty–related tasks, I had been looking forward to this one the least. I've never been handy with makeup and have never worn much; just the word "eyeshadow" sends me right back to the hapless inadequacy I felt in the makeup aisle of Eckerd's before starting the seventh grade. I had been convinced, however, by the argument many brides are plied with in this department: on your wedding day, you "need" to wear more makeup than usual *for the pictures.*

"It's like being a model on a fashion shoot," one woman said, likening the aisle to the red carpet or the runway. (I came across the phrase "the white carpet" more than once.) Friends of mine who still worked in television meaningfully reminded me that the camera, that other enemy of a woman's self-esteem, was never kind. Never mind that I usually only wear under-eye concealer, mascara, and lipstick and look fine in pictures; never mind that the reason so much makeup is necessary on television is because television lighting is harsh enough to make J-Lo look washed out; never mind that I was not a fashion model but myself, getting married. I still bought into the "for the pictures" logic because while I may look fine in pictures, like most women I know I don't particularly like looking at pictures of myself, and I wanted to like looking at these.

"For the rest of your life people will be saying, 'Oh, can I see your wedding pictures?'" said Tia, a graduate student in Virginia. "They never say, 'Can I see that one picture of you at that random happy hour where you happened to look great?'" The wedding photo is the photo that endures, and according to the Fairchild Bridal Group, couples increased the money they spend on photography and videography 100 percent between 1999 and 2005. Clearly, the extremely media-savvy members of the wedding-boom generation have absorbed the idea that weddings are mini-movies starring themselves, and are easily persuaded that looking good in photographs and videos is more important than looking like yourself at your wedding when appearing *live.* Again, as with my wedding dress, I was determined to find that elusive but much-discussed balance between looking like myself and manufacturing my most beautiful self, and hoped that one of the white-coated women I was scheduled to see would reveal fairy godmother wings.

The first of these women, however, was less like a fairy godmother and more like a prison nurse. She was Slavic, bosomy, and about six feet tall, and she had been assigned the task of "shaping" my eyebrows. Having never had my eyebrows shaped, I had no idea what the etiquette for the situation was, but it did seem odd to me that she insisted upon having me stand in front of her, legs spread shoulder-width apart, so she could be absolutely certain that she got my eyebrows "even." She also insisted on doing all the work with a pair of tweezers, though one painful yank of wax seemed more appealing to me. She scowled as she towered over me, and plucked and plucked.

As time passed and I began to accept the wincing pain that already had tears running down my cheeks, tears of which my assailant was openly disdainful, I began to feel increasingly paranoid. I couldn't possibly have this many hairs around my eyebrow area to pluck, I thought, *I must be entirely eyebrow-less by now!* Visions of over-pluckers from the 1960s, with grease-penciled arches where eyebrows should be, filled my head, and I found myself saying, "I like them full, *full*, please, not too thin!" a plea that was met with grim, impervious silence and finally with a curt, "It's your first time, you don't worry, you will like." I realized I probably should have had an eyebrow trial run, too; one woman told me a friend of hers had Botox injected into her face the day of her wedding and one eyebrow got "stuck up." (Not so great for the pictures!) At least, I thought, whatever this woman is doing to my eyebrows will not be permanent.

Finally, it was done. Oops, one more hair! Then it was done. A hand mirror was ceremoniously handed to me. I held it up to my face. And there they were, my eyebrows, not too thin, not over-plucked or over-arched, only slightly, in fact, different from how they were before. I had no idea how this was possible—what the heck had she been *doing?*—but aside from some considerable redness and a discernibly less hairy patch on the bridge of my nose, for thirty-five dollars my eyebrows looked just about the same . . . but a tiny bit better.

"Thank you," I said with great sincerity. "You will be *beauty-ful* bride!" my newly maternal eyebrow plucker said, pulling me into her chest for a hug.

I left the treatment room and thought, perhaps my makeup artist will achieve the same thing: I will look just about the same, but a tiny bit better. It was too much to hope that I would look just about the same, but a *whole* lot better, which of course was what I really wanted.

The dark-haired woman of indeterminate age who showed me to a long marble counter filled with colors in creams, powders, sticks, and glosses clearly had no fairy godmother wings either, and was not even willing to humor my desire to be thought unusually afflicted by the dark circles under my eyes ("We all have those, darling, see all these concealers? See what I have to wear under *my* eyes?"). But as she patiently instructed me, one layer at a time, in the arts of foundation, powder, eyeliner, and blush, I soaked up the information as I always have whenever I've been convinced—sometimes for very shoddy reasons, like that Kristen Meadows's mother wore blue eye shadow without looking trashy and therefore Kristen Meadows must have been right when she told me I should wear purple, a "fact" I have never forgotten, even when I can't remember the name of a book I just read—that somebody was telling me the *real* scoop, that somebody, finally, was telling me what I so desperately needed to know.

This woman also spent a full hour-and-a-half looking at me. Staring at me, holding a magnifying mirror up to my pores, making decisions and careful choices (or carefully choreographed "careful choices") tailored to my looks, my skin, my eyes, my cheekbones, my face. This was gratifying because I felt I was going to get the answers I'd always sought, but it was also gratifying purely because it is hard to get anybody to pay attention to you so thoroughly if you are not paying them—and I was paying her. Another craving I acquired in puberty was the craving to be looked at (something I had a love/hate relationship with, wanting to be looked at, hating being looked at), a particularly feminine want. Beauty is a way for women to command attention—still the only way, perhaps, they command it completely—and brides know this very well.

As my face began to take on more contour, more definition, and more color, my hope that I would be looked at, long, hard, and to applause, increased. Perhaps this is why, at the end of the session, I bought two hundred and fifty dollars worth of makeup, brushes, makeup removers, makeup brush cleaning solutions, and other makeup-related gear—me, a woman who had previously only bought mascara at the grocery store.

"Ninety-four percent of brides invest money in new beauty products," Rosie Amodio, editor at theknot.com, told the *Pittsburgh Post-Gazette*, "and ninety-three percent pamper themselves with professional services, spa treatments, manicures and makeup." The beauty industry has brides right where they want them as they prepare for their wedding day, and clearly aims to acquire them as customers for life. This is an industry that spends 1.18 billion dollars per year on advertising. When women say they spend thousands of dollars on these products "for themselves" (money they could be saving) they greatly underestimate the impact this ad blitz has on them. When they say they do it for men, they greatly overestimate how much the average man cares if a woman wears anything but minimal makeup and nice, flattering, clean clothes. The beauty index fashion magazines offer is "no direct template of men's desires," wrote Naomi Wolf, "any more than beefcake photos tell the whole truth about women's desires. The magazines are not oracles speaking for men. . . . What editors are obliged to appear to say that *men* want from women is actually what their *advertisers* want from women."

I could not honestly say, in other words, that I bought all that makeup for Andrew, or even for the pictures. I bought all that makeup because after twenty-seven years of being bombarded with messages telling me that beauty products—the *right* beauty products, the perfect products for *me*, products which, of course, as per their makers' greedy agenda, are always changing and must always remain just out of reach—would make me wanted, loved, happy, and secure, I believed it. In that sense, I did buy all that makeup "for myself," and walking around town that afternoon, eyeliner, lipliner, and lipstick still perfectly in place, I experienced the spike in self-confidence that so many women referred to when I pushed them to explain the investments they make in beauty.

"How much I like my outfit, haircut, or hair color dramatically effects how happy and comfortable I feel with myself," said Dana, a thirty-year-old historian from Dallas. A thirty-two-year-old executive in Silicon Valley, who estimates she spends between twenty and thirty thousand dollars a year on her appearance, told me, "I now make more money [than I used to] and I don't save any of it, but that rarely bothers me. I would rather feel good about myself." And Virginia, a lawyer in Texas who "did the Quicken pie chart" to find that beauty-related items made up 50 percent of her spending, not including clothes, said, "Retail therapy is great. Nothing like charging huge amounts on the credit card." She later said, "But I know it's not therapy . . . [and] I just figured out that I could have my one hundred foot boat by now with [a] cabana boy named Sven."

Indefensible? Not if it's a "choice"! With classic sandwiched panache, women my age use feminist rhetoric to defend the money they spend on beauty. In its most egregious and ridiculous form, this logic permits a woman who has her pinky toe sliced off (or "trimmed") to better fit into pointy-toed shoes (portrayed as "the" summer beauty treatment by a magazine in New York) to defend her decision as a "right," and, because it is a choice, a decision exempt from others' judgment. (As though the idea of women *choosing* to partake in modern-day foot-binding weren't almost as frightening, albeit in a different way, as women being forced to do it.) Many women mix their rhetoric in a more sincere effort to sort out their conflicted feelings about beauty and their bodies, saying one thing when the issue is kept general, but turning around and saying another when they consider their personal situation. "Too many of us start at too young an age worrying about having small breasts, or not small enough waists, or skin that isn't perfect," one woman said. She then went on to add, "I just recently started thinking about getting bigger breasts." Another woman asked: "Whatever happened to accepting yourself for your inner qualities, and demanding that the men in your life do the same? To violate the self with a scalpel shows a lack of self-respect," and then said, "I would get surgery . . . I have a double chin I could do without."

These comments, it should be noted, came from women who were not currently engaged—for whom a march down "the white carpet" was not imminent. Imagine, however, what happens when a woman similarly torn between her efforts to say (and feel) the "right" things about her body, and the temptation to saw off her double-chin, finds herself a *bride*. Suddenly she is dropped into a world where it seems that everyone around her (that well-funded chorus again) is urging, even *commanding* her to focus on everything about her appearance that she most despises, and then to make use of the golden, once-in-a-lifetime "opportunity" to declare war on those things, and fast. Again, the deeper issues with which a woman may be struggling as she approaches her wedding day are expertly diverted into the purchase of face creams and, more and more often, of major surgery. As Francine Prose also observed in her critique of online women's websites, "There's plenty of advice about how to change ourselves—woman by woman, pound by pound, wrinkle by wrinkle—but not a shred of guidance on how to change our situation."

If there were billions to be made by offering women guidance about changing their situation with regard to basic issues of power, equity, and economics, as Prose suggests, perhaps things would be different. But as it stands, it's the classic bait-and-switch. Lure your customer by sympathizing with her over-stressed, overworked, sandwiched-woman plight, then ensure her eternal dependence on you by convincing her that the solution lies not in examining the roots of this plight but in "making herself feel good" by buying more of the stuff you're selling (*give yourself a break today!*), and finally—last and best of all—laugh all the way to the bank.

At the end of my beauty day that June, however, I did not feel I'd been had. Quite the opposite—I had no doubt that I'd been *made*, and that it had all been well worth it. I had been professionally highlighted, styled, outfitted, and made up; I felt confident, happy, proud. I was beautiful, and loaded up with bags of things I'd bought to help me stay that way. I thought I noticed more people looking at me admiringly. I smiled at them with the slight mix of condescension and thanks I thought befitted a beautiful woman as she passed schlumpier mortals on the street.

Then, late in the afternoon, I arrived home. I walked into my bathroom—which was lit by natural light from a skylight—and looked in the mirror for the first time since I'd left the makeup counter. And I couldn't believe what I saw. I looked awful. Grotesque. Spackled, as a friend of mine likes to say. Painted, too-thickly, too-dark, too-blushed, too much! I rested the heels of my hands on either side of the white porcelain sink and stared at my face for awhile, leaning in, backing away, trying to see if from *any* angle this made sense, trying to recognize myself under all that unrecognizable stuff. I sat down on the toilet seat across from our wall-mounted, full-length mirror, and, confronting my visage, felt a mix of emotions surge: disappointment at having gotten a bad makeover; anger at having paid so much for it; humiliation at having felt so impressively made-up all afternoon; amusement (briefly) at my folly; but then, sweeping away all others, a sharp, aching, utter despair.

What was I *doing*? Who was this person I was looking at? What had I been thinking? What the fuck, I suddenly found myself asking urgently, was going *on*?

Impulsively I reached for the toilet paper and tore off pieces to wipe against my skin. Eventually I got it together enough to splash water across my face, and watched dumbly as foundation and mascara drizzled down my cheeks. Makeup meltdowns are common to brides: one woman told me that a friend who normally wears almost no makeup at all was so distressed when she saw her professionally done face just before her wedding that she had to be held down and fed Xanax ("it was like bathing a cat"). Another woman reported running out of a Sephora in tears after a makeover, totally undone. My makeup meltdown was a moment of clarity: physical evidence of the façade I had committed myself to constructing in order to be a perfect bride.

Wiping the makeup off was cathartic, and, I thought, enough. (I was very glad I'd done it before Andrew came home.) The next day, emotions in check and my head clear, I made an appointment at another makeup place nearby. I resolved to tell them what had happened, to ask them to make me look natural, please—like *me*, please, only a tiny bit better. I told myself I had simply made a classic bridal error: I had missed that sweet spot between being myself and being my bridal self, so I would try, try again.

Another hundred and fifty dollars later, I felt I'd gotten it right. But I never did a "trial run" before the wedding—never, as I'd been instructed, practiced doing my makeup alone since I was planning to do it myself. I kept scheduling a trial run, then procrastinating; I kept meaning to undertake it, then putting it off. I just didn't want to do it. *I just didn't want to!* Even with my new, more "natural" makeup regimen at the ready, it just didn't feel right. But the day of my wedding I did it anyway, and the pictures do look nice. Was my store-bought blush the reason? I doubt it.

"I've never seen a bride who wasn't beautiful," one woman told me. "They're beautiful because they're *happy*." Not all brides are happy, of course. But on my wedding day, I was. And I think that I—and the pictures—would probably have looked even better if I'd put my faith in that, and passed on that purple eyeshadow.

MORE than anything, my makeup meltdown startled and embarrassed me because it seemed so juvenile. Not since I was a teenager had I experienced such rage and despair about the way I looked. Crying over the wrong foundation seemed dangerously close to insanity to me, and gathering myself together, putting things in perspective, and heading out to the stores again to find the right foundation felt like a reassuring reassertion of control. The elephant in the bathroom with me that afternoon, of course, was the idea that I was not crying over the wrong foundation but something that ran much deeper, something I wanted to run away from. "I've seen some of my friends totally freak out and not have any fun [on their wedding days] because they are so worried about their appearance," said Marlo, a marketing executive in California. "But I think it is more of an issue of them being freaked out in general, and it's channeled into how they look."

This is the popular wisdom—brides are freaked-out in general, and this manifests itself in mini, specific freak-outs about things like makeup, place settings, flowers, or whatever is on hand at the moment that the general freaking-out happens. The idea of being beautiful for one's wedding, however, sparks a *particular* kind of freak-out, with deep ties to women's experiences as adolescents, the time they learn what it means to be feminine, and the time they learn that femininity and beauty—along with the behavior "beauty" prescribes—are inseparable commodities.

What do girls learn about beauty, and the behavior it demands, in adolescence? First there is the discovery of oneself as an object for boys to evaluate. Many women told me vivid stories of the please-use-his-name-because-he-deserves-to-rot-in-hell variety: the popular kid with the white blond hair and perfect "1970s wings" who told a girl her teeth were yellow and spotted; the handsome teenage tennis instructor who announced, every time his eight-year-old pupil walked onto the court, "Here she comes, fish-belly white!"; the boy who didn't believe his neighbor's newbie breasts were real and yanked off her bathing suit top at a swim party in front of everyone. Girls do not do this to boys, and it is not because they are the nicer sex. It's because they don't have the *right* to do it. If you think girls are nicer, just think of what they do to other girls—sometimes with twice the venom because they can't do what they may really want to: rip the shorts off the mean boy at the pool party to expose his flawed, vulnerable body, too.

Then there is the discovery of yourself as an object for *you* to evaluate—when girls stop thinking of their bodies as instruments for activity in the world and instead begin picking themselves apart into pieces, each in need of being attacked until they are made "right." Mia, a literary agent in New York, recounted a list many women make in adolescence as they come to view their bodies as treacherous enemies: "too small boobs, too skinny, too big mouth, too much bush, underwear not sexy enough for adolescent guys, not tall enough, problem skin, not tan enough, too tan, hair too curly, hair too straight, hair not the right color, hair too damaged, no fingernails to speak of, cellulite, crooked nose, one ear higher than the other, one leg slightly longer, etc. etc. etc." As Joan Jacobs Brumberg observed in her book *The Body Project: An Intimate History of American Girls*, modern American girls now learn that a good girl is defined by good looks, rather than by good works, and Mia's "list" is about feeling not good enough.

And then there is the acceptance of the behavior beauty prescribes: consenting to wear shoes that cut into your feet when you walk, making it impossible to run; accepting that one "can't leave the house," i.e., move about freely in public, without demonstrating some attentiveness to beautifying (a poll by W magazine found that 60 percent of women wouldn't leave their homes without mascara or lipstick); internalizing the notion that being pleasing to look at is paramount, and entitles a woman to friendship, love, promotions, sexuality, and orgasms. (Many women report feeling sexually inhibited when they don't feel "beautiful.") "There are people who say beauty is not important, that what's important is what's inside," said one beauty pageant director. "But who is going to get close enough to an ugly woman to ask what's inside?"

One of the worst things about weddings is the way they resurrect and reinforce these lessons. Women who have worked hard since adolescence to reject the idea that they are physical objects for others to evaluate are told that one of a bride's most essential tasks (the most essential task?) is doing "everything she can" to make herself into a beautiful object for all to pass judgment upon. Women who have worked hard to love their bodies are told that in order to be a beautiful (a.k.a. deserving) bride, one must stand in front of a mirror and scrutinize skin, shoulders, teeth, and hair with pitiless exactitude, and label one's self an apple or a pear. And women who have worked hard to feel entitled to friendship, love, promotions, and orgasms not because of how they look but because of who they are find themselves reduced to how they look once again.

Women sense this when they become brides. They know they are obsessing over their looks more than they have since the seventh grade. They know they are regressing to an adolescent fixation on appearance, but many women do not resist this regression, just as I did not. Why? Because—in what forms perhaps the strongest evidence that most of us never *really* recover from the lessons of adolescence, even though we say the "right" things—many women actually view it as a *golden opportunity!*

Part of me thought this! Part of me was full of "I'll-show-them" zeal, eager to have everyone in my life, from every era of my life, see that I was all grown up . . . as a beauty. To show that I had mastered the game at last. As a bride, a woman is permitted to mount the most thorough, expensive, professional defense against the constant judgment levied against her looks she will ever muster, and I could hardly wait to muster it—to banish, at least for one day, that awkward girl who could never get her outfit right by showing up as a full-on knockout, dressed better than anybody in the room, unassailable at last. (Women who were beautiful girls probably feel a different sort of pressure/opportunity: to maintain their reputation as beauties.) In a way, being a bride seemed like a chance to travel back in time and redeem that all-wrong teen, as in the classic fantasy movie where the adult, sophisticated, well-defended woman has a chance to go back to seventh grade and do battle with those mean boys (and girls) who hurt her.

So back I went, and regress I did, all the time forgetting one thing: in those movies the adult woman always comes to the same realization. Seventh grade sucked! No sane person would revisit it willingly! It is horrible because everyone is awkward and insecure and cruel—but mostly it is horrible because it is the time when everyone, boys and girls alike, learns that social survival depends on creating two selves, a public and a private one, and two lives, an inner and an outer one, and it is the time in life when the confusion about which of these selves is authentic, and which of these selves is false, is at its peak—making everyone in pre-algebra a totally unpredictable, moody, hormonal miniature schizophrenic.

Something like the description of the typical bride.

"Adolescence," writes Mary Pipher in *Reviving Ophelia: Saving the Lives of Adolescent Girls,* "is when girls experience social pressure to put aside their authentic selves and to display only a small portion of their gifts. This pressure disorients and depresses most girls." This description could easily apply to women preparing to marry. Brides experience social pressure to display only a small portion of their gifts, and this pressure disorients and depresses most brides. The problem isn't wanting to look beautiful the day you get married—*of course* you want to look beautiful the day you get married—the problem is the pressure on women to set aside their authentic selves and display only a small portion of their gifts. The relentless emphasis on appearance is part of this pressure. Brides are asked to elevate the false, stereotypically feminine self above the complex, mature, varied, and authentic selves one hopes they have developed since adolescence, to concentrate all their efforts on the tasks of femininity (beauty, shopping, party planning) as though they constituted their only interests, even if this is a lie.

The construction of the bridal self, the clothing, the makeup, the hair, the arduously built presentation for "her day," is in many ways the ultimate elevation of the false self. Again and again, women I talked to described the pursuit of perfection—the perfect wedding, the perfect dress, the perfect hairdo, the perfect *you*—as the most difficult thing about being a bride. "Perfect," of course, really means "false," and the endlessly referenced anxiety about how to be a bride while still being yourself underscores how difficult women my age find it to be *feminine* while still being themselves, and at the same time how much they want to be both, as they ought to be able to do ("femininity," obviously, is in dire need of being redefined)—and how hard it has been for them to find this balance while the ground is still shifting beneath them.

I didn't find that balance. Instead I coped with my anxieties and contradictory feelings as I had in adolescence, by studying the role I was supposed to play and then working hard to play it—perfectly. The donning of a costume and the making up of one's face is, obviously, a form of acting, and act I did. Men act when they play the part of groom, too. But again, the slave always acts more than the master.

THERE is also a prerogative, of course, for the master to act like the master. Andrew loves clothes, shoes, and most things decorative more than I do, and yet when it came time for his big moment he could find very few ways to express himself through his physical appearance beyond wearing a very fine white and gold-brocade vest under his elegant black tuxedo, which he went to some lengths to choose and have fitted to his shape. As a man, he was not permitted to explore the full range of self-expression a woman enjoys when she selects her clothing, and if

I felt constrained by the beauty demands put upon me, Andrew was just as constrained—if not more—by the inflexible, unimaginative rules regarding a man's possibilities for self-presentation.

Again, women often suggested to me that grooms prefer not to shop or pay much attention to their appearance because, well, they're men—forgetting that for centuries diamond rings, high heels, and tights that showed off shapely legs were the provenance of kings. Historians have pointed out that the industrial and capitalist revolution shifted men's clothing toward its current aesthetic of no-nonsense usefulness, and the modern-day groom's sober suit epitomizes this shift. The question that would overhang a man enrolled in "groom boot camp," or who hauled his groomsmen into "Suddenly Slender" to reduce their "measurements," would either be: "Are you *gay?*" or, "Shouldn't you be at *work?*" or both. Women in the professional world must contend with this barely concealed question, too: as Nazneen, a physician, told me, "female physicians who spend too much time on their appearance are judged as not working hard enough . . . [if] I wear a tailored suit, fix my hair and wear makeup, people think I am a pharmaceutical rep instead of a doctor!"

Andrew, I think, would have enjoyed some more freedom in this department, and he ought to have had it. As it stands, however, as Anita, a legal secretary in California, put it, "when men emphasize their looks, they're categorized as gay or metrosexuals bordering on gay." My friend Jessica believes that if the social stigma were lifted, many men's inner-peacocks would immediately spring forth, and "they'd have padded tighty-whitey's on the market faster than you could say 'Miracle Member!'" Men are not innately, biochemically opposed to self-decoration; they are supposed to be sexual predators, in the business of perpetrating sexual aggression rather than inviting it, as beautiful women are supposed to do. Giving straight men the freedom to clothe themselves in ways intended to sexually entice women, letting them explore that part of them that is receptive to sexual advances, could be a good thing.

As with so many of these issues, of course, "freeing" men to adopt some of the worst things about stereotypically feminine beauty behavior—a vain and narcissistic obsession with one's looks; an insecurity that pits a person against her own body as an enemy; the misplaced waste of resources in pursuit of "perfection" as defined by greedy cosmetics companies; and an emphasis, especially acute as the culture has belittled self-sacrifice in favor of self-gratification, on good looks rather than good works—makes little sense, just as it would make little sense to tell women to stop buying creative, fanciful clothing, to cut off all their hair (if they didn't want to), stop brightening their lips with color, and eschew all jewelry. Yes, men should be freer to express themselves and enhance their appearance without being emasculated, but no, it is not a sign of progress that increasing numbers of men are getting nose jobs.

And there was something affecting, authentic, and just right about Andrew's beauty day, which followed a few weeks later. It really was a "beauty hour," and it consisted of the two of us making our way through the aromatic, crowded, summer streets of Chinatown to visit the tailor who had been charged with making the last adjustments to his special wedding-day vest. We held hands, and we did it together, which was very nice. After a quick and satisfactory fitting behind the makeshift curtain in the corner of the shop, we brought the vest home so he could try it on with his black tuxedo. I sat on the bed and watched him dress until he was done.

He was a beautiful groom. I teared up at the sight of him, showered, shaven, and smelling very nice. And he was pleased with himself, too—glowing, in fact—properly pleased with his elegant, special clothing, and ready, just like that, for our big day.

I envied him.

nine

cᗣᘛᗢᕲ

My Proposal

At Last

I resolved to propose to Andrew almost immediately after he proposed to me in Boulder. At the time, I assumed I'd do it the next
time we were together in New York. But after several attempts at writing to him the way he'd written to me, I gave up and wrote him a plain
old love letter instead—feeling obliged to explain that I needed an extension, since I'd been dumb enough to proclaim my *intention* to propose in an attempt to get credit for the thought without actually having
done anything. "This is less than it should be, and less than it ought to
be," I began. I wasn't ready yet.

I'd never thought of proposing until after I was proposed to, and
when I contemplated asking Andrew to marry me I found myself flus-
tered, stymied and shy. I'd written to him before. But the pressure to
write something unforgettable, to say everything and say it right, was immense. Beneath the pressure to perform, of course, lay a deeper anxiety,
a question about my readiness, about what I wanted. As the days and
weeks passed and I continued to delay, I felt impressed with Andrew and
his proposal in a whole new way, and I came to empathize with his

stalling in a whole new way, too. I also began to see how important it was to push myself to ask for his hand, to formally ask him back.

Having failed to make my declaration in New York, I sat down to work in earnest when I went home to Texas for the winter holidays. I imagined proposing to Andrew on the narrow strip of roof outside my bedroom window, a place I'd spent a lot of time sitting and talking with my sister, my brother, and the boyfriends who shimmied up the wiry oak tree that grazed my window with its branches—a place that had meaning for me the way the mountain trails had for Andrew. (My meaningful spot came with a view of my front yard, a suburban street, and Marvin Porter's house, but it was what I had.) I'd also read that a "super-bright moon" would be visible on the twenty-second of December, a moon unlike any moon seen in one hundred and thirty-three years, and this seemed like a propitious time to do my thing—not to mention a way to glam up my hometown roof. But the reports of the moon's brilliance turned out to be greatly exaggerated (somewhere on the Internet a fact from the 1999 *Farmer's Almanac* had been inflated to the point of fiction), and my attempts at writing to Andrew were not brilliant at all. When I found myself poaching lines from a poem I'd read as part of the subway's "Poetry in Motion" series, I closed my notebook and delayed again.

In the end, I waited just about as long as I possibly could. I still hadn't done it in July, a month before the wedding. And then one night I found myself lying in bed alone, listening to a terrific rainstorm. The fat drops hitting the hollow box of our window air-conditioning unit sounded like popcorn popping when it really gets going, and as I stared up at the skylight watching the water wash across its curving surface in the dark, something wonderful happened. Visions of centerpieces, place cards, and invoices, which for months had deprived every other thought in my brain of much-needed oxygen, suddenly disappeared. And for the first time another kind of vision filled my head.

I could *see* it.

I could see it! Our wedding—saying the things we were going to say, in that place, on that day, marrying each other. I felt a rush of joy. And for the first time, I felt like I couldn't wait another minute.

It was a feeling of complete affirmation, a letting go, a yes, and this yes made me ready to ask Andrew for his. I got up, went to my computer, and wrote to him at last. The next morning I flew to LA, where we were meeting to collect our car (he had been, once again, in Japan) and drive it out to Boulder to be ready for our honeymoon road trip. When he picked me up from the airport, I told him I wanted to get a bottle of champagne and head straight for the beach near his old house in Santa Monica. I think he knew what was coming, but it didn't matter, just as it hadn't mattered when he asked me.

"Let's find a spot the way we used to," I told him, and we took off our shoes and walked from the Venice boardwalk into the sand, negotiating the beach with the awkward, wobbly steps you take as you counter the resistance of the heavy, slippery grains under your soles. The sun was setting, and the light was grabbing hold of the particles of smog in the air to fill the sky with color. We found a spot somewhat out of sight of the pale blue lifeguard's box (technically you are not supposed to bring bottles onto the beach), and tucked our tailbones into the slope of the beach.

The water was calm. I opened the champagne and poured two plastic glassfuls. I was a little shaky. He smiled hard. I blushed.

"I have a poem for you," I said. We each took a swig of champagne, grabbed each other's hands, and I pulled out my folded-up piece of typing paper and began.

"I never said I wouldn't stand on a table for you," I said, and we both laughed at that one, "but from the second of our first touch, I said that I would marry you." (Incredibly, this is true. That Andrew did not run away screaming is much to his credit, but it helped that we were in the middle of making out.) "Even so," I went on, "it took so many years for me to understand what I meant." Andrew sucked in his breath sharply, and looked down. I thanked him for all he'd done to help me learn to love and be loved. And I kept telling him. And I almost put everything into words, though not quite.

"Marry me?" I asked him. He said yes.

"I have a gift for you," I said. It was a silver picture-frame locket, about two inches by three inches in size, engraved with the words

"Marry Me" on the front and our wedding date on the back. "As long as the grass grows, the wind blows, and the river flows," I'd written inside. He fingered its surface, beaming with pleasure. I'd surprised him with that, at least. And I'd given him a gift to keep for as long as he lived, to carry with him everywhere—though of course he was allowed to carry his in private. At last we were properly engaged the way we ought to have been from the start, *both of us.*

ten

"Bachelorette" Is Not a Word

... And Lollipops Are for Chicks

I gave myself away at the fabric store. It was June, about two months before the wedding, and my sister and I were shopping in the garment district for material to make the chuppa. She was in town for my bachelorette party. She arrived a few days early, so we decided to use our pre-bachelorette-party time to run wedding-related errands. We were examining bolts of creamy silk and white lace when Kimberly spied something out of the corner of her eye, turned to me, gave me a funny little smile, and said, "Can you like, go over to that other part of the store for a minute?"

"Why?" I asked, returning her funny little smile, which made her smile wider.

"Don't be difficult! I didn't have time to . . . you know, take care of something I wanted to take care of before I got here and . . . will you just go stand over there please!"

"Fine!" We were both laughing outright by then. I turned on my heel and just as I did she said, "Oh who cares anyway. We're not twelve. I need to buy some white tulle to make you a big ugly wedding veil for your bachelorette party. Okay? But I guess I should ask, do you *want* to wear a big ugly veil?" I shrugged and avoided making eye contact. Noting this, Kimberly finished off her speech by saying: "It's fine if you don't want one! Nobody's going to make you do anything you don't want to do."

"Well, I don't want to be a bad sport or anything," I said, finally looking up. And as soon as our eyes met I released the goofy, undeniably pleased expression that had been welling up since she said she was going to make the veil. She laughed.

"You do want one but you don't want to say so because you'll feel stupid!"

"I don't care!" I said. "If you want to make me one, I guess you should just make me one! Okay?!" We regarded each other.

"I'm gonna make you a huge, hilarious veil," she said. I grinned. Great.

Minutes later we had forgotten all about the chuppa, and were combing every fabric store we walked into for stiff, white, ballerina-tutu tulle. I'd been outed. It could not have been more obvious. I was dying to participate in any and all embarrassing bachelorette-party-related customs. I was eager to abet my sister's party planning in any way possible. I was not, by a long shot, going to be a blushing bachelorette.

THE bachelorette is the only truly new wedding ritual to come into existence since baby boomers got married a generation ago. In days of yore (like the 1950s), the closest thing to bachelorette parties were "personal showers," thrown for the bride by close friends, excluding mothers-in-law and great-aunts and featuring naughtier presents, along with, presumably, naughtier conversation. The bachelor party, however, dates back to ancient Sparta, when a man's military comrades would toast and feast him the night before his wedding. It is unlikely (though possible) that this toasting and feasting involved drinks with names like "Red-Headed Slut" and "Slippery Nipple" (from bachelorpartyfun.com's "Top 20 Drinks") or featured strippers who could pick up dollar bills with their hoo-hoos. But it is very likely that the themes of alcohol and loose women were present, which means bachelor parties have a long history indeed.

Most women I talked to saw the advent of the bachelorette as a sign of female empowerment. Bachelorette parties show that women are "more in touch with our sexuality and our bad-girl side," said Corrie, a thirty-three-year-old food writer from San Francisco, "and more willing to show that we value our female friendships." Laurie, a dance instructor in Denver, said, "Maybe we are finally getting away from the antiquated sex roles we've clung to for generations, despite everything. If women can go out and act crazy just like men can, it's a sign that we're not relegating women to the prim and proper Mrs. Cleaver wife role anymore. Here's hoping!" Melinda Gallagher, president and founder of Cake, LLC, a New York–based company that creates erotic entertainment for women, told the *Wall Street Journal* she believes sexual assertiveness is a lagging indicator of female empowerment, and that the trend toward increasingly bawdy, rowdy bachelorette parties (the *WSJ* headline read, in part, "In a *Sex in the City* World, Brides Are the Wild Ones") is a sign that the lagging is over.

I believed this hype. I, too, thought it would be a sign of my emancipation and modernity to wear a veil as I drank, smoked, and caroused all night like one of the boys. The rebellious symbolism of wearing one in *that* context was clear to me, while wearing a veil on my wedding day was more complicated . . . or so I thought.

The thing is that for all the hype, most traditional bachelorette parties—meaning those that involve a lot of booze and sexually themed antics—often end up being weird, boring, weirdly boring, or just plain awful. "I can't imagine a more depressing way to spend an evening," one woman said. "I do not look forward to them," said another, "and I have a sneaking suspicion that lots of other women don't really want to be there, either." Part of the problem, of course, is that the bachelorette has become yet another stop on the obligatory, forced, perfect-bridal-experience world tour, another event to plan, accessorize, and photograph, complete with yet another accompanying, pre-written script. (There are endless "how-to's" for all that "phallic fun!" as one website put it.)

This script is an awkward fit for many brides, but many of them try to shoehorn themselves into it anyway, feeling that if they don't, they will have missed out. One woman described a bachelorette party where she and five other women marched through the streets of New York drunk, pooped, and annoyed, soldiering on to a strip club at the bachelorette's insistence because without visiting one, the party would not be up to snuff. Upon arrival the bachelorette spent most of the time looking squeamish and alarmed, but apparently it was more important to this particular bride to *say* she went to a strip club than to *want* to go to one. Contrary to popular belief, plenty of men find bachelor parties uncomfortable too. "I don't think men necessarily look forward to these things," said Mia, the literary agent in New York. "I think it's actually stressful for a lot of men, and is often very, very expensive." Leslie, a thirty-seven-year-old mom in LA, said her husband begged off the whole thing and went bowling, and was much happier for it.

I, however, did not want to go bowling, or, for that matter, do a modern version of the personal shower, which has lately taken the form of a relaxing spa weekend with the girls, with evenings spent indoors watching romantic comedies and drinking white wine. When my friend Clarissa (who should have opted for the relaxing spa weekend) had her bachelorette, we ended up at a bar where women traditionally dance on the bar, and while Clarissa was too shy to take part, I climbed right on up because it was a bachelorette party, for Pete's sakes, *somebody* had to dance on the bar! (Better yet, it gave me an excuse!) I may have been unprepared to answer the question: "How have you always envisioned yourself walking down the aisle, ever since you were a little girl?" but since adolescence, I'd had no problem at all envisioning my bachelorette. I watched MTV. I did not want a hired stripper, that I knew. But I had no trouble seeing myself on top of a bar/stage/parade float, in a sexy outfit being cheered on by sweaty men, dancing my ass off. A bachelorette party acknowledged that I had a sexual, single life before I became a Bride and that I often really enjoyed it. It meant the opportunity to have all the women in my life that I love together in one place, at one time, partying. It seemed like *me*.

Me. Except normally I would not go out to clubs wearing a big ugly veil. In fact normally I would not go out to clubs, ever. (Bars, yes, clubs, no.) But that's what bachelorettes do, and I was eager to follow the script as I imagined it, simply with amendments like "no strippers, please." Taking the word "bachelor" and sticking an "ette" on it, however, turned out to be harder than I thought. As Microsoft Word's spelling checker and the *Oxford English Dictionary* will both tell you, "bachelorette" is not a real word. And as I found out over the course of my bachelorette party weekend, it probably shouldn't be.

On the way back to the apartment, Kimberly and I ran into my friends Suzy and Gabi on the street. They were each carrying armloads of grocery bags. Running into two of my best friends on the street where I lived—one of whom had recently moved to Holland after falling in love with a Dutch man, and the other of whom lived in San Francisco—made me incredibly happy. Suzy had, upon her arrival from Holland, announced that she would be cooking the Friday night dinner I had promised to deliver, and I did not protest too much. "This is what I do in Holland," she said to me, "I go to school in Amsterdam and take Dutch classes and then I go to the market and come home and cook for Mark. It's great. We drink delicious French wine, get totally shitfaced, and then we go to bed at like, ten o'clock."

"I'm going to chop things," Gabi said. "'Cause I don't cook."

That night everybody else rolled in, and the apartment filled with women and the smell of cooking onions and chicken and lamb, and Suzy opened up some of the expensive bottles of red wine Andrew and I had bought years before in Napa and handed me a glass, saying, "Hey lady. If you drink this fancy shit you won't have such a bad hangover tomorrow morning." Sounded good to me.

Six out-of-town guests were staying with us and we'd borrowed several air mattresses for the occasion. This gave the evening a slumber-party atmosphere, and as we leaned back in our chairs after stuffing ourselves with Suzy's delicious dinner, the atmosphere was relaxed, happy, and warm. I, for one, felt all this wedding stuff was paying off at last. By unanimous agreement Andrew had been invited to dine with us and stick around afterward, and so he had. In my mind this was an irrelevant breach of the bachelorette-party rules because this was not my *real* bachelorette party, this was just the night-before party at home. Still, I was hopeful that some portion of the script would be followed that evening, and within a few minutes Devon, my best friend from high school, obliged.

"All right," she said, grinning, "Any of you ladies wanna explain why I get so horny when I'm on my period? Do the cramps turn me on, or is it the bloating?"

Ah hah! Frank, funny, all-bets-are-off woman-talk! Andrew listened in, occasionally letting out his quick blast of a laugh and commenting briefly when prodded. My sister offered up the latest installment of her tragicomic relationship with her ex-boyfriend, whom she'd broken up with at business school. "He's started dating a woman I'm going to live in a house with next year!" she sputtered. "I'm going to have to get up in the morning and see him wandering into the bathroom in his boxers!"

This is the kind of drama I will be permanently excusing myself from by getting married, I thought. It's so depressing.

It was, dare I say, a perfect evening. There was poker playing, with two bags of peanut M&M's substituting for poker chips, there was dancing in our bare feet, during which my sister ran over and stuck the big ugly veil on top of my head, there was extremely immature peer pressure, applied by me, for everyone to do shots. Andrew announced his departure around the time "Our Lips Are Sealed" came on, and while we all argued, he shook his head sagely like the sweet dad you have a crush on—mostly because he doesn't turn out to be the freaky kind of dad that would take off his shoes and dance with his daughter's friends at her slumber party.

We stayed up till three. During a dance break my sister related our grandmother's despair over her lack of a husband. "When I was in college she thought I was going for my MRS. Then she thought I applied to business school so I could find a husband there. Now I think she'd settle for a park ranger or a grizzly bear." She laughed. She was working at Yosemite National Park that summer before returning to business school. "There *are* some cute park rangers. Maybe I should make one of them my boyfriend for the summer. Otherwise Nana is going to decide I'm a lesbian."

"Oh no," I said, "Nana is not cool enough to come up with that." Gabi, who is a lesbian, was one of the women present who was in love at the time, but her girlfriend was not invited because the evening was very much about us all being there without partners, freeing us, for one night, from the lines that get drawn between the coupled and the uncoupled, the married and the single, and, ultimately, those who become parents and the childless. (As many women pointed out, that's the *real* divider, but marriage portends it.) Marion, a thirty-year-old playwright in New York, said she looks forward to bachelorette parties "not for any of the cheesy rituals, but because I love seeing my female friends. I so rarely get to see them now without babies and/or husbands."

There were no babies and only one husband between all the women at my house that night, and this partly explained my pressing desire to have a wild party—I wanted to show that I was not going to be a "boring married," both to reassure my friends (one woman described a wedding shower as a time when "you get to sit around one last time with your friends of the same sex who may or may not stay your friends once you're married," an idea that scared the hell out of me) and to reassure myself. I did not want to say goodbye, or encourage my friends to "let go of the attachments" they had to my "old," unmarried self (as in a ritual described in *The Conscious Bride*); instead I wanted to solidify those attachments, to hold onto my "old" self too.

Coming from a soon-to-be-married woman, however, there was something condescending about my feeling the need to "reassure" all my single friends that I would still be around. Subconsciously, I was seconding the notion that for a woman marriage is forward movement, and unmarried women are left behind. The idea is deeply ingrained. The only reason my situation was reversed (I feared being left behind—or being left out—because I was *getting* married, not because I was remaining single) was because I was one of the first of my friends to marry. If I'd been one of the last, I probably would have felt relief at finally arriving in married-lady-land with everybody else. Either way, a woman's impending marriage is traditionally treated as a triumph to celebrate, while a man's impending marriage is treated as imprisonment to mourn, and this is one reason showers and bachelor parties were such apt counterparts for so long: as Jaclyn Geller put it in *Here Comes the Bride*, "the female bridal shower joyfully anticipates the beginning of a monogamous relationship . . . [while] the bachelor party appears to celebrate sexual licentiousness, lamenting the loss of male freedom that wedlock entails."

To the extent that bachelorette parties recognize the loss of female freedom that wedlock entails, and the change in friendships it may bring about, they *do* represent progress. Bachelorette parties admit that for modern women, marriage isn't everything—that it wasn't before the engagement, and that it won't be even after the deed is done.

"Sisterhood runs deep," Suzy said when I asked her about how being married has changed her friendships. (We didn't talk about friendships with men at all, which says a lot—if the divide between the married and the unmarried is great, the divide between non-romantically linked men and women is even greater. As a woman who, at one time, had more male friends than female friends, the fact that none were at my bachelorette party spoke volumes about how strongly those friendships are discouraged in adulthood, when romantic relationships are expected to trump all others.) "Plus," she added, mentioning the unmentionable, "what if the marriage doesn't work out?"

A realistic question, and one, in this day and age, that charges single-sex pre-wedding parties with an added dimension of anxiety—as women wonder not only whether they will still be friends once one of them marries, but whether they will still be friends when one of them marries, divorces, remarries, or never marries at all.

I hoped that the answer would be yes, but who knew? At that moment, however, with my arm around my sister's petite, slender frame at 3 a.m., I vowed to nurture the closeness I felt to her and to all those women, a closeness that needed Andrew's absence, at times, to breathe and thrive. It was right and proper to focus on each other as individuals and not, as Elizabeth Cady Stanton once put it, as "relational creatures," a.k.a. women defined by their relationship to a man, or a partner, or a child.

There was one small hiccup in my philosophical, self-satisfied musings, of course: the only reason we were all gathered together celebrating ourselves as individuals and not as relational creatures was that I was about to get married.

"We should do this every year," I said to my sister, "on general principle."

"Fine," she said. "But I sure as hell am not going to plan it."

Iᴛ was a great night. But it was a chick night, a ladies night, a night at home with my girls. It was not my Bachelorette Party. I wanted more, and I was gonna get it.

At around six o'clock the following evening, Andrew packed up his bag and got ready to leave. Unlike the night before, he was going to stay at his friend Tim's house to make himself completely scarce. Bag slung over his shoulder, he gave me a wry smile. "Have fun tonight," he said. "Don't do anything I wouldn't do." I smiled back.

"In other words, do whatever I want," I said, with light, taunting warning. Andrew had already had his bachelor party a few weeks before. He and his friends had all gone to Tahoe together, modeling their weekend in part on the guys' weekends he and a group of fraternity brothers took every summer for years—weekends mostly focused on outdoor activities like hiking, rock-climbing, and rafting—until a critical mass got married, and the guys' weekends stopped. Andrew's bachelor party, however, had also dutifully followed portions of the bachelor-party script, the full extent of which I will not disclose here. Let's just say the time-honored traditions of alcohol and loose women were involved. I heartily approved of it all—a bit too heartily, perhaps, telling every one of his friends how totally, unreservedly supportive and enthusiastic I was about the whole affair, partly because I wanted the freedom to cut loose at my own party, but mostly because although I wasn't really worried about Andrew getting too friendly with a stripper, I was *really* worried about being seen as the bossy, managerial, room-monitor wife.

If there's one thing I can't stand, it's when a man says, "Better not tell my wife or I'll be in big trouble, har har har," or when a man calls his wife from a bar, hangs up, stands up to leave, and says, "Sorry guys, just got a call from the boss, har har har!" This irks me for so many reasons, beginning with the idiotic idea that men are eternal children while women are eternal mothers. I began to feel this burden in adolescence when, as a girl, I was supposed to be mature, responsible, and well-behaved, sexually and in every other way, and—if this weren't bad enough—to assume responsibility for keeping the irresponsible, irrepressible boys I hung out with in check. (When girls act as freely, wildly, and, yes, as stupidly as your average teenage boy, the censure is the worst.) Not only that, but, as an adult, I soon discovered that women who did not strike the perfect balance between playing this role while appearing not to play it (implicit in *The Rules* #16, "Don't Tell Him What to Do!" is *"At Least Not Directly!"*) could expect to be labeled either as domineering bitches for being overly controlling, or pushovers for being too "easy" in every way.

Many women, of course, build up huge stores of resentment about this situation, and can't wait to become wives because when they do, the authority they've been saddled with since about age ten—whether they liked it or not—is finally socially sanctioned and, theoretically, officially recognized by their husbands. (In this case *The Rules* ought to read: "Don't Tell Him What to Do . . . So You Can Be His Wife and Tell Him What to Do *Forever!*") For these women, having some control over what happens at their fiancé's bachelor party takes on immense importance, and (unsurprisingly) this adds to the immense importance their male counterparts attach to defying this control and honoring the code of male secrecy that makes bachelor parties so threatening to some women.

"It is impossible to know what really happens at a bachelor party unless some guy there is completely honest with you about what happened, and what are the odds of that?" one woman I interviewed declared. "The purpose of a bachelor party is to get laid one last time before you get married, and to prove your manhood by getting your friends laid as well. It's about showing off your aptitude for debauchery," she added. "Any woman who doesn't think this is what happens at a bachelor party is lying to herself." This is an extreme view. I'd be willing to bet that most bachelors do not actually get laid at their parties. The *fear* that they will, however, drives many women mad.

This fear is a recurring theme in wedding magazines and on wedding websites, as worried brides wring their hands over bachelor parties gone wild. Weddingchannel.com's bachelorette-party-planning advice reads like one of those dating manuals that counsels women to "pretend" (to be busy, to be having fun, to have a life) in order to get what you really want from a man (for him to busy himself only with you, for him to have fun only with you, for him to be your life), suggesting, for example, that a woman plan a skydiving trip for her party not because she actually *wants* to go skydiving, but because such a plan might trick the groom into skydiving, too—rather than diving into a stripper's pants. "Let your plans slip to your groom," the authors suggest, with conniving, passive-aggressive aplomb, "and he might be jealous enough to suggest a change in his bachelor party plans to his best man."

It goes without saying (or it should) that playing these kinds of games is no way to start life as a husband and wife. "The event becomes a self-fulfilling prophecy," Geller observes in *Here Comes the Bride.* "Angry at her groom's participation in an event that treats marriage like a punishment, the modern bride punishes him, acting the part of the stern disciplinarian." Angry at his bride's attempt to assert her newly acquired authority over him, the modern groom acts the part of a horny thirteen-year-old who's snuck out of the house with pockets full of cash. This dynamic by no means confines itself to the battle over the bachelor party—instead it is an excellent indicator of the patterns that will dominate the marriage to come.

I wanted no part of this. But if I had no interest in playing the parent/child role, Andrew had even less, and I'm happy to say our bachelor/bachelorette parties were not aimed at *each other*, as the parties of mother/naughty-boy pairs often are. The least fun bachelorette parties are those that exist solely as a response to the bachelor's night out, and are as pathetic and unconvincing as the woman who sees her love interest dancing with someone else at a party and quickly grabs the nearest man to make out with him with contrived, vengeful pique. "Some future brides can be vindictive and want to get even with the groom," said Anita, a thirty-four-year-old legal secretary in Whittier, California, "especially if she knows that he's having strippers and going barhopping."

Weddingchannel.com primly discourages this tactic, which might be labeled the "anything you can do I can do better" bachelorette (the article suggests having a "talk" to avoid this kind of one-upmanship), and in its article the *Wall Street Journal* thinly disguises its disapproval of this as well, describing bachelorette parties as "rampaging" through the streets while reporting that men have maturely toned things down in recent years, trading blow jobs for comradely inter-generational golf weekends. This strains credulity, but a strong case can certainly be made that when groups of women travel to strip clubs in shuttle buses playing pornographic videos on the monitors, noshing on gigantic Rice-Krispie treats in the shape of penises (as in one party described by *WSJ*), it is a clear case of sticking an "-ette" on the end of "bachelor" and failing. Parties like these certainly bring my mother's question to me—*do you think feminism is about women being "liberated" to imitate stereotypical male behaviors no matter how depressingly bereft of compassion or dignity they are?*—quickly to mind.

Once again, I wanted no part of this, either. Naïvely, perhaps, I had high hopes of having a party that was authentic, genuine, and appropriate for a *woman*—while still being over the top and highly photographable. A tall order, true. But one of the reasons I'd unequivocally vetoed strippers of any sort, despite some last-minute lobbying by Suzy to have a willing and, according to her, very able friend of hers come by the apartment and entertain me, was that I felt having one would be more about having one—and about the fact that *men* have them—than about me or my desires. This idea had taken definite shape at one of the two bachelorette parties I'd been to before, at Chippendales.

That night was the first time I'd been there or any place that featured, among other things, beefy men prancing around in tight shiny thongs doing one-armed push-ups on stage and pretending to hump the floor. All I knew was: I did not want to be the floor. I did not even want to be the purple velvet pillow that one of the greased-up Mr. Olympia candidates was cupping in two hands and licking in a very suggestive, utterly ridiculous manner. But the whole time I was open-mouthed, laughing, and generally fascinated, particularly by the way the other groups of women (who were without exception—or so it seemed—attending bachelorette parties) were reacting to it all: as though it were one big hilarious fraternity prank.

"When women go to see male strippers, I honestly believe it is all a big joke, very tongue in cheek," said Sophia, a thirty-year-old doctor in San Diego. I couldn't agree more: twelve-year-olds in the front row of Backstreet Boys concerts, eyes rolled up in their heads, swooning in individual, rapt trances, take the sexuality of those singers more seriously than these women took the dancers' at Chippendales. You could have taken a photo of the crowd, cropped out the action on the stage, and told people the women were watching a friend ride a bucking bronco or even, when a clap-along got started to "Let's Get Physical," that they were standing on the outskirts of the hora cheering on funny Uncle Morty. It was the complete opposite of the enthralled concentration so many men exhibit as they watch women strip-tease. I was tempted to do the wave.

At the same time I found it very disheartening. It was depressing and puzzling to see grown women rendered so childish and silly, as though they were scandalized by the guy with the purple velvet pillow when I was willing to bet that most of them had been on the receiving end of the oral sex he was miming, and had enjoyed every minute of it. It was clear, however, as some of the women were called up onto the stage for personal treatment, that the dancers didn't take these women's sexuality seriously, either. (Perhaps because they didn't share it?) They bound their hands to chairs, gyrated in front of them, and occasionally grabbed their breasts—another insulting reminder that it was all a joke, since when female strippers make contact with their male clients, it is generally with the idea of getting them off. Female strippers "perform" sexuality too, of course, but the men in the audience are genuinely aroused. By contrast, *everybody* in Chippendales was putting on a show, and nobody was convincing. As the bachelorettes, chained to their chairs, reacted to their harassment with everything from nervous laughter to staged sexuality to stark drunk immobility I thought, "Note to self: this is not for me."

Which is one reason I was a bit nervous when my sister told me that while she had booked two cars to pick us up at 9 p.m., I was to report to the living room at 8 p.m. for my first bachelorette party surprise. "No strippers, right?" I asked my sister again as she helped me don what turned out to be the official year 2000 bachelorette uniform: a backless, sleeveless top, strung around my neck and tied to my body by the tiniest of threads, along with three-inch mules and a nice pair of tight, ass-hugging pants.

"A little trust, please?" she responded, heading upstairs. I was quite pleased, of course, that bachelorette-party pranks were afoot, anticipating good times ahead.

By seven-forty-five I was in the living room with one hand cuffed to a kitchen chair, everybody else (it seemed at a glance) was seated on the purple couch next to me, and Devon handed me a shot of tequila. "You're going to need this," she said. I tossed it back. I had no idea what was about to happen, but I was already giggling. I decided giggling was all right because, though handcuffed, I wasn't at Chippendales.

"Kamy," Devon said, her pale freckled skin and cropped sandy hair looking summery and smashing, "since you told us you didn't want a stripper tonight, we decided we had to come up with something else. Something good. Because you are not the kind of girl we had to worry about freaking out at her bachelorette party." This freaked me out. "So we decided maybe you would like something that was as much like Andrew as possible." Devon shot a quick glance to my right and I noticed, for the first time, that the bathroom door was closed and a light was on inside it. Oh my god, I thought, they have convinced Andrew to do a striptease for me. I believe at this point I let out a shriek.

"I think we did a pretty good job," Devon said, "but *you* will have to be the judge!" And with that, she walked over to the stereo and hit play.

The opening bars of "Hit Me Baby One More Time" thundered forth, and the bathroom door opened.

Out of it walked two people in suits. Andrew's suits. Andrew's shirts, Andrew's shoes, Andrew's ties. But neither one of them was Andrew.

"Oh my," I heard Gabi say. I couldn't say anything. I was laughing so hard I was already crying. The "strippers" made their way over to me, holding a bottle of tequila (clearly they needed the liquid courage more than I did) and somehow they maintained expressions of unbroken seriousness, even though they both had hobo-clown reddish brown beards drawn onto their faces with lipliner. As soon as they reached my chair, Hank and Frank, known by day as Suzy and my sister Kimberly, exchanged a look and soundlessly dropped into the funniest, most dead-on stripper parody I have ever seen.

Their hair was slicked back à la the Robert Palmer girls. Their Armani ties, once removed, were slung around my neck and sawed suggestively back and forth. I slapped some boxer-clad butts when they were offered up to me. Suzy kept making this mugging, lip-curling, chin-thrust-forward face that somehow reminded me of a French gangster, and Kimberly turned out to be wearing the Joe Boxer briefs I'd bought for Andrew years before, black with a big yellow smiley face printed onto the crotch, which he had never worn since because they have no fly. I was already laughing so hard my stomach hurt when Hank and Frank, in a coordinated move coinciding with a lull in the music, began to unbutton their Saks Fifth Avenue dress shirts. I tried not to imagine what was going to happen next. They kept the shirts closed, swaying to the beat, until suddenly the music burst forth again and the shirts flew open to reveal . . . chests completely plastered with clown-red, thick, fake curly chest hair. Andrew's head hair used to be curly and red until it started falling out and turned brown. But his beard was still red, and apparently Hank and Frank had made the inference from there.

Weird? Yes, definitely. But also witty, silly, and daring—a million times better than hiring a greased-up muscleman to shake his fake-and-bake ass in my face. It made a complete mockery out of the whole thing, and by that time, after months of playing the painfully humorless, earnest role of proper-engaged-lady, and after months of feeling trapped, strange, and not a little bit uncomfortable as a fiancée, it was just what I needed. And as Britney faded away, and Hank and Frank retreated to the dressing room to freshen up for the rest of the evening, I could not imagine how on earth we were going to top it. But I was ready to try. I wasn't done with this bachelorette thing yet.

THE cars, which turned out to be two minivans rented for cheap, took us from SoHo to the East Village, where we pulled up in front of a place called Lucky Cheng's, the "Drag Queen Capital of the World" where "delicate drag queens serve luscious Pan-Asian cuisine and spicy entertainment." So said the website, which does not explain how it came to be the bachelorette party capital of New York.

Maybe all those women who'd been going to Chippendales decided that if they were going to laugh at the entertainment, they might as well go somewhere funny. Maybe there was some collective realization that the "bachelor" + "ette" model was flawed, and something had to be done to rewrite it—why not go to a place where men dressed as women did the dancing and strip-tease? (The drag queens at Lucky Cheng's do not, thankfully, actually strip.) Hard to imagine a bachelor choosing to go to a place where gay women dressed as men sing pop anthems while wearing stuffed Speedos, making it hard to argue that the women at Lucky Cheng's were trying to out-bachelor the bachelors. Just what they (and we) *were* trying to do, however, remained unclear.

We walked in at about 9:50, through red double doors that led into a rather narrow bar area. Large pink Chinese lanterns hung from the yellow-painted ceiling, and behind the black lacquer bar the brick walls were slathered in metallic gold. The bar was jam-packed with women, all of whom, it seemed, were wearing backless, strung-together tops like mine. A platinum blonde drag queen holding a clipboard stood at the top of a flight of steps, surveying us all as we waited like penned cattle for the 10 p.m. seating. The 8 p.m. seating was enjoying its last cabaret number. We could just barely see the show taking place over the hostess's shoulder. A fat drag queen was charging the tables, shouting with nasal New York camp: "Come on you drunk bitches! Clap! Are you too drunk to clap, you little whores? You don't fool *me* with those cheap white veils."

I wanted to laugh. I really did. I get it! *Lucky Cheng's!* Where a bride, via an unceremonious hail of drag-queen abuse, could drop the good-wife routine she'd been expected to assume as soon as a ring had been put on her finger, and hear somebody shout out loud the contradiction that most modern brides carry around with them—the split between their *real* lives and the virgin-bride, centuries-old rite they were ready-ing to play! Or . . . a place where adult women come to be insulted and heaped with abuse by a fat, hostile drag queen who appears to hate them—perhaps because they are not there to celebrate their sexual, sin-gle past but because they are ashamed of it? Hmm.

"This place is fucked up," Suzy said to me under her breath. I smiled and shrugged, trying to see the bright side, but already seeing that my enthusiastic insistence on having a "real" bachelorette party, a party that would be clearly differentiated from a regular night out with the girls, had been severely ill-informed.

Hypothetically, another thing to recommend Lucky Cheng's would have been the opportunity it represented to bond with other harried, modern brides with a sense of humor. I briefly entertained this notion until moments later the drunk bitches in their cheap white veils, along with their friends, began filing past us. For the most part, they did not smile. Instead, they looked me up and down. So I looked them up and down too.

"Is it me," I asked, turning back to Andrew's sister Erin, "or is there like a mean, competitive, evil cheerleader-tryout vibe in this place?"

"Yeah," Erin said. "I feel like everyone's really hostile. It's *weird.*"

"It's not weird," Suzy said. "These chicks go to Cancun for MTV Spring Break and shake their tits for the camera." There was a high in-cidence of big hair and big makeup. "They've got their war paint on, man. They ain't all gettin' married."

Clearly there would be no bonding. Instead the "I won" theme that had characterized too many of my experiences as a bride pervaded this sweaty, cramped bachelorette holding pen, too, and it seemed as though everyone there was looking to see who had lost the most weight on their bridal diets, who was the hottest (and therefore, most deserving) bride in attendance, and who was going to present the biggest impediment to the principal goal of the night-out bachelorette party: attracting male attention. (There were groups of men at Lucky Cheng's, something I couldn't fathom at first but quickly understood in light of the hundreds of women roaming around with "scavenger hunt" lists almost exclusively composed of tasks involving sexually themed dares and men.) The hostility between women was so intense it seemed to go beyond a gang-like standoff between bachelorette-party groups. Disturbingly, one got the feeling that some of these brides were the object of their *friends'* barely concealed anger.

I never felt this, but maybe I tuned it out. Certainly the hazing and humiliation that characterizes many "traditional" bachelorette parties often has an undertone of anger. Devon later told me she wouldn't want a bachelorette party at all because it involves "all that stupid stuff that women do to embarrass each other. Why would you want to make your friends look like such idiots? When I see girls at bars with dildos and that fake veil, it just embarrasses me." I don't know what she thought of my party, but I'd thought of the fake veil, at least, as a joke *I* was telling on myself, on the whole wedding thing. But often the fake veil and other crude accoutrements of bachelorette parties are jokes being told on, or about, the bride. "I think [the party props] are a great way to embarrass a friend that is a prude or uncomfortable with sexuality," one woman said. As for the anger, it isn't hard to imagine some of its origins: women tired of being bossed around by a bride (and tired of shelling out hundreds of dollars for each mandatory pre-wedding event) eager to boss her around for a night instead; single women angered at the instant status, protection, and sanctity bestowed on a woman just because she's marrying when they may feel she doesn't deserve it, or at the least that they deserve it, too; and finally women just plain jealous of the attention heaped on bachelorettes by opportunistic guys.

I couldn't wait to get to our table, and finally, thankfully, our party's name was called. As we walked up the steps, a Lucky Cheng's–related person shoved a small cardboard box into my hands, which I carried with me to our booth. The dining room was also done in glistening gold brick, with a red Chinese dragon hanging from the ceiling and booths and chairs covered with turquoise, magenta, lavender, and orange fabrics. Our booth was next to a room with a square elevated stage, where a black transsexual in hip-hugging silver lamé was gyrating to Pink's "There You Go."

"Can we go home and play poker now?" asked Gabi.

"No!" I yelled, resolutely shaking off the bar-area vibe. I was determined to have fun—*fun*, dammit. "This is great! It's totally hilarious and ironic and I would never come here if I weren't having my bachelorette party, and that's what it's all about."

"What's in the box?" my sister asked as we settled in.

The box was an official Lucky Cheng's bachelorette party kit. It contained: one dinky white veil (the veil I'd seen on all the drunk bitches); one hot-pink feather boa; one candy necklace; one fleshy pink penis straw; one Jolly Rancher red penis lollipop; and a bunch of other penis-related items that I cannot now recall. (A phone call to a Lucky Cheng's employee yielded only this description: "I don't know exactly what's in it! Toys! Penis-shaped toys!") I noticed that a bachelorette at a table near me was wearing a penis-shaped *hat*. I was glad this had not come in the kit.

"Do you think guys get bachelor-party kits with vagina straws in them?" I asked my sister. "No," she said. Mia, the literary agent, answered a similar question this way: "I can imagine men sucking on vaginas at bachelor parties, but lollipops are for chicks. See the difference?"

I was completely unaware of the bachelorette-party-penis-paraphernalia industry until that moment, but I was in the minority, and since my night out the business has only grown. Alan Lasky, vice president of the company that runs bachelorpartyfun.com and bacheloretteppartyfun.com, told the *Wall Street Journal* that brides purchase four times as many "naughty novelty items" as men do, and theknot.com, in its article

"Bachelorette Parties: 7 Must-Have Party Props," advises party planners fearful of a trip to the sex shop to "make a bee-line for the penis sipper (a.k.a. 'dickie sippie')"—the tone of this helpful hint as chipper and banal as the suggestion that brides should make a fake bouquet out of the bows they receive at their wedding showers. Online, you can find penis-shaped lipstick; penis earrings; penis *pacifiers* (suck on that one); penis party whistles; penis squirt guns; bachelorette cor-*sausages* (featuring black or white "sausages" in the middle); penis candles; penis pasta; penis Jell-O trays; penis ice trays; penis tooth*dix*; penis forks, knives, and spoons ("pecker ware"); penis snack trays; and, of course, the six-foot inflatable penis, also known as "Captain Pecker."

"If women ruled the world," my friend Franny said to me after I told her about the penis gear, "guys would be wearing vagina earrings and we'd be getting lap dances."

Clearly this is part of what underlies the bachelorette-party penis-accessories business. Even at an event ostensibly celebrating a woman's libido, she is not permitted real sensuality, or even real flirtation with transgression, but is left with a lollipop because our culture still tells us that women and their bodies are for male use, and not the other way around. Penis toys are also appropriate, however, considering that girls learn early on in their sexual educations—as Naomi Wolf observed in *Promiscuities*—that the penis is their responsibility. Why not tote a penis around like a ball and chain all evening, in homage to the duties of your sexual past, and perhaps, your sexual future?

The props are also intended, however and as always, to humiliate. (The website *Bachelorette Party Fun* refers endlessly to humiliation, its "Bachelorette Party Oath" committing participants, among other things, to embarrassing the bachelorette "at least once per hour.") This also makes sense, of course, considering how deeply sex and humiliation are bound together for women. The age-old connection between the two has only grown more confused for women my age, raised as they were with wildly mixed messages like "sex is great!" (sexual revolution talking), "sex is deadly!" (AIDS-scare talking), "women love sex as much as men do!" (feminism talking), "women who love sex are whores!"

(centuries of male control over female sexuality talking). Considered this way, it could easily be argued that penis props, along with the humiliating games requisite to the "typical" bachelorette, are not at odds with modern female sexuality, but instead perfectly represent the *culture's* view of it. (They *are* at odds with many women's private notions of their sexuality, which also stem from the culture—a contradiction that underscores, again, how wildly the messages are mixed.)

The fact that the only lap dance I got at my bachelorette was called a "drag-box" dance, administered by a six-foot-tall male transvestite named Hedda Lettuce who hoisted me into the air, turned me upside down, sawed me up and down his crotch, and then propped me, arms and legs spread, up for display as I came into close and convincing contact with the evidence of Hedda Lettuce's manhood, *and* that my other likely option in this department would have been to have a gay man pretending to be a straight man harass me mockingly at Chippendales, said a great deal about just how confused society is when it comes to dealing with the "sexual assertiveness" women have supposedly been liberated to express. In a way, I felt this drag queen was teaching me a lesson. "Want to say goodbye to what it's *really* like to be an openly, publicly sexual woman without a boyfriend or a husband to protect you and vouch for you? No problem! I'll touch you and manhandle you and call you a slut to your face!"

"This shit is reeeally bizarre," Suzy said after my drag-box dance had ended.

"But after this," I said, hopefully, trying to find a purpose to the evening, "I will be totally cured of my desire to go out to cheesy clubs full of mean drunk women."

"No," my sister said, "you will be cured of your desire to go to Lucky Cheng's and watch really tall drag queens swing around strip-club poles."

She was right. I was dissatisfied. I was buzzed. And I was itching for action. My bachelorette party still had something missing, for all its penis party toys. Sexiness, *real* sexiness, the randy, the titillating, the erotic, the naughty. I may not have wanted to go to Chippendales, but I did want a whiff of sex that night. Just a whiff!

Jessica and Caroline had written up a things-to-do list for me (titled "Mission Impossible: Kamy") that included having a guy put on my lipstick and kiss my bare back. It also included having a guy braid my hair. Suddenly I felt a strong inclination to do some flirting with men of the straight variety. "Maybe I should check off some stuff on my list," I said, eyeing a group of cute (I had champagne goggles on at this point) guys on the far side of the room. Just then, however, Caroline approached me with eyes alight. "Kamy," she said. "Downstairs . . . they've got *karaoke*."

As it turned out, these were the four words I'd been waiting to hear.

THERE, on the karaoke runway in Lucky Cheng's karaoke lounge, I found it. I'd known it all along—the one thing I'd told my sister that I absolutely *had* to do for my bachelorette party was dance—but it wasn't until I was dancing and singing on that little strip of stage, four feet off the ground and packed on all sides with people, that I realized exactly what it was, for me, that would feel like a real send-off to my single, sexual past.

For men—and only for some men, I know—the bachelor party is about staring at, appreciating, lusting after, and otherwise interacting with sexy women. It is about dancing around, supposedly for the last time, with a gorgeous naked woman who is not your future wife. For women—and only some women, I know—the bachelorette party is about *being* stared at, *being* appreciated, *being* lusted after and otherwise desired. It is about dancing around, supposedly for the last time, with a bunch of guys (not always gorgeous and usually not naked) who are not your future husband. "I've heard more about women tearing off their own clothes at bachelorettes and finding that more sexy than any male strippers," said April, who hired a stripper for a bachelorette party she planned and ended up, along with the rest of the group, sharing mojitos with him because they found his performance so un-arousing. As another woman put it: "For women the thrill is luring guys to them, while for guys, the thrill is having women placed at their feet—or on their laps." For better or for worse, this went for me, too, and dancing like a stripper was a lot more fun, and more like it, than having one.

Like many women my age, I had long confused this kind of display with feminist empowerment. I was "appropriating" the role of "stripper," I told myself, and thus taking charge of it—obviously this was empowering! But as Ariel Levy put it in her 2005 *Washington Post* article "Raunchiness Is Powerful? C'mon, Girls," the strippers and porn stars women increasingly look to as role models (Jenna Jameson, feminist icon?) are paid to "fake lust, to imitate sexual arousal." "We're supposed to imitate an imitation of our own sexuality and call that empowerment?" Levy asks. "Seriously?" Did I think it was empowering to dance like a stripper because I didn't actually strip, and I didn't actually get paid? I was still the seller after all. At bachelor parties men literally play the buyer, paying women to strip or service them. At bachelorettes women do not literally sell (though the ever popular "Suck for a Buck" T-shirts essentially do this), but they usually put on quite a show for free. Once again, women have not yet truly broken the mold, crossing over to play buyer in the transaction of sex and relationships, and still have trouble experiencing lust freely instead of performing it. Instead, women my age have been "freed" to sell more brazenly, openly, and strenuously than ever before.

I was no exception. Consider some of the dance moves I demonstrated on that karaoke stage! Bumping and grinding with my female friends, shaking it like a Polaroid picture. This was how I learned to dance in high school and college, with Madonna as my primary idol and tutor; it's how my cousin, fourteen years my junior, learned to dance when she was in the *fifth grade*, with Madonna's brain-dead inheritors, from Britney to Christina, as her guides. (As least Madonna can be credited with some real grasp of social rebellion, some flicker of cultural wit.) It should be said that this wasn't all a show, because I do find it arousing to "sell," so to speak. If men were freed to cross over and play the seller sometimes, they'd probably benefit sexually and otherwise, and they'd definitely be much better dancers. And it was especially fun to sell it, as I'd hoped it would be, as a bachelorette—because for one night and one night only, I had a free pass. The big white veil on my head protected me from the fears that usually plagued me when I went out, danced, and drank: *Will people get the wrong idea about me? Will any of these guys try to grab me or hurt me or say something horrible? Will I be embarrassed or humiliated tomorrow? Is this okay?* Bachelor parties afford men the chance to escape the ever-monitoring eye of women. Bachelorettes give women the chance to escape the ever-monitoring eye they are raised to train upon themselves.

I had not only been freed from this constant, internal self-monitoring, however. I'd also been freed from the constraints placed upon me by the ever-trickier, ever-more-complicated double standard I'd struggled to live up to during my sexual coming of age: the notion that a modern woman is supposed to be as sexy as a porn star and as marriageable as somebody's stay-at-home mom (the infamous MILF, or Mother I'd Like to Fuck). Pop stars like Britney Spears and Jessica Simpson illustrate the almost laughable (if it weren't so pathetic) lengths women go to as they attempt to be both: these two dry-hump pythons and muscle cars in their music videos while pleading to be seen as squeaky clean, even *virginal* good girls at home, then lamely trot out feminism when defending their "right" to earn their livings as glorified strippers without being treated that way.

And they do have a point—women *should* have the right to be sexy and, yes, to put on a show from time to time, without being censured or treated crudely. That was part of what I enjoyed about my bachelorette. On the other hand, is Jessica Simpson's right to wear Daisy Dukes *and* play happy housewife (for awhile) really a sign of progress? Or have women simply found themselves working harder than ever to become the ultimate male fantasy: "a lady on the street and a freak in the bed?" According to one of the young women Meghan Daum interviewed for her article "Why Have These Girls Gone Wild?" (*Glamour*, July 2004), this is what men want. But as Daum reported from her experience of Spring Break in Cancun, an appalling number of college-aged women seem to believe that they have to prove their ability to be freaks in bed by being "freaks" on stage, licking whipping cream off each other's bodies, for example, or entering contests that require them to suck beer out of a bottle held between a strange man's legs in order to win a T-shirt . . . and lots of male attention.

Increasingly, women are pressed into being more exaggeratedly, performatively sexual than ever, but they continue to be denied the deeper, more substantive cultural changes in attitude and environment necessary to meaningfully ratify their sexual freedom. Girls may now have thongs sticking out of their low-rise jeans, saline-filled bras (or saline-filled breasts, as more and more teenage girls do), and the "freedom" to give blow jobs in the seventh grade, but until they are given the right to be sexual actors rather than re-actors (along with the right to say "Marry me," not just "Yes"), and are given the right to have sexual lives that are not male property, lives *men* have the right to publicly define (as in "marriage-material" or "one-night-stand"), the appearance of sexual freedom will continue to be a far cry from the reality that underlies it.

It's one thing to do karaoke with your friends and dance like a semi-professional seductress for a night; it's another thing to confuse the democratization of pole-dancing, not to mention the horrors of Spring Break, with female liberation and power. But it should also raise a red flag that the line between being empowered ("you go, girl!") and being demeaned ("you're gross, girl!") has become so damn hard to see. Toward the end of our evening at Lucky Cheng's, however, I had the good luck—or the misfortune—of having that line suddenly leap into view with alarming clarity.

My wake-up call came in the form of a fellow bachelorette, pushed up onto the stage by her friends around the time I was coming down from my party high. (Suzy had just taken things down a notch by pulling up a chair and crooning "Once, Twice, Three Times a Lady" to me in classic Japanese karaoke style.) This woman was totally hammered, wearing a handkerchief-on-a-string top like mine and that puny Lucky Cheng's veil . . . and she was holding a five-foot-tall inflatable penis, complete with bulging, flesh-colored testicles at its base, in her hands.

"Look at that thing!" I suddenly yelled to anybody who would listen, feeling a sharp burst of outrage. "What is this all *about*?" Written in black marker on the penis, like the scribbles kids make on each other's casts, were: "The Great Cape Escape II," "Sue, Ku Man Chu, Love, Duck," "Where were you this morning?," and "BOOZE."

At that time, I did not know how pervasive penis props had become. But as I sat in Lucky Cheng's karaoke lounge watching that vacant, lost-looking woman holding onto her Captain Pecker on the stage, I sensed it. I sensed it very clearly.

The phone rings, in the middle of the night, my father yells what you gonna do with your life, Oh daddy dear you know you're still number one, but girls, they want to have fun, oh girls just want to have. . . .

Cyndi Lauper. The words flashed across the karaoke screen, but Inflatable-Penis Chick stood immobile, penis propped on her hip with one hand, microphone hanging lamely from the other. She mumbled. She was barely making a sound. But I was tapping my feet. I love that song . . . and, more important, I'd just started a fresh beer. Her friends came over to me. "Do you think you could help her out?" they asked.

I think they asked. I may have made an executive decision. I jumped up on the stage. "Come on!" I shouted, grabbing the second mike. "This is a great song!" Inflatable-Penis Chick stirred. She managed: *That's all they really want, oh oh, when the working day is done oh girls, they want to have fun, oh girls just want to have fun. . . .*

The song settled into its musical bridge. I looked out at the crowd, about a hundred people by then, men and women both, clapping along and perking up as the irrepressible, light eighties beat tripped along. I looked at the girl standing next to me, swaying vaguely, holding onto that stupid, insulting, fleshy-pink plastic penis. And something snapped.

"Hey!" I yelled into the mike. "This is some *bullshit*!" The inflatable penis jiggled, its owner winced. The crowd flinched. "Don't you think? Isn't this some *bullshit*, ya'll?" I raised my hands in the air, as though I were Ludacris exhorting the crowd at a televised beach party. I turned to my on-stage companion. "Why don't you tell me about yourself," I said.

"I bet you have a great job. I bet you *work*. I bet you take care of your business. I bet you don't base your entire identity on earning a positive response from huge inflatable *penises*." I held my mike beneath her startled mouth, which mustered something about a law firm. "See! See?!" The lyrics kicked in again. *That's all they really want, some fun, when the working day is done oh girls, they want to have fun, oh girls just want to have fun. . . .*

"Can you see the *irony* in this song!?" I ignored the inflatable penis and started pacing the stage. It appeared to me that every single person in the crowd was totally with me. "It's a *joke*! Girls just wanna have fun? Anybody ever hear of Madeleine Albright, secretary of state? How 'bout Janet Reno, the attorney general of the *United States of America*?!" (Obviously this was in the last months of the Clinton administration. It wasn't time to give it up for Condi yet.) *I'm raising the roof!* I thought.

That may not quite have been the case, but nobody booed, anyway. The part of speech that followed is a little hazy to me now. Jessica says I went through every female member of the senate I could remember. I think I said some more stuff about penis worship. I wish I had said that I was sorry that we'd all acted like catty competitive children earlier. I wish I had called upon the group to help me figure out how the hell bachelorettes had ended up wearing penis hats. But I didn't. I just seriously killed the mood.

Soon after my speech, we walked out of Lucky Cheng's, piled into cabs and went to a club. The evening was beginning to take on the character of a bachelorette-death-march, but I'd said I wanted to go dancing at a club, and insisted we put a check next to that box. So we went, and it was hot and sweaty and strange creepy men rubbed against me and twenty minutes into it, I wanted to go home. At that club, where we all looked out for each other, forming a pack to defend ourselves from unwelcome advances, I remembered how smelly, awful, and just plain scary being a single woman out in the big city at 2 a.m. could be. One reason women's pre-wedding festivities "joyfully anticipate the beginning of a monogamous relationship . . . [while] the bachelor party appears to celebrate sexual licentiousness," as Geller complains? Because for women being "free" in the sexual marketplace can be demoralizing and downright dangerous.

"Getting older and being married is a relief," said Corrie, a thirty-three-year-old food writer from San Francisco. Elbowing my way out of that swordfight and escaping into the night air, I knew exactly what she meant. Corrie also added, however, that as a married woman she sometimes felt "invisible" because she was "less of a sex object," and that sometimes she lamented her loss of status as a sexy, single girl. I knew exactly what she meant by this, too. As relieved as I felt to be committed to Andrew, no longer "out there," as Carrie Fisher memorably put it in *When Harry Met Sally*, I also feared becoming invisible once I became a wife. In a culture that emphasizes women's sexual attractiveness so much, I feared being put out to pasture, and felt a kind of urgency about showing myself off "in my prime" not just as I walked down the aisle, but out that night in the dating-and-mating trenches. Another reason I wanted to be a bachelorette? To be ogled and admired, in *that* way, by as many men as possible, one last time.

Arriving back at my apartment that night at two in the morning, however, as I headed for the bedroom only to find the bed dark and empty, and remembered that Andrew was staying at Tim's place that night, I immediately called his cell phone. "Come home," I told him, weary and filled with longing. "Please, please come home."

I'd had enough.

As it turned out, Andrew had had a rough night, too. His friend Tim had taken him to dinner and then told him that he and Jennifer, his wife of three years, were getting divorced. Their cliff-top wedding, with a beautiful view of the beach, was one of the first we'd ever gone to together. We'd known Tim and Jennifer had been having problems, but they'd kept the separation to themselves for months, and the announcement of the official divorce came as a surprise to both of us. I kept thinking of Jennifer saying goodbye to us on her wedding night, giddy, glowing, and laughing after having been tossed in the pool—no joke—

in her parents' backyard after the wedding reception. Andrew, obviously, was thinking of Tim, who he said was lonely and depressed.

It had been very good for Andrew to get away and spend the evening with Tim, who was suddenly single, and suddenly in a different position in relation to certain of his guy friends. We'd spent the previous New Year's with Tim, Jennifer, and two other couples, and now Tim would not fit into the couple social equation anymore. He still had single guy friends, however, and soon resumed a rhythm of friendship and closeness with them that echoed his past. Tim, in fact, was about to reclaim and rejuvenate male friendship in his life as a single guy, while Andrew, as a married man, was likely to find himself increasingly isolated as he focused on work and family. When I asked Virginia, a lawyer in San Antonio, Texas, whether she thought women risked losing their friends when they married, she said, "Hell no. But men? Different story."

"Most of my friends are men," Virginia continued, but "when they get married, I never see them again." It isn't too difficult to see why a wife might be threatened by her husband's friendships with other women, though one would hope that such friendships would be possible in a strong marriage. But many wives are jealous of their husband's friendships with other *men,* too, intent on establishing clear ownership of their husband's emotional lives. This jealousy, coupled with the demands of work, can isolate married men. "The increasingly rigid demands of the workplace and the social expectations of family life radically limit the time that American men can devote to cultivating friends," writes Jaclyn Geller in *Here Comes the Bride,* citing several convincing studies charting the difficulties heterosexual men face in maintaining their male friendships.

Geller also theorizes, very convincingly, that the frenzied excess of bachelor parties is driven more by the deeply buried, ever-present knowledge that marriage often signals the end of male emotional intimacy, and less by the more obvious themes of sex and debauchery. "The bachelor party takes an overtly hostile derogatory stance toward marriage by celebrating hyperactive masculine sexuality," she argues, "because recognizing the degree to which wedlock impedes male friendship would be too painful." Andrew once observed that many bachelor parties he's attended seem fueled more by the married men, intent on seizing a rare opportunity to "escape," than by the groom in question. Seen this way, the ball-and-chain, one of the few bachelor party props, represents not just the end of sexual freedom but the beginning of wifely domination of a man's social life. With this in mind, however, the female stripper is a bachelor-party prop, too, and the horny antics of the guys in the audience are as performative (or at least as self-consciously exaggerated) as the giggles of the bachelorettes at Chippendales.

I knew Andrew was afraid of losing the close relationships he'd always nurtured with his male friends, and I'd like to think my hearty approval of Andrew's guys' weekend (modeled on the guys' weekends that now, post-weddings, babies, and so on, no longer happen) was not just my way of resisting the role of room-monitor wife, but also my way of encouraging him to keep up his male friendships. I wanted to resist the tyranny of togetherness that isolates not just men but couples, too. I didn't want our wedding to be a goodbye or a send-off as we retreated into wedlock, but an affirmation of our friendships and our family relationships, a statement of our commitment to them for life.

And in total, my bachelorette party weekend succeeded in this way, especially taking Friday evening's festivities into account. "Friday night was the best," Gabi said over pizza in Little Italy on Sunday. Everyone but Gabi and Suzy had gone home by then, and Andrew had left that evening for a business trip. Suzy agreed, proceeding to unleash a tirade about Lucky Cheng's that had me rolling. "Those women!" she concluded with flourish. "They were so mean and haggard and made-up!" This seemed a little harsh as I thought fondly of the groups of women I'd danced and sung with the night before. But there was no denying that Saturday night had suffered from some serious "bachelorette-is-not-a-word" complications. Friday's relaxed, lovely fun would have been better followed by a night out that included karaoke—the perfect activity for me—just not at a bar packed with drunk bitches sucking dickie sippie straws.

For all its flaws, the bachelorette *is* an important sign of progress. It gives a bride a chance to acknowledge that life alone had its joys, thrills, freedoms, and pleasures, and that marrying means sacrificing them, not just for men, but for women, too. The intense pressure on women to marry sometimes obscures this point, preventing them, as they work single-mindedly to secure commitment from a man, from really thinking about what commitment to a man will mean, and what, when committed, they will miss.

"Our friends Tim and Jennifer are getting a divorce," I told Suzy and Gabi, seemingly, to them, out of the blue. I was actually imagining Jennifer, who was a prodigious partier, out on the town again till 4 a.m., and felt a little wistful at the idea—despite the fact that at 8 p.m. the day after my party, I was still hungover.

"If they were unhappy, then good for them, man," said Suzy, with characteristic straightforwardness. "Divorce isn't always a bad thing."

Gabi, catching a look in my eye that she may have misinterpreted, put her hand on mine. "Andrew's a good man," she said.

"Yeah," said Suzy, chagrined. "If anyone's going to make it, it will be you guys."

I smiled. I hoped so. In three weeks, seven months of hard labor were going to result in the biggest party Andrew or I had ever thrown, and the public announcement of the most important commitment we'd ever made. I believed we were going to make it as a husband and wife. How well I was going to fare as a bride on my wedding day, however, was an entirely different matter.

eleven

The Wedding

The Rest of My Life Will Never

Be Long Enough

There were signs, a few weeks before our wedding, that for all my planning, note-taking, three-ring binders, and things-to-do lists (not to mention prolific check writing), and despite the fact that for many months I had expended the better part of my talents and brainpower on constructing a perfect three-day weekend for me, Andrew, our family, and our friends . . . things were not going to go exactly as we had planned.

Two weeks before the wedding, for example, the copy place I'd chosen to assemble our wedding favors—books I put together containing quotes, song lyrics, movie lines, poetry, and original thoughts about love and marriage, solicited (strong-armed) from our guests—failed to use the cornflower blue paper I'd provided, churning them out on good-old white typing paper instead. And then there was the owner's insistence, when I walked in to pick up the corrected books, on saying: "Don't do it!" (He'd had a bitter divorce, he said. The woman who provided the chuppa fabric, on the other hand, told me to enjoy the wedding because "it's all downhill from there." Apparently she had a bitter marriage.) A week and a half before the wedding, Andrew forced me to sit down with him and have what he termed a "logistics" session, which involved drawing diagrams and making extremely detailed schedules, and I felt so agitated, overwhelmed, and over-weddinged that I could barely sit still, and squirmed and bristled and felt totally trapped until I finally stood up and said, "Why are you making me do this!? I hate this! I can't take this for one more minute!" and it took two glasses of wine and a lot of kisses to calm me down. (Still we couldn't figure out where everyone should sit.) A week before the wedding, there was the snafu regarding the bathroom trailer, as crucial an item as could be for our rustic-but-elegant mountain wedding—it had been double-booked, and our booking had gotten the boot. A few days before the wedding United Airlines had a pilots' strike, nullifying in one fell swoop the travel plans of at least a quarter of our guests. It also wasn't promising that Montana and Idaho—the primary destinations of our honeymoon road trip— were being ravaged by forest fires, and at least one hotel had already called us to cancel. And the day I arrived in Boulder, a week prior to Andrew in order to prepare, I opened my suitcase with Caryl standing by my side to discover that my oily makeup remover had leaked inside my black faux-leather cosmetics case, and my soaked black cosmetics case had in turn left a blackish-blue stain the size of a fist on the right shoulder of the tuxedo shirt Andrew had had specially tailored for our wedding.

And then there was the dream I had that we'd ordered our officiant from a company that shipped them—tiny doll-sized men in little gray suits—to the soon-to-be-wed via UPS, but when ours arrived I opened the box to find that he was dead.

It could have been worse, of course. One of my favorite stories of the "what can go wrong will go wrong" variety was the bride who took her dress to the dry cleaners but misplaced the ticket and, incredibly, *forgot which dry cleaners it was*, resulting in her sister and her best friend knocking on the doors of every dry cleaners in Boston the day before the wedding saying, "Do you happen to have a wedding dress here for Sarah?" Another was the bride having a small, intimate wedding who was pressured into sending an invitation to her husband's ex-step-mother's sister, and received a reply card two weeks before the event with twelve, count 'em, *twelve* people listed on the back as this person's guests. (Two of the uninvited guests turned out to be swingers who propositioned the best man and his wife.) Still, I thought the missing bathroom trailer and the United Airlines pilots' strike were pretty darn good, in terms of being pretty darn bad.

But, as we all know, things have a way of working themselves out, especially if you are willing to part with money, which, in the case of the bathroom trailer, we were. Marci Barton, of Perfect Planning International, could never explain to me how we had failed to prevail upon the owners of bathroom trailer number one to provide it to us and not the other people who needed it (surely we needed it *more!*), but for more money, a company in Denver was willing to drive another one up the mountain. (Throughout the process Marci had been impeccably nice, and undoubtedly helpful, but had never made me feel that she was *in charge*—which was probably as it should have been, but fell far short of my wedding-consultant-as-wedding-savior fantasy.) Almost all of our guests whose flights had been canceled by United found ways to fly to Denver anyway—without parting with too much of their money, I hope—and a dry cleaner earned my eternal gratitude by rescuing Andrew's shirt, though it took numerous attempts. Also very auspicious was the fact that our officiant, a former congressman whom Andrew had worked for and whom we both greatly loved and admired, arrived in Boulder alive.

Perhaps more important were the numerous signs that it was all going to be as wonderful, meaningful, memorable, and just plain fun as I'd hoped—like finding myself on the same flight with old friends of ours as I flew out to Denver (they were making a week of it with their two children) and running into others around town before the festivities even began, which was a delight. "It's so rare to get all these people that you love and wanted to meet each other together in one place, and I loved that," Terry, a thirty-five-year-old account director from Colorado, recalled. On the flight out I wrote letters to my mother and to my father, who'd been so generous and supportive, trying to make use of the opportunity to say things that ought to be said in handwriting, for keeps—and crying a lot as I did. Sitting around the kitchen table tying white ribbons into the programs with my parents, sister, cousins, and aunts, I learned that my six-year-old cousin Sam, our ring bearer, thought I said ring *bear* when I asked him to be ours a few months before, and had been discovered walking around his house growling to practice.

And a few days before our wedding, Caryl and my mother presented me with the photographs I'd asked for, to place on a table in the reception tent. They were old photographs, a few in color but most in black and white and sepia, of Andrew's and my mothers, fathers, grandmothers, grandfathers, great-grandmothers, great-grandfathers and even a great-great-grandmother or two, many of them taken just at this moment in their lives, on their wedding days. It was a great gift. My mother also gave me another gift, one I hadn't anticipated or known about, something she'd kept to herself all that time—a wedding hankie made from my baby bonnet, with this bit of explanatory verse attached:

> *I'm just a little hankie, as square as square can be*
> *But with a stitch or two they made a bonnet out of me.*
> *I'll be worn from the hospital or on christening day*
> *Then I'll be carefully pressed and neatly packed away.*
> *For her wedding day, so we've been told,*
> *Every well-dressed bride must have something old.*
> *So what could be more fitting than to find little me,*
> *A few stitches snipped and a wedding hankie I'll be.*

My baby bonnet, placed into my hands to hold as I walked down the aisle. When my son was born a year ago, my sister made one just like it for him from the fabric we used for our chuppa. (The poem goes on to explain that if the bonnet is for a boy, his bride can carry it down the aisle, but I don't see why my son can't carry it himself someday. As Andrew later observed, he could have used one since he was a "bawling mess.") This is what weddings are all about, I thought—this is what makes it all worthwhile.

Except if I'm honest I'll admit that although I was touched by the hankie, and moved by the photographs, I was light years away from being relaxed, or even, dare I say it, happy. On Thursday, with a series of things slated to take place beginning Friday morning that I could hardly hold together in my head all at the same time, and a mania about having them all go perfectly that I couldn't shake, the pressure of being a hostess and a party planner made it tough to absorb the good, and easy to obsess over the bad or even the bumpy. Andrew could see this quite clearly, as could perfect strangers, and that morning, on our way to the county clerk's office in Boulder to get our marriage license, Andrew laid his hand on my shoulder, squeezed it, forced me to look at him, and smiled with clear, steady, admirable, and extremely annoying calm.

Finally he said, "I got some good advice about this."

I looked at him with interest and skepticism.

"What was it?" I asked.

"Somebody told me that we should pick a moment when we let all of this fall away—all the planning, all the worries about who walks in where when, all the stress about centerpieces and bottled water and buses, and especially all the people who couldn't be here with us—that we should pick a moment to let all of that go and look at each other and nothing else, and focus completely on what we're doing together, here."

I wish I could say I reacted well to this beautiful sentiment.

"Pick a moment? Pick a *moment?* I don't have a moment to pick a moment! Do you realize how many things we have to deal with for this whole thing to happen in even remotely the way we planned? Do you realize that nobody but me, me, *only me*, not even Marci Barton, *our professional wedding planner*, being an exception, knows exactly what all these things are?" In a way, I felt like Andrew had just said that all the stress I felt was unnecessary, made-up, even, and that this was an easy thing for him to say because while he had been a Super Groom, he hadn't had to be The Bride. Not only that, but half of what was stressing me out were *his* insane wedding obsessions, like his concern that the buses would not clear the "Cushman Ranch" sign, a concern repeated over and over again even after the elderly (but hardy) Mr. Cushman climbed up a ladder and measured the damn thing to be sure, along with his worry that the caterers would forget his instructions that the salads *not* be placed on the tables until the guests sat down—ironically, à la my dad, because he was concerned about attracting flies.

But as I was unloading I was laughing, and Andrew was laughing too. The advice he'd just passed along made a great deal of sense. It was wise. Both of us determined, right then, to find that moment; and both of us felt sure that we would.

Pretty sure, anyway.

The county clerk's office, with its wide, quiet, fluorescent-lit hallways, orderly cubicles, lethargic elevators, and unflappable government-building torpor was the perfect antidote to my agitation. Everything within those walls proceeded at an orderly, plodding pace from 8:30 a.m. to 4:30 p.m., and as Andrew and I filled out our application, swearing that we were over eighteen, not currently married to anyone else, or related to each other, we both felt a sense of satisfaction and purpose. It was just the two of us, alone, no muss no fuss, doing paperwork because we wanted to be married to each other.

Of course it was not just the two of us, really, it was just the three of us: me, Andrew, and the State—the arbiter of official marriage in this country for the last several centuries. And we didn't only want to be married to each other—we wanted public, legal endorsement of our union by our government. Acquiring this, for us, was easy: we came, we filled out our application, our application was granted, we left the building with a license and, once we were married, mailed it back and received a certificate of marriage in return. By applying to the state to marry, however, what, exactly, had we assented to? Were we agreeing to the *state's* definition of what it meant to be a husband and a wife?

I didn't think so, but about half the country, depending on which polls you read and how the question is asked, disagrees, as evidenced by the heated debate over gay marriage. The argument against gay marriage, in many ways, is an argument *for* the state's right to define its adult citizens— those who marry, anyway, which is almost all of them—according to their gender. As Adam Haslett wrote in the *New Yorker* in May 2004, soon after the Massachusetts Supreme Court granted same-sex couples full civil marriage, "No other expansion of the marriage franchise, to the sterile, to slaves, or to interracial couples—has required an alteration in the basic definition of the term: the union of a man and woman as husband and wife. To discount this as mere semantics misses what the definition points up: that marriage, through all its incarnations, has been a procedure that assigns people a new identity based on their gender."

In other words, gay marriage threatens the state's ability to make men into husbands, and women into wives. It undermines the notion that "wife" comes with an agreed-upon definition and that "husband" does, too. (What does it mean to be a husband, asks Haslett, in a world where a man can have his own?) As Haslett and others rightly point out, however, most heterosexuals have been rejecting the interference of the state in defining husbands' and wives' roles for a while now. Wives work and support their families, husbands raise children, married couples choose not to have children at all, couples have demanded and acquired the right to divorce when they wish. And I, for one, was immensely glad these changes had taken place, and I sure as hell was not in that county clerk's office to accept a state-mandated definition of what it means to be a wife.

On that point, I was not in the least confused, and perhaps this was one reason I never even considered requesting that other set of government forms most women fill out after receiving their certificates of marriage: the forms required to change one's name.

"When you want to define something, you name it," said Alexandra, a former television anchor who is now a stay-at-home mother of three. "I did not want to be defined as belonging to my husband. Joining him on the path through life was my choice, but at thirty-six, with a large chunk of life and a career under my belt, I couldn't accept being annexed, and that is how it would have felt to change my name." Alexandra, in other words, did not want to be made a *femme couverte*, to be absorbed, as she legally would have been in the past, into her husband's citizenship. Despite the fact that this is no longer legally the case, changing her name, she felt, would tacitly endorse this view. Mary, a thirty-eight-year-old writer in New York, based her decision to keep her name less on being defined as a wife, and more on preserving her identity as an individual. "Why should I take on my husband's name and be folded into his family . . . when my family is very important to me?" she asked. "Why should my identity change and not his?"

I related to both Alexandra's and Mary's reasoning. I didn't like the idea of being annexed; I also could not imagine "Kamy Wicoff" ceasing to exist. Felicia, a thirty-three-year-old television executive in New York who does not plan to change her name when she marries, had a unique take on the significance of changing one's name: when she was six, her stepfather (the man she considers to be her real father) wanted to adopt her, and she wanted to be adopted . . . until she found out that it would mean changing her name. "Change my name?" Felicia remembers thinking, "'Oh, hell no!' I announced to my parents that I did not want to go through with the adoption because I didn't want to change my name. My dad assured me that this did not mean I was not his daughter and that he would respect whatever decision I made." (Husbands should tell their wives the same thing.) Many years later, Felicia produced a television documentary about a Hollywood celebrity, an experience that strengthened her determination never to change her name, as she tried to track down her subject's sorority sisters and couldn't because they'd all gotten married and, as she put it, disappeared.

"If I had any doubts before working on that show, I certainly didn't afterward," she averred. "The day after my wedding, Felicia Hamilton will *still exist.*"

What about the argument, however, that when a woman marries her identity does change, because as a wife she is a new and different person, and she should embrace this transformation in a formal, public fashion? Sheryl Nissinen, in *The Conscious Bride*, goes so far as to suggest that refusing to take your new husband's name—and, down the line, potentially having a last name different from one's children—signifies a troublesome resistance to what it means to be married. Retaining one's maiden name, she writes, "bypasses one of this culture's few rituals for transformation. To change one's last name and take on the name of one's spouse assumes an element of surrender. It also concretely acknowledges that a change of identity has occurred."

Nissinen contends that "feminists" fail to understand this, and thus fail to see that women who resist the transition from maiden to wife often suffer the consequences in their first year of marriage and beyond. To be fair, Nissinen does not say that changing one's name is necessary to successfully making the transition; she simply says that the transition is necessary, and that assuming a married name helps facilitate it.

This is an interesting argument, and while I object to it for numerous reasons—principally that men are not asked to become new people when they marry—I appreciate it for being an argument of some kind, rather than the sort of non-argument, "this isn't an issue" approach that has come to dominate discussions of whether or not married women should change their names. Katie Roiphe, in an article for the online magazine *Slate*, captured the attitude of many women I spoke with when she said, "Today, the decision is one of convenience, of a kind of luxury—which name do you like the sound of? What do you feel like doing? The politics are almost incidental. Our fundamental independence is not so imperiled that we *need* to keep our names." This is the classic statement of a sandwiched woman: feminism freed me to choose, and as long as I choose freely, any further examination of the choice I make—or of the fact, for instance, that only 2 percent of American women keep their birth names when they marry (if you count hyphenation and other forms of keeping it, as a middle name or a second name, the percentage goes up to 10)—is irrelevant and, worse, insulting.

On the other hand it would be insulting for me to question the sincerity of women like Lori, a thirty-six-year-old academic dean who changed her name ("I wanted us to be a family unit"), and told me that doing so in no way undermined her identity or her independence. "I do not feel it has changed my identity at all," she told me. "It was not a big decision at all . . . I am who I am regardless of my name. If I had married earlier on, when I was not as sure who I was, I might have kept my name to hold on to whatever identity I had. But in my thirties I knew who I was and didn't worry that the change of name would erode my sense of self—and it hasn't." (Lori's feeling that it was easier to change her name when she was older was unusual; more women echoed Emmy, a twenty-three-year-old from Philadelphia who was taking her fiancé's name partly, she said, because she was not yet established in a career.) Lori is far from being alone: sandwiched women, in fact, seem to find the issue so "irrelevant" now that according to a study conducted by a Harvard economics professor, college-educated women—the group who have always kept their names at the highest rate—recently reversed the three-decade long trend toward keeping their names that began in the 1970s.

Unquestionably, women like Lori are capable of maintaining their identities while changing their name to their husbands', and do. This does not, however, make the issue irrelevant. Because there is still a lot to learn from asking the question: why is it still only *women* who agonize over this decision—or don't agonize over it, but are still charged with making it? And why is it that of all the women I spoke with, only one of them told me her husband changed his name to hers ("That was one of the greatest gifts my husband gave to me," Laurie, a dance instructor from Denver, told me, "I got to keep the name I'd grown up with, but we share the same name")—an act that caused so much uproar that her uncle attempted to interrupt the wedding ceremony, and her husband's mother told her son that the rain that fell that day was his dead father spitting on him?

And why is it that even Laurie, clearly comfortable with unconventional thinking, described her husband's family as being "understandably upset" when he changed his name? Very few people would describe a woman's family as being "understandably upset" when she does the same. Some women I interviewed did say that their mothers or fathers wanted them to keep their names in some form, particularly if they were the last of a family line, and a small number of couples both hyphenate their names, and an even smaller number make up a new name entirely. But when it comes down to it, there is a deeply embedded sense that a woman can and should have a "married name," and a man shouldn't. And this means something about men, women, and marriage.

Consider, for example, that gay couple who I believe will one day have the right to marry legally, as Andrew and I did. If this couple wants to share a name, which partner will change hers or his? Which partner won't? How will they decide? Will the person who makes the most money keep his or her name? Will the person who plans to assume primary responsibility for either bearing or raising the couple's children keep his or her name? Will the person with the nicest name prevail? The person with the ethnic name? The person with a well-established career where name recognition is important? If women really were free to choose when it came to this issue, this is the kind of discussion every couple would have when they got married. As it stands, the discussion focuses almost entirely on *one* partner's decision: the woman's. This is certainly more freedom to choose than women had before, but this reality calls into serious question Roiphe's popular but patently false statement that for modern women, "at this point . . . our attitude is: Whatever works." I have never met a woman who, when confronted with this decision, simply mused, "Which name do I like the sound of?" as Roiphe describes. It would be more accurate to say that for modern women, the attitude is: "Whatever works . . . that does not involve the man changing his name when he gets married."

For the most part, I have found that keeping my name works. But it is occasionally annoying to have a different name from Andrew, and now that we have a child, the complications, both practical and emotional, have increased.

For many women, it is the idea of children that propels them toward taking their husband's names. Cary, a thirty-seven-year-old writer in New York, didn't change her name when she married, but now that she has two children, "I'm queasily thinking I should change it. . . . I don't like having a different last name from my kids." I feel a pang at this too, and while I was unconventional enough to never consider changing my name, I was much too conventional to consider giving my son any name but his dad's. In a way, this was part of how I apologized for keeping my name when talking to people who flinched at my choice: "Oh, but our children will have his last name, and I'll answer to it when I'm a mom, I'm not going to go around correcting my kids' seven-year-old friends." Keeping my name is something I feel I have to make other people feel comfortable about, but now that I have a child it's become something I have to work harder to make myself feel comfortable about, too. I took some inspiration from Mary, the thirty-eight-year-old writer, who recently had a daughter and told me, "I have no problem having a different last name from my husband and even my children. . . . I want my daughter to get comfortable early on with the idea that some traditions can and should be broken." She's right.

There is little escaping the fact, of course, that due to the numerous practical difficulties that would arise if all people insisted on keeping all their names all of the time, somebody will always have to be willing to compromise. But I'd be kidding myself if I didn't acknowledge the significance of the fact that I, not Andrew, am the one who compromised when it came to giving our son his father's last name. (He does have my last name as one of his two middle names, saddling him with a name that requires two lines on his social security card, all parts of which I plan to tell him are totally optional.) And I'd be missing an opportunity to learn something about myself and the world I live in if I ignored the fact that I, not Andrew, felt I had to consciously consider and defend my identity throughout our engagement.

On Friday morning, the day before the big day, Andrew's father, David, led a group bike ride around the plentiful and lovingly well-kept bike trails of Boulder. My mother and father chose to ride a tandem bike—an experience they will never repeat, as they could never properly coordinate the starting and stopping—and all of us (about twenty people) dutifully donned bike helmets, which meant we all looked ridiculous. It was the first group activity of the weekend, and as we cruised along together on that sunny, dry mountain morning, taking in the sights under David's able direction, I began to feel the joy of having all those people I loved in one place . . . until all those people I loved, traveling along a winding path in single file, each braked slightly harder and more abruptly than the person in front of them when David stopped at a red light, and this braking, by the time it got to me, became more like a slamming on the brakes of the twenty-bike pile-up variety, forcing me to squeeze my brakes so hard and fast that my back tire flew straight up into the air behind me, and I went right over my handlebars.

Thank god I was wearing that helmet.

I will never forget the expression on my mother's face as, after leaping off her tandem bike (leaving my father tilting to who knows what fate) and running toward me at unparalleled warp-maternal-instinct-speed, gasping with horror as visions of black-eyes and body casts raced through her head, she got down on the asphalt, leaned into me and cried, "Kamy! Kamy! Are you all right? *Are you all right?*"

I think I actually laughed. (It was pretty funny.) I was all right! No black eyes, no facial lacerations, and no broken bones, either. Just a badly bruised hip (an annoyance on the honeymoon, during which I could only comfortably sleep on my left side) and some seriously scraped elbows. I, for one, ended up relishing the result that in our wedding photos, I, in all my veiled, petticoated finery, am also sporting two big, visible scabs as my final bridal accessories. I think Andrew got a kick out of it too, though he did not find out about the incident at all until a couple of hours later, because he wasn't there. Instead he was holed up in our hotel room writing his wedding vows. Surprise surprise, he had procrastinated, with Andrew-aplomb, until the absolute last minute.

Yes, we wrote our own vows. This was something we knew we wanted to do from the beginning. Throughout our relationship we'd both gotten a lot of happiness out of writing to each other, and being written to, and it seemed like a natural extension of our courtship to write to each other on this most sacred of occasions. It also seemed like a good way to achieve what we most desired for our wedding ceremony: authenticity, thoughtfulness, an element of surprise (we'd agreed not to share our vows with each other until the ceremony), a rejection of the generic and the rote. Like many couples, we set out to "create" our wedding ceremony, and writing our vows was an integral part of doing it. Like many couples, however, we did not simply want to make our wedding ceremony up. We wanted to incorporate traditional elements, familiar language, and ritual practices in order to signify our participation in a cultural rite of passage that is historical and socially shared. Doing this, we thought, would remind us not only of the importance of the world beyond our lives as individuals; it would acknowledge that our lives were, as they always are, utterly inseparable from it.

Coming from two different religious backgrounds, Andrew's Jewish and mine protestant (I was actually raised as a Unitarian Universalist, which is no longer a denomination of protestant Christianity, but which has protestant roots), precluded us from doing a traditional religious ceremony—something we probably wouldn't have done anyway—but we very much wanted to find a way to infuse the ceremony and the day with a recognition of the spiritual. In particular, we wanted to express our belief that human beings are part of something far greater than themselves and their private concerns, and that marriage, in this sense, is a spiritual act. As the scholar and writer Joseph Campbell put it in his series of interviews with Bill Moyers, *The Power of Myth*, "Marriage is a recognition of a spiritual identity . . . not a simple love affair. It's an ordeal, and the ordeal is the sacrifice of ego to a relationship in which two have become one . . . a mythological image signifying the sacrifice of the visible entity for a transcendent good."

For Andrew and me, incorporating symbols like the Jewish chuppa, using most of the traditional protestant wedding vows, and performing the exchange of rings common to both traditions all signified our wish to wed in a way that emphasized that which was greater than ourselves, while our conscious choices about which of these symbols to use signified our wish to wed in a way that emphasized our shared philosophies about life. Unlike my experience with the wedding dress, however, mixing these two elements to compose the ceremony never freaked me out, or threatened my sense of self, or presented problems of identity or concerns about hypocrisy or play-acting. And one of the main reasons for this was that Andrew and I coauthored our ceremony together.

In writing it together, and in focusing on marriage and on our feelings rather than on weddings and diamond rings, there was so much less gender-based *stuff* in our way, and for once we were not sent off into separate rooms marked Bride and Groom, or burdened with the falsity that imposed on us from the start. In a way, however, I also think that coming from different religious backgrounds was helpful to us, because neither of us felt pressured by family, an officiant, or our pasts to say words we didn't believe, or perform acts purely for the sake of ritual even if we did not comprehend their meaning. (This is hugely to our families' credit, as many other interfaith couples face some of the most stressful and trying times of their lives trying to balance each of their family's religions, feelings, wishes, and traditions.) Yet we also created something that felt connected to our ancestors and to God in the sense that we understood and wished to recognize and honor them both.

There were ways, of course, in which being cut loose from a traditional religious model was difficult and a little scary. One of the principal things we risked losing was the advice, guidance, and confidential counsel of an officiant who was part of our spiritual lives. But David Skaggs, the former congressman and friend who agreed to marry us—a first for him, not incidentally—undertook his duties with seriousness and great care, traveling to New York from Washington, D.C., three times to sit down and talk to us about marriage, children, religion, money, family, and whatever else he or we thought needed discussing before taking such a big step. Unfortunately fewer and fewer couples have this experience: my brother and his wife, for instance, who had a destination wedding, were married by a caring, well-spoken minister—whom they'd never met before that afternoon. (He also took wedding photos—twofer!) As Adam Haslett observed in writing about gay marriage and about modern marriage, period, "in an era of low civic participation and high economic insecurity, spouses are ever more relied upon as the sole providers of continuity and human solace." Disconnected geographically or otherwise from the networks of family, church, and neighborhood upon which couples used to rely, couples find themselves increasingly isolated, and weddings sometimes reflect this, seeming disconnected or isolated, too.

Perhaps Andrew and I sensed this and feared it—in the "statement of principles" we composed as our first step in creating our ceremony, we talked not just about our commitment to each other but about our commitment to our community, our families, and our friends. We wanted to reject the "it's *our* day" ethos that can make a wedding a gaudy narcissistic bore, and which selfishly ignores the fact that weddings, in a world with fewer and fewer shared rituals, are much-needed times for all those in attendance to mark the passage of their own lives. When I got married, my mother was not going to cry because I'd finally been redeemed from the ignominy of singlehood, or because she was going to be redeemed from the ignominy of having unmarried daughters. (Well, maybe a little.) She was going to cry because she'd be given an opportunity to grieve and to celebrate the changes in her life that her eldest daughter's wedding signified. And my father did not want to walk me down the aisle just because he was hung up on "giving me away" in a traditional fashion. He'd always dreamed of walking me down the aisle because he'd lost his father when he was four years old, and his loss added poignancy and depth to the ritual, making it deeply important for him to enact.

You could also argue, of course, that Andrew and I were not *really* interested in rejecting the "it's our day" ethos, or showing our commitment to spirituality and community, but instead were desperately trying to concoct some kind of plausible, high-minded excuse for what many may have found inexcusable or at least very tacky: Andrew had eight groomsmen, and I had nine, yes, *nine*, bridesmaids.

Showing our dedication to family and friends? Or showing we had lost all sense of propriety and scale? I have offered various explanations, depending on who was asking, chief among them that Andrew was the one who wanted eight groomsmen and once I went beyond my sister and his sister I got involved in "friendship groups" that quickly took the number in my bridesmaid posse even higher than his. Whatever the reason, it made for quite a pilgrimage to the wedding site late Friday afternoon, as we corralled no less than twenty-five people to head up to the Cushman Ranch to rehearse.

I was a bit of a wreck, and for the first forty-five minutes of this exercise I was the epitome of the stressed, tense, no-nonsense, event-planner bride. I tapped my clipboard impatiently when unnecessary horsing around took place; I obsessed over exactly when, where, and how it was all going to go (convinced that none of it would go that way when the time came); I brusquely told my father where to stand without feeling even a fraction of the emotion that would overwhelm me so completely the following day when I laid eyes on him (and he on me) that I would actually have to ask him to talk to me about Spurs basketball all the way down the aisle.

But then, just as I was going down my list with manic concentration, surrounded by a relatively obedient and patient bridal party politely listening to my instructions, I came to this: "And then Andrew and his parents will walk down the aisle."

And in the time it takes to take a breath, before I had even finished the sentence, a sob so total, unexpected, and undoing that I could have stifled it as well as I could have stopped a tidal wave, burst forth. And for nearly five minutes, with everyone startled, concerned, moved, and/or amused, I stood there holding my clipboard and cried. Really, really hard. Andrew put his arms around me. I was embarrassed and utterly unable to stop. I had not chosen my moment. My moment had chosen me.

I let go. And that night at our rehearsal dinner, as Andrew and I listened to toasts and roasts, watched slides and video tapes, heard original haikus and took in everything and anything else our resourceful guests had brought for us, I knew what Lori meant when she told me how her rehearsal dinner made her feel. "It was an amazing thing to look at [all those] people and realize every one of them meant something to us," she said. "I cried for hours afterward thinking about it, because I have never felt that amount of warmth and love and happiness for me—for us—all in one place."

We went to bed that night feeling enormously grateful and happy. We went to bed together, since spending the last night of our unmarried lives together seemed as important, momentous, and right to us as spending the first night of our married lives together. And then we woke up, and it was our wedding day.

My aunt hosted a bridesmaids' brunch and gave everyone Kleenex and waterproof mascara. And despite continuing to feel a bit sheepish, I realized that the smartest thing I'd ever done was ask all nine of those women to be my bridesmaids, because there was nothing better than having them all with me that day. Andrew hung out with the guys, and the time passed quickly, and the next thing we knew we were headed up the mountain again. But this time, it was for the real thing.

At four o'clock, I put on my Vera Wang gown in the master bedroom of Lee and Lewis Cushman's mobile home. I'd had my hair done in front of the full-length mirror Marci Barton, who was in fine form that day, had wisely thought to provide. My mother slid her periwinkle garter—which she wore for her wedding and which she swore had once been blue, thus fulfilling the "something blue" requirement—over my ankle, and I pulled it up snugly around my thigh. (It was not to be seen again, since to my mind and Andrew's, the garter-throwing thing was out of the question.) Sarah, one of my bridesmaids, kept rolling around on the Cushman's waterbed, lazily procrastinating about getting ready and creating a sound that unnervingly resembled thunder—the last thing I wanted to hear as I stared and stared out the windows at the cloudy sky, praying it wouldn't rain. I did my makeup for the first time since I'd had it done by someone else at that shop in New York. I put on the pearl earrings that Andrew gave me that fateful day in Napa. My sister laid my long, airy veil across her forearm, lifted the white comb over the crown of my head, and fit its tiny teeth snugly into my hair. She looked at me.

"Oh my god," she said. She started crying. My mother started crying. Nine women were trying to do their makeup in a place with the square footage of a storage locker, and upon the sight of me, each and every one of them started crying. I was ready first, so in order to give the rest of them a chance to walk down the aisle without cheeks smeared with mascara (several of them had unwisely chosen not to wear the waterproof), I went out to the Cushman's living room, rested my backside gingerly onto the arm of an easy chair, and stood there by myself for awhile.

I was standing next to a glass door that opened out onto the Cushman's small deck, and this deck had a view of the wedding site: the pond, tranquil with the afternoon cloud cover's blue-gray sheen reflected on its surface, the pine trees and the aspens a rich green around the pond and beyond it, and the mountains beyond them, still cupping fields of snow in their uppermost valleys. In the foreground sat two hundred empty white wooden chairs, an empty white aisle runner laid lumpily across the dry August grass to divide them (the bride's side, the groom's), and to the left, on a little hill, the white reception tent where I could see the first busload of guests milling around in suits, dresses, and tuxedos, sipping champagne, talking to each other, helping each other around, waiting. (The sight of Andrew's ninety-two-year-old Grandpa Irv, in his fedora and his bow tie but without his dear Sally, who'd died a few years before, filled me with joy and sadness.) Waiting for Andrew, waiting for me. Waiting for us to get married.

We were going to get married. And I suppose this is as good a time as any to ask: *Why?*

In her book *The History of the Wife*, Marilyn Yalom poses this question, once unthinkable, but which now hovers over most people marrying today. "Why bother marrying at all," she asks women in particular, "when you don't need a husband to have sex, economic support, shared residence, and even children?" I'd come up with various reasons at various times before my engagement and during it. One of them was well-put by Yalom, when she suggested that more young people ought to marry with "the conscious expectation that they will become kinder and wiser by virtue of choosing a decent, generous mate." I believed my marriage to Andrew had the potential to make me kinder and wiser— my relationship with him had begun to do that already. I also believed, however, that being married would simply make me happier and more secure. And in the most practical sense, I believed marriage would make life easier: financially, when it came to having children, and in all kinds of other day-to-day ways.

Good reasons, all. But I'm not sure that these sensible answers to the question "why marry?" would have set my heart thumping with antici-pation as I stood alone by that window, waiting to marry Andrew at last. I'm not sure aspirations to goodness or socioeconomic benefits would have filled me with the unwavering, awesome belief that what I was about to do was right. But this was what I felt. And my answer to the question "why marry?" was written on a scrap of paper I was holding fast to in my hand.

Andrew. I have promised to spend the rest of my life with you. But the rest of my life will never be long enough. Because I will never tire of your laugh, that boyish burst, or of your jokes, some of which we have already been laughing at together for years. I will never stop smiling like an idiot when I know it is your blue eyes that will meet me around the next corner. I will never stop buying flowers to meet you when you come home. I will never stop craving the low rumble of your voice on a telephone line, or better yet in my ear as you whisper our world to me. I will never be handed enough torn-out squares of magazines, with quotes, restaurant recommendations, or poems on them.

I will never hold you enough. I will never look at you enough.

Andrew, my life will not be long enough to tell you all the things I want to tell you. To go all the places I want to go with you. To cherish you as much as I must cherish you. But this is my vow to you: give me your life, and I will try. Stay with me always, and I will not waste one single minute.

Why marry? Because you feel like this.

Andrew answered this question that day, too, with his vows to me. But in a way he answered me most completely with a single command, uttered with urgency and tenderness as, newly married, we turned our backs to the mountains to walk back up the aisle. Giddy and unsteady, I had eyes for the aisle runner alone. But Andrew was looking over his shoulder. And suddenly he snapped to attention, gripped my hand, and tugged on it. Uncomprehending I resisted, continuing to walk away, until he finally touched my chin and turned my face back toward the mountains.

The clouds, hovering thickly all afternoon, had parted. Beams of sunlight were shooting through them in white, bright shafts, falling on the mountains, falling everywhere. "Sweetie," Andrew whispered, *"look at the light."*

And I did.

EPILOGUE

Mysterium Coniunctionis

We had always envisioned our road-tripping, free-wheeling, loosely planned honeymoon as an antidote to the highly organized, highly planned, highly complicated enterprise of our wedding. What we never imagined was that we would have a second wedding, a wedding that, in the end, would feel like a kind of antidote too.

Toward the end of what turned out to be a nearly perfect journey—despite the specter of the terrible fires, which were always just on the horizon as we alternated between camping and staying in fancy hotels in the spectacular but stricken country of Idaho, Wyoming, and Montana—we headed for the southwest corner of South Dakota, home of the Pine Ridge Indian Reservation and the Oglala Lakota Nation. Almost exactly ten years before, Andrew had driven alone to Pine Ridge from Stanford, with a grant to spend the summer studying the educational system there. He'd arranged the trip with Basil Braveheart, the superintendent of the schools at that time, a former paratrooper in the Korean War and an educator and spiritual healer in his community. Over that summer, Basil became a spiritual counselor, teacher, and guide to Andrew, too.

I'd heard about Basil and about that summer at Pine Ridge for as long as I'd known Andrew, but I'd never been, and as we drove through the

Badlands to the home Basil shares with his wife Charlotte (the stone and wood house he was born in, onto which a mobile home has been attached), I tried to imagine Andrew's first weeks on the reservation, spent alone in a dirt-floor cabin that Basil's family owned with no power, a cold-water pump outside, and herds of cattle that rumbled by his door each morning at dawn. Pine Ridge is a huge place, two million acres, much of it wide grass prairies where buffalo graze. The Badlands are only part of the reservation, but they are unforgettable: an other-worldly landscape of striated, multi-colored peaks and valleys, buttes and spires, an ancient seabed pushed skyward over time. Seeing the Badlands for the first time, the architect Frank Lloyd Wright felt "an indescribable sense of mysterious elsewhere—a distant architecture, ethereal . . . an endless supernatural world more spiritual than earth but created out of it." I sensed this too, and Andrew always had. It was the perfect setting for the experience we had our last morning in Basil and Charlotte's home.

We woke up early that day, got dressed and gathered together the few things we'd brought in for our stay. The night before, Basil had burned sage and told us of his recent vision quests—spiritual talk, as he put it, talk he knew Andrew would understand, and hoped I would too. Andrew hadn't seen Basil in ten years, but the connection between them was palpable and unbroken; over that summer, Andrew had become like a member of Basil's family, and that morning as we walked into the kitchen Charlotte and Basil were there waiting for us. Basil held a large, heavy, woolen Indian blanket in his arms. I immediately understood it was theirs, and that they were giving it to us. Andrew had explained to me many years before that on the reservation, people celebrate momentous occasions with "give-aways," giving away something they own to everyone who shows up to celebrate with them. He explained this to me when his first birthday gift to me was a vase he already owned. I received it with some skepticism, thinking: *Nice appropriation of Native American spirituality to get out of buying a girl a present!* But now, particularly after our wedding, the registry, and the whole bit, the idea of the "give-away"—even though it must be said that the tradition is also driven by the grinding poverty many of the residents of Pine Ridge suffer—was very moving to me.

Andrew and I exchanged a glance as we walked toward Basil and Charlotte, smiling at each other happily. As we approached, Basil lay the blanket across one arm and, with his two outstretched hands, wordlessly stopped us and positioned us together on the linoleum floor, shoulder to shoulder, facing him. "Charlotte and I would like to give you this blanket," he said in his low, quiet voice, which brought us nearer to him, "in honor of your wedding day." He wrapped the blanket around both of our shoulders, so that it enclosed the two of us. He then tied a cloth around our wrists. "Now I'm going to say a prayer in Lakota. It's the prayer we say when a couple marries." And as Andrew and I stood before him, he spoke for a minute, maybe two. We held hands, and held our breath. "There," he said. "Now you are married." He and Charlotte kissed us both. He untied the cloth, and handed it to us. We were married.

It was that simple, and it was real.

It didn't matter, at the time, what the prayer meant—we understood it. But years later, Andrew and I asked Basil to tell us anyway. "It's hard to put it into English," he said, after some thought. He told us he had asked the spiritual powers to the west to witness the coming together of this woman and this man. He said that the blanket, and our being wrapped inside it, symbolized our immersion in the "divine, unmerited assistance" we rely on at every moment, which takes every form, from the air we breathe to the blood in our bodies, a gift from a divinity so compassionate that it is given freely and constantly, without expectation or demands. "Did I tie a cloth around your wrists?" he asked us. We said yes. "That represents the mystery of opposites coming together— the total mystery of the masculine and feminine coming together. I like the Latin term, the term from Jung, you know Jung?" Basil paused. "*Mysterium coniunctionis*. The mystery of coming together. It's very holy. And a wedding is a surrendering to it."

Weddings, as modern American couples currently conduct them, are not about this. They are more about differentiating men and women (not to mention gimmies instead of give-aways) than the mystery of the masculine and the feminine coming together. When Basil wrapped us in that blanket, he urged us to acknowledge this mystery. And though we didn't know it, he was also asking us to honor this divine concept in our marriage by working to break down the barriers that separate women and men. Our experience of wedding, however, threw up and even exaggerated these barriers at almost every turn, with almost every custom and rite, and rather than feeling supported in our efforts to come together we felt pried apart, sometimes by the people around us, very often by commercial interests who profit from insecurity and stereotyping far more than they do from self-confidence. Americans my age cling to the concept of "soul mates," but seem far from understanding it: as it is attributed to Plato, soul mates are two halves of a whole, once androgynous being split-apart by Zeus, and when soul mates (or "split-aparts") find one another, it is a miracle of wholeness that transcends gender. It is not a time to find ourselves split apart all over again in the process of becoming Man and Wife.

REFERENCES

Alison, Marielle. *How to Be a Bride and a Flower Girl, Too!* New York: Little Simon, 1999.

Andrews, Edmund. "Survey Confirms It: Women Out-juggle Men." *New York Times*, September 15, 2004.

Bachelor Party Fun. "Top 20 Drinks." http://www.bachelorpartyfun.com.

Bachelorette Party Fun. "Bachelorette Party Oath." http://www.bacheloretteparryfun.com.

Barash, Susan Shapiro. *The New Wife: The Evolving Role of the American Wife.* Lenexa: Nonetheless Press, 2004.

Barletta, Martha. *Marketing to Women: How to Understand, Reach, and Increase Your Share of the Largest Market Segment.* Chicago: Dearborn Trade Publishing, 2003.

Barron, James Douglas. *She Wants a Ring—And I Don't Want to Change a Thing.* New York: Quill, 2001.

Bartolomeo, Joey. "Hollywood's Twenty-Five Most Romantic Proposals." *US Weekly*, December 9, 2002, 58–69.

Bayot, Jennifer. "For Richer or Poorer, to Our Visa Card Limit." *New York Times*, July 13, 2003.

Beauvoir, Simone de. *The Second Sex.* New York: Alfred A. Knopf, 1952.

Beckerman, Ilene. *Mother of the Bride: The Dream, the Reality, the Search for a Perfect Dress!* Chapel Hill: Algonquin Books, 2000.

Behrendt, Greg and Liz Tuccillo. *He's Just Not That into You: The No-Excuses Truth to Understanding Guys.* New York: Simon Spotlight Entertainment, 2004.

Belkin, Lisa. "The Opt-Out Revolution." *New York Times*, October 26, 2003.

Bratten, Millie Martini. "Bride's Basics." *Brides*, February/March 2000, 6.

Brodsky, Daniella. "Cosmo's Engagement Survival Guide." *Cosmopolitan*, June 2004.

Brophy, Mary-Beth. "Planning the Bachelorette Party." *The Wedding Channel*, www.weddingchannel.com.

Brumberg, Joan Jacobs. *The Body Project: An Intimate History of American Girls.* New York: Random House, 1997.

Campbell, Joseph and Moyers, Bill. *The Power of Myth*. New York: Doubleday, 1988.

Caplan, Jeremy. "Metrosexual Matrimony." *Time*, October 3, 2005.

Collymore, Terrie. "The Simple Life." *Brides*, November/December 2005.

Condé Nast Bridal Infobank. New York: Condé Nast Bridal Group, 2001.

Corral, Jill and Lisa Miya-Jervis, eds. *Young Wives' Tales: New Adventures in Love and Partnership*. Seattle: Seal Press, 2001.

Cott, Nancy F. *Public Vows: A History of Marriage and the Nation*. Cambridge: Harvard University Press, 2000.

Cruz, Melissa de la. "Wanted: $mart, $uccessful, $ingle Men." *Marie Claire*, March 2003.

Daily, Lisa. *Stop Getting Dumped! All You Need to Know to Make Men Fall Madly in Love with You and Marry "The One" in Three Years or Less*. New York: Plume, 2002.

Daum, Meghan. "Why Have These Girls Gone Wild? Thousands of Young Women Spend Spring Break Getting Wasted, Getting Groped and Getting Naked—In Broad Daylight. Writer Meghan Daum Went to Cancun to Ask: What's Up with *That*?" *Glamour*, July 2004.

DeNavas-Walt, Carmen, Bernadette D. Proctor, and Cheryl Hill Lee, U.S. Census Bureau, Current Population Reports, P60–229, "Income, Poverty, and Health Insurance Coverage in the United States: 2004," U.S. Government Printing Office, Washington, D.C., 2005.

Dowd, Maureen. "Men Just Want Mommy." *New York Times*, January 13, 2005.

Ehrenreich, Barbara. *The Hearts of Men: American Dreams and the Flight from Commitment*. New York: Anchor Books, 1983.

Elliott, Amy. "Bachelorette Parties: 7 Must-Have Party Props." *The Knot*, http://www.theknot.com/ch_article.html?Object=A00706121120.

Epstein, Edward Jay. "Have You Ever Tried to Sell a Diamond? An Unruly Market May Undo the Work of a Giant Cartel and of an Inspired, Decades-Long Ad Campaign." *The Atlantic Monthly*, February 1982.

Essig, Laurie. "Same-Sex Marriage: I Don't Care If It Is Legal, I Still Think It's Wrong—And I'm a Lesbian." *Salon*, July 10, 2000.

Fairchild Bridal Group, "Bridal Spending Tops 125 Billion, a 4% Increase over Last Three Years: 2005 'American Wedding' Survey Reveals," news release, May 25, 2005.

Fein, Ellen and Schneider, Sherrie. *The Rules: Time-Tested Secrets for Capturing the Heart of Mr. Right*. New York: Warner Books, 1995.

Field, Genevieve and Liz Welch. "Quick—What Do You Want in Life? A Dream Job? A Man You Love? Or Just the Ability to Look in the Mirror and Like What You See?" *Glamour*, September 2005, 350–355.

Fields, Denise and Alan Fields. *Bridal Bargains: Secrets to Throwing a Fantastic Wedding on a Realistic Budget*. Boulder: Windsor Peak Press, 2005.

Flipse, Robyn, R. D., and Jacqueline Shannon. *The Wedding Dress Diet: Lose Weight and Look Great on Your Wedding Day*. New York: Doubleday, 2000.

Forero, Julian. "A Bevy of Teeny Beauties, Minds Set on Being Queens." *New York Times*, April 15, 2000.

Friedan, Betty. *The Feminine Mystique*. New York: W. W. Norton and Company, 1963.

Gardyn, Rebecca. "Here Comes the Bride's Checkbook." *American Demographics* 23, no. 5 (2001): 12.

Geller, Jaclyn. *Here Comes the Bride: Women, Weddings, and the Marriage Mystique.* New York: Four Walls Eight Windows, 2001.

Gerstman, Bradley, Esq., Christopher Pizzo, C.P.A., and Rich Seldes, M.D. *Marry Me! Three Professional Men Reveal How to Get Mr. Right to Pop the Question.* New York: HarperCollins, 2000.

Ginsburg, Madeline. *Wedding Dress, 1740–1970.* London: Her Majesty's Stationery Office, 1981.

Greenfield, Casey. "More Women Are Popping the Question." *Cleveland Plain Dealer,* October 20, 2000.

Greenwald, Rachel. *Find a Husband after 35: A Simple 15 Step Action Program.* New York: Ballantine Books, 2003.

Hacker, Andrew. *Mismatch: The Growing Gulf between Women and Men.* New York: Scribner, 2003.

Hart, Matthew. *Diamond: History of a Cold-Blooded Love Affair.* London: Fourth Estate, 2002.

Haslett, Adam. "Love Supreme: Gay Nuptials and the Making of Modern Marriage." *The New Yorker,* May 31, 2004, 76–80.

Hayt, Elizabeth. "It's Never Too Late to Be a Virgin." *New York Times,* August 4, 2002.

Heaner, Martica. "Here Comes the (Buff) Bride." *New York Weddings,* Spring 2005.

Hochschild, Arlie Russell. *The Commercialization of Intimate Life: Notes from Home and Work.* Berkeley and Los Angeles: University of California Press, 2003.

Horyn, Cathy. "Perfect Wedding: $5000 Cake, Hold the Simplicity." *New York Times,* June 6, 2004.

Hudepohl, Dana. "Is Marriage the New Dating?" *Marie Claire,* March 2005, 113.

"If It Were All up to Men . . . Here's What Jake Thinks Women Would Be in For." From "Ask Jake," *Glamour,* September 2004, 162.

Jones, Daniel, ed. *The Bastard on the Couch: 27 Men Try Really Hard to Explain Their Feelings About Love, Loss, Fatherhood and Freedom.* New York: William Morrow, 2004.

Kanfer, Stefan. *The Last Empire: De Beers, Diamonds and the World.* New York: Farrar, Straus and Giroux, 1995.

Kazanjian, Dodie. "The Rules of Engagement: Choosing the Right Ring Inspires Almost as Much Trembling among Grooms-to-Be as the Proposal Itself. Relax, Gentlemen: Today's Options Are Endless." *Vogue,* March 2004, 380–84.

The Kinsey Institute. "Frequency of Sex." In *Frequently Asked Sexuality Questions to the Kinsey Institute.* http://www.indiana.edu/~kinsey/resources/FAQ.html.

Kirshenbaum, Rich and Daniel Rosenberg. *Closing the Deal: Two Married Guys Take You from Single Miss to Wedded Bliss.* New York: William Morrow, 2005.

The Knot. "Invitations: Top 6 Trends." http://www.theknot.com.

The Knot. "Proposals: He Finally Asked! How You Reacted." In *Ask Carley.* http://www.theknot.com/ch_printarticle.html?&Object=AI990506000027. (accessed December 5, 2003).

The Knot, "Your Wedding Consultant: 13 Questions to Ask."

Kulish, Nicholas. "Turning the Tables: Bachelorette Parties Are Getting Risque." *Wall Street Journal,* September 3, 2002.

Lagorce, Aude. "The Gay Marriage Windfall: $16.8 Billion." *Forbes,* April 5, 2004.

Levy, Ariel. "Raunchiness Is Powerful? C'mon, Girls." *Washington Post*, September 18, 2005.

McBride-Mellinger, Maria. *The Wedding Dress*. New York: Random House, 1993.

McMahon, Cindy Murphy. "Take a Look at That Rock: Sparkling Tips." *Omaha World-Herald*, January 16, 2000.

Miller, Laura. "State of the Single Woman: Unmarried Gals May Be the Freest People Around. But to Fully Enjoy Their Lives, They Need to Stop Paying Attention to Society's Instructions." *Salon*, December 12, 2002. http://www.salon.com/books/feature/2002/12/12/single.

Minkowitz, Donna. "Wedding Vows: How to Have Our Family and Smash It Too." *The Nation*, July 5, 2004, 36–38.

Mitchell, John. *What the Hell Is a Groom and What's He Supposed to Do?* Kansas City: Andrews McMeel Publishing, 1999.

Modern Bride. "Bare Essentials." October/November 2005.

Modern Bride. "Indulge! Modern Bride Editors Sample the Best Big-Day Beauty Treatments." October/November 2005.

Mother Jones. "For Richer or Poorer," January/February 2005, 24–25.

Murphy, Evelyn and E. J. Graff, *Getting Even: Why Women Don't Get Paid Like Men—And What to Do About It*. New York: Touchstone, 2005.

The National Marriage Project. "The State of Our Unions." edited by David and Whitehead Popenoe, Barbara Defoe. Piscataway: Rutgers University, 2001.

Nissinen, Sheryl. *The Conscious Bride: Women Unveil Their True Feelings About Getting Hitched*. Oakland: New Harbinger Publications, Inc., 2000.

Nussbaum, Emily. "Is *This* Girl Power? Men Are Dogs, Men Are Babies, Men Are Stupid. Come On! Man-Bashing May Be Good for a Laugh, but It's No Good for Women." *Glamour*, June 2004, 120–31.

Omelianuk, Scott. *Esquire's Things a Man Should Know About Marriage: A Groom's Guide to the Wedding and Beyond*. New York: Riverhead Books, 1999.

Orenstein, Catherine. "What Carrie Could Learn from Mary." *New York Times*, September 5, 2003.

Peacock, Mary. "The Rock." *Womenswire*. http://www.womenswire.com/weddings/rock.html.

Peterson, Karen S. "Romance of 2000 Creates Wedding Glut: Brides Forced to Scramble for Sites or Wait Till 2001." *USA Today*, December 20, 1999.

Pipher, Mary. *Reviving Ophelia: Saving the Selves of Adolescent Girls*. New York: Ballantine Books, 1994.

Pollitt, Katha. "There They Go Again." *The Nation*, November 17, 2003, 9.

Proctor, Robert. *Agate Eyes*. (Forthcoming)

Prose, Francine. "A Wasteland of One's Own." *New York Times*, February 13, 2000.

Reiter, Amy. "Elegant Bride: The Magazine That Makes Martha Stewart Look Liberated." *Indiebride*, Summer 2002.

Roiphe, Katie. "The Maiden Name Debate: What's Changed since the 1970s?" *Slate*, March 16, 2004.

Roney, Carley, ed. *The Knot Book of Wedding Gowns*. San Francisco: Chronicle Books, 2001.

Rothstein, Ronald, Mara Urshel, and Todd Lyon. *How to Buy Your Perfect Wedding Dress.* New York: Fireside, 2002.

Rozhon, Tracie. "Competition Is Forever." *New York Times,* February 9, 2005.

Rubenstein, Hal. "A Dress for Every Figure." *InStyle,* Spring 2000, 183–91.

Sandell, Laurie. "No Guts, No Guy: Listen up, Women! You May Be Only One (Nail-Biting) Question Away from Finding the Man You Want. The Secret: Ask *Him* Out. Be Unafraid, Be Very Unafraid." *Glamour,* October 2004, 146–48.

Saranow, Jennifer. "To Have and Hit Up." *Wall Street Journal,* May 6, 2005.

Shropshire, Corilyn. "Exercise Classes, Teeth Whitening, Even Cosmetic Surgery on a Growing Number of 'To-Do' Lists Before Wedding Day." *Pittsburgh Post-Gazette,* September 20, 2004.

Siegel, Deborah. "The New Trophy Wife." *Psychology Today,* January/February 2004, 52.

Sporkin, Elizabeth, ed. *People: The Greatest Weddings of All Time.* New York: People Books, Time Inc., 2002.

Steinem, Gloria. "What It Would Be Like If Women Won." *Time,* August 31, 1970, 22.

Story, Louise. "Many Women at Elite Colleges Set Career Path to Motherhood." *New York Times,* September 20, 2005.

Treistman, Ann. "Ring Anxiety: What Do You Call a Confident Career Woman Who's Lusting for a Band of Gold? Totally Normal. What to Do When You're Between a Rock and a Hard Place." *Glamour,* October 1999, 158–62.

U.S. Census Bureau. "Statistical Abstract of the United States." Washington, D.C., 2001.

Waite, Linda J. and Gallagher, Maggie. *The Case for Marriage: Why Married People Are Happier, Healthier and Better Off Financially.* New York: Doubleday, 2000.

Wang, Vera. *Vera Wang on Weddings.* New York: HarperCollins, 2001.

Wedding Channel. "Who Are You?" www.weddingchannel.com/ui/buildArticlePreview.action?assetUID=3453.

Weinstein, Ellen. "Where Are the Women?" *Fast Company,* February 2004, 52.

Wolf, Naomi. *The Beauty Myth: How Images of Beauty Are Used Against Women.* New York: Anchor Books, Doubleday, 1991.

———. *Misconceptions: Truth, Lies and the Unexpected on the Journey to Motherhood.* New York: Vintage, 2001.

———. *Promiscuities: The Secret Struggle for Womanhood.* New York: Fawcett Columbine, 1997.

Women's Wear Daily. "Strength in Numbers." October 2002.

Yalom, Marilyn. *A History of the Wife.* New York: HarperCollins, 2001.

Zamiska, Nicholas. "College-Educated Women Adopt Spouse's Surname." *Wall Street Journal,* July 15, 2004.

ACKNOWLEDGMENTS

A biographer friend once told me that no one likes being written about, whether it's good or bad. But someone gave me an incredible gift when I was seized by the need to tackle this subject in writing: my husband Andrew. Andrew so utterly, totally, unhesitatingly said yes to this book, and to the personal approach I took to writing it—even though it meant a very public outing for a very private man—that I am embarrassed to say I never even asked his permission. I am humbled and deeply touched to say that I never had to. Andrew's unflinching confidence in me, even when I was sure I could never write another word, his loving praise and careful criticism as my first, best, and most constant reader, and his intellectual and analytical contributions to the ongoing conversation we have been carrying on about these issues for years, all made this book possible. His love and friendship make my life better than I ever thought it could be.

Andrew is not the only person, of course, who didn't-exactly-agree to be written about in this book. My mother consented to remain in the dark for years as it took shape, and gave me the space and time I needed to write freely and honestly without insecurity or fear. So much of *I Do But I Don't* is the fruition of conversations we've been having since my childhood, and my mother's brilliant mind, quick intellect, and wry humor inspire and guide me still. My father may believe he performed his greatest service by helping my mother restrain herself as she waited to see just what I was up to, but he did much more than that. He is also a writer, and the unabashed pride, delight, and passion he takes in my work—even when it makes him wince, as he puts it—gave me strength and lifted me into delight when I most needed it, too. My sister Kimberly has served as my sounding board, my PR person (many of the women interviewed here are friends of hers), my comfort, and my rock. My brother Reid, who also snaps into a state of rapturous intensity when discussing writing or books, has followed my progress with great interest and love. I am also grateful for the support and valuable input of his wife, Miranda. My aunts, uncles, and cousins have all given me love, encouragement, and their two cents regarding just about everything discussed here—I thank them.

Andrew's family—his sister Erin and her partner Dario, his parents David and Caryl, his aunts, uncles, cousins, and beloved grandparents—also generously gave me their input and their consent as I wrote this book. Not everyone acquires a second family they love and admire as much as I do mine. I am also indebted to a special group of women who have been like family to me for many years now, many of whom helped me get through my wedding as it was happening, and contributed their ideas and enthusiasm to my book about wedding, too: Allison Axtell, Amy Fox (also one of my best and most trusted readers), Anne Tramer, Hillary Heath, Lisa Ling, Monica Novotny, Pam Mourouzis, Saydeah Howard, Sitarah Pendleton, Tracy Smith, and Jennifer Wang. Arielle Miller, Anne Knudsen, Gina Bianchini, Lisa Reisman, Mandy Rice, and Sarah Saffian (also a great editor) were also key parts of my support system. I owe Gina in particular a debt I can never repay—she knows what it is.

I will be forever grateful to the more than eighty women who filled out my detailed and, yes, *long* series of questionnaires regarding all things wedding-y. A writer's job is an isolated one, but the voices of these women kept me company, and their stories constantly surprised, enlightened, tickled, and educated me. (All of their names have been changed here, but they will surely recognize themselves.) It has been said that labor is the only gift more precious than love, and these women—some of them total strangers—gave it freely and amply. Without their work, this book would be much less than it is.

I have also been very fortunate in the group of mentors and readers who have entered my life over the years. Diane Middlebrook and Nancy K. Miller are hugely important to me both personally and professionally—their critical input eased my mind as I wrote, and their love kept me going. Hope Edelman and Francine Prose were shrewd and encouraging teachers and editors, and are good friends, too. Colin Harrison and Richard Locke shepherded me through the thesis phase, along with my fellow students in Columbia's MFA program. Erin Hosier, my agent, has proven to be a dream come true—without her I would not be writing an acknowledgments section of any kind, something I can never acknowledge sufficiently. Her dedication, unswerving commitment, and smarts amaze me. I am also grateful for the guidance and confidence of my editor, Marnie Cochran, and the rest of the team at Da Capo Lifelong Books. Lauren Hunter also helped get this book across the finish line; thanks to her, too.

Finally, I would like to thank Grace Brignolle. I got the contract for *I Do But I Don't* when my son Maximilian was just five days old. Three months later, when I began to take baby steps toward working again, Grace came into our family and became, as she put it, "Max's personal assistant." She is much more than that. Without her labor, and the peace of mind she gives me by caring for Max with such love, creativity, and intelligence, this book would, quite simply, not exist.

As for Max, I can only imagine what it will be like when you are able to read this. Perhaps I would rather not. For now, thank you for lifting me completely out of myself and my troubles with your awesome growth, and your irrepressible sense of wonder. One of your first words was "Wow." Thank you for making the world new again.